AQUATIC READINESS

Developing Water Competence in Young Children

Stephen J. Langendorfer, PhD
Bowling Green State University

Lawrence D. Bruya, PhD
Washington State University

Human Kinetics

Library of Congress Cataloging-in-Publication Data

Langendorfer, Stephen.
    Aquatic readiness : developing water competence in young children
/ Stephen J. Langendorfer, Lawrence D. Bruya.
        p.   cm.
    Includes index.
    ISBN 0-87322-663-1
    1. Swimming for children.   I. Bruya, Lawrence D.   II. Title.
    GV837.2.L36   1995
    797.2'1--dc20   93-42159
                                                      CIP

ISBN: 0-87322-663-1

Developmental Editors: Sue Mauck and Holly Gilly; **Assistant Editors:** Sally Bayless, Jacqueline Blakley, Dawn Roselund, and John Wentworth; **Copyeditor:** Wendy Nelson; **Proofreader:** Steve Wrone; **Typesetter:** Julie Overholt; **Text Designer:** Keith Blomberg; **Layout Artist:** Denise Lowry, Tara Welsch, and Denise Peters; **Cover Designer:** Jack Davis; **Photographer (cover):** Wilmer Zehr; **Illustrator:** Patrick Griffin; **Mac Artist:** Gretchen Walters; **Cover Models:** Benjamin Gilly, Meredith Gilly, Lori Matthew, Mallary Matthew, Tyler McElwee, and Amy Moden; **Printer:** Braun-Brumfield

Printed in the United States of America   10 9 8 7 6 5 4 3 2 1

Human Kinetics
P.O. Box 5076, Champaign, IL 61825-5076
1-800-747-4457

Canada: Human Kinetics, Box 24040,
Windsor, ON N8Y 4Y9
1-800-465-7301 (in Canada only)

Europe: Human Kinetics, P.O. Box IW14,
Leeds LS16 6TR, England
(44) 532 781708

Australia: Human Kinetics, 2 Ingrid Street,
Clapham 5062, South Australia
(08) 371 3755

New Zealand: Human Kinetics, P.O. Box 105-231, Auckland 1
(09) 309 2259

Contents

Preface

Aquatic Readiness provides the aquatic instructor with a comprehensive source for developing or revising an aquatic program for young children. This text is written as a challenge to all aquatic instructors, but especially to those who teach children. Basically, we are challenging the way that most instructors, parents, and even kids view the aquatic learning process. In that sense, we are trying to turn the aquatic world upside down.

With the dramatic rise in the availability of swimming facilities since World War II has come an equally dramatic increase in the number and types of aquatic programs offered. For instance, some emphasize water safety for infants and offer classes to enhance "drownproofing" skills; other programs emphasize "water orientation" and fun classes for parents and their young children. Still others try to foster early swimming and stroke skills.

Infant and preschool swimming has been a particularly controversial topic, partly because there are so many philosophies and approaches. Such prestigious organizations as the Council for National Cooperation in Aquatics (CNCA), the American Academy of Pediatrics, the American Red Cross, and the YMCA of the USA have all been a part of the furor over the past 2 decades. Despite the controversies, many new programs have been created for teaching swimming to the young child. Within the past 7 years both the YMCA and the Red Cross have developed their own nationally standardized programs for infants and young children, and there is a plethora of other programs and books available to instructors and parents.

However, we have noticed that there is a general lack of scholarly treatment of aquatics for young children and that aquatic instructors often receive insufficient training. This book is a start at remedying both situations.

The first chapter introduces the concepts of water competence and aquatic readiness. The water competence model urges you to teach broader sets of skills; the aquatic readiness format presupposes a new set of fundamental skills for young children and identifies children as the center of the learning process.

Chapter 2 describes the misinformation regarding the role of aquatics in the child's overall development, the acquisition of aquatic skills by young chil-

dren, the teaching methods and strategies for working with young children in the water, and the health and safety of infants and young children during aquatic experiences.

Chapter 3 challenges you to evaluate your measurement and testing procedures, your instructional assumptions, and even the games-and-fun environment of your swimming pool, while chapter 4 presents the aquatic readiness model to provide you with a new way to observe aquatic skills in children. Instead of comparing a child's movements to an adult stroke, we show how skills change progressively and sequentially.

To teach aquatics to children, you need more than simply an efficient class organization and a commanding style of disseminating information. You must also be skilled in movement education, play, and developmental games—indirect methods of presenting and reinforcing skill learning that are crucial to effective communication with young children. Chapters 5 and 6 help you develop such methods.

Without motivation, learning is slow. Chapters 7 and 8 show you how to use large equipment and games in the aquatic environment to increase motivation and learning through active play.

Aquatic instructors must also begin viewing the aquatic environment for what it is: a wonderful, exciting learning environment replete with hidden dangers and risk. As an instructor, you must be familiar with the preventive principles associated with risk management in the aquatic environment. This means more than simply having good lifesaving and first aid skills and an emergency plan for the pool. Chapter 9 shows you how to actively inspect your facility and program, looking for risk situations and keeping an effective documentation system.

The appendix is a compilation of over 100 aquatic games, organized according to skill level and aquatic readiness skill categories.

Whether you are an old hand of 20 years' experience, a new instructor whose ink on the WSI is still wet, or a parent working with your own child, all of the information on child development, aquatic learning and development, teaching, risk management, and games in this text is for you. We think your children will benefit from and enjoy the aquatic readiness approach. Read; experiment; have fun!

Acknowledgments

Aquatic Readiness is the result of many people having shared their ideas with us over the years. We are particularly grateful to all of our mentors and colleagues who have passed along their wisdom, especially Marguerite Clifton and Lolas Halverson. We are equally appreciative of those undergraduate and graduate students who have contributed to this effort in many ways and of all those youngsters and their parents who have taught us so much about how they learned to swim. Finally, and most importantly, our special thanks to Jeanne and Lorna and the kids for their patience and encouragement during all the late nights and conference trips while this book was developed and written.

We also would be remiss if we didn't acknowledge Rainer Martens's special brand of motivation in making this book a reality and our developmental editors, Sue Mauck and especially Holly Gilly for her infinite patience and gentle guidance.

Chapter

1

An Introduction to Aquatic Readiness

Exciting things are going on in aquatics these days. The field is rapidly changing, especially in instructional programs for children. In fact, there are so many developments that an instructor can easily miss many of them or be overwhelmed and confused. *Aquatic Readiness* addresses new ideas, activities, and techniques in working with children in the water to assist you, the swimming instructor.

THE SWIMMING WORLD IS A-CHANGIN'
CONCEPT 1.1

The aquatic community in the United States is rapidly changing and broadening to accept new ideas and perspectives.

Aquatics in the United States is undergoing a remarkable renaissance. The primary agencies offering swimming and water safety programs and instructor certifications, such as the American Red Cross and YMCA of the USA, have expanded their aquatic audiences and what is being taught. Traditionally the focus of aquatic instruction has been on swimming strokes: learning how to perform them, perform them safely, and perform them faster. The broader scope of aquatic skills has remained secondary to the emphasis on learning and performing specified swimming strokes. The main source of information about performing swimming skills has come from persons who already knew how to do strokes, to lifeguard, or to swim competitively. These people have passed along their own beliefs, observations, and understandings of aquatics. Unfortunately, the prevailing folk wisdom handed down from teacher to student often perpetuates fictions and misinformation along

with the truth. As one example, until recently almost everyone taught that a swimmer's hand is used during stroking like a canoe paddle to produce forward movement. Recent evidence suggests that the hand acts more like a propellor or airplane wing to produce lift as a major component of swimming propulsion. As another more developmental example, most American swim instructors still attempt to teach all students an idealized, adult stroke pattern, usually emphasizing the crawl stroke. Evidence is presented later in this book showing that strokes change over time and must be individualized to the size, strength, and experience of the learner. Practical experience and observations in Europe and Asia suggest that strokes other than the crawl can be learned first. Finally, while it is generally accepted that vigorous exercise is not recommended after eating a full meal, there is no evidence that food in the stomach causes stomach or any other kind of cramps. Yet this folk fiction is passed along even today by parents and instructors.

Contemporary aquatic professionals have turned to a wide variety of fields to bolster their arsenal of teaching and learning tools. Research literature from pedagogy; curriculum; motor learning, motor development, and motor control; biomechanics; medicine; public health; and even anthropology are being incorporated into aquatic programs and activities. A new dedication to the scientific method has meant that claims, hunches, and hypotheses are subjected to tests and checks to verify their accuracy. Many professionals have sought to adopt a critical mind-set, a willingness to question and wonder about the things we believe.

The integration of these new knowledges and methods is exciting! They rejuvenate and expand aquatics. As aquatic professionals become more highly trained in such specialized areas as infant and

Misinformation in aquatics (such as poor diving learning progressions) has been perpetuated along with accurate information.

preschool swimming, lifeguarding, coaching, and kayaking, they are able to debunk traditional misinformation. And as learning, developmental, and biomechanical principles are applied across many aquatic areas, including learn-to-swim, competitive and synchronized strokes, diving, scuba, and boating, they help support a broader understanding and appreciation of many facets of aquatics.

WATER COMPETENCE: MORE THAN JUST THE SAME OLD STROKES
CONCEPT 1.2

A water competence model for aquatics broadens the traditional scope of aquatic activities and should be included within the total aquatic program.

One way aquatic professionals can expand their perspective is by adopting the concept of water competence as a primary goal. Water competence, traditionally called watermanship, is proficiency in a wide variety of aquatic skills, knowledges, and values that come from a variety of fields and subdisciplines. A water competence model of aquatics recognizes that there is more to swimming than learn-to-swim and competitive programs and opens aquatics up to the vast knowledge explosion occurring in fields from neurophysiology to pedagogy. There is much we can learn by broadening our understanding of aquatics.

The water competence model of aquatic activity used in conjunction with aquatic readiness implies participation and proficiency in many aquatic skill areas. From a water competence perspective, success in swimming lessons for the young or elementary school child does not mean automatically continuing on to work on strokes or to begin competitive swimming. In the water competence model (see Figure 1.1), anticipated outcomes to swimming lessons may include synchronized swimming, aquatic exercise, diving, leisure activities, underwater activities, boating, water games, and water safety activities.

The water competence model for aquatic activity has profound implications for aquatic professionals. It is no longer adequate for a skilled aquatic person merely to have mastered six basic and advanced swimming strokes or to be proficient in lifesaving. Expertise must be developed in lifeguarding, water safety, and boating as well as in aquatic instruction and competitive and synchronized swimming principles and skills. Today's consummate aquatic professionals must be at once generalists across aquatic areas and specialists within several areas.

The water competence model poses similar challenges for our aquatic programs and their administrators. It is no longer sufficient merely to offer learn-to-swim lessons and an age-group swimming team. Aquatic programs must offer personal water safety, synchronized swimming, aquatic exercise, recreational and leisure swimming, exercise, weight control, boating, and boating safety. Children and adults of all skill levels need these programs. Providing adequate staffing, pool time, and resources will be a great challenge, but your aquatics program and its participants will benefit.

AQUATIC READINESS—BEFORE THE CHILD GETS "INTO THE SWIM"
CONCEPT 1.3

Aquatic readiness includes foundational skills, attitudes, and understandings that precede the acquisition of more advanced aquatic skills such as swimming strokes (advanced locomotion) and water safety.

Proponents of instructional learn-to-swim programs long have viewed formal swimming strokes (e.g., crawl, elementary backstroke) as the foundation for aquatic skill development. Based on years of experience with learners of all ages, experienced swimming teachers have claimed that there are skills to be learned that are more rudimentary than, and funda-

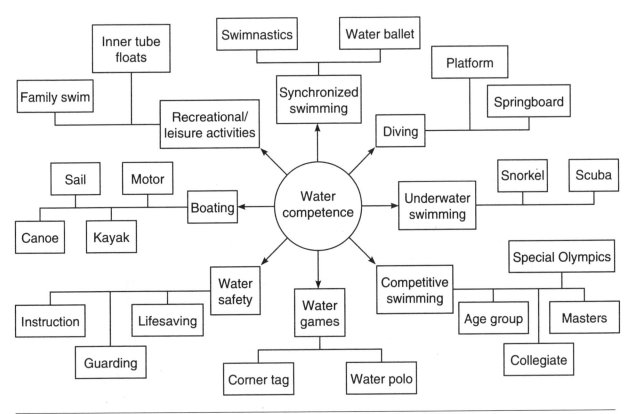

Figure 1.1 Water competence model for aquatics implies participation in several aquatic skill areas.

mental to, swimming strokes (Bory, 1971; Newman, 1983; Murray, 1981; Prudden, 1974). Such observations are not surprising. Developmental research suggests that for skills in many areas, including the cognitive and social domains, there are prerequisite readiness skills that must be acquired before acquiring the advanced skills (see Figure 1.2) (Roberton & Halverson, 1984).

We believe that before any learner, but especially a child, works at becoming competent in traditional strokes (which we will call "advanced formal strokes"), a set of fundamental skills, attitudes, and understandings must be acquired first. We call this developmentally appropriate process of addressing prerequisite needs "aquatic readiness" (see Figure 1.3a). In this model, such basic psychomotor skills as water entry, water balance, water buoyancy, breath control, arm movements, and leg movements are all prerequisite to later advanced formal strokes (see Figure 1.3b). In addition, the aquatic learner should acquire several important attitudes such as respect for the water, adherence to water safety principles, and following facility rules for safe participation (see Figure 1.3c).

Finally, all aquatic learners need to formulate cognitive understandings about such aspects of the aquatic environment as class procedures, pool rules, language of instruction ("Turn your head and breathe

to the side"), games and activity rules, and basic mechanics (buoyancy, relaxation, submersion, and propulsion) (see Figure 1.3d). These concepts can be acquired at a level of sophistication appropriate to the learner's age, and cognitive, psychomotor, and social development.

The acquisition of these aquatic readiness skills, attitudes, and understandings may radically alter a person's direction, rate of progress, and ultimate achievement level in water competence. This is true especially for children. As Figure 1.4 suggests, aquatic readiness skills are a developmental foundation for basic strokes as well as for such specialized water competence areas as synchronized swimming, competitive swimming, and water safety skills. Developmental researchers have suggested that early fundamental learning can improve the quality of later skills (McGraw, 1935/1975; Seefeldt, 1980). Early readiness also helps the aquatic learner develop faster and more completely, because early learning establishes a strong base (Schmidt, 1975).

Importance of Aquatic Readiness

Some persons argue that young children acquire aquatic skills with little emphasis on readiness. We suggest that they may be acquiring these aquatic skills in spite of current practices. Two major tenets of this

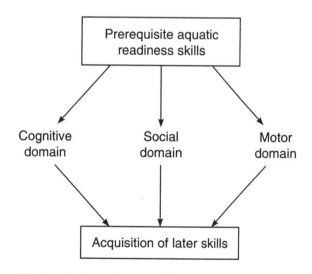

Today's aquatic professionals must be both generalists across aquatic areas and specialists within several areas.

Figure 1.2 Prerequisite readiness skills are required in all domains of human development.

text are that focusing solely on strokes may result in poor-quality water competence skills, and that combining aquatic readiness skills with subsequent stroke teaching will produce more optimal progress in aquatic learning for children. Certainly, promotion of aquatic readiness will encourage, and not discourage, the development of good aquatic skills, including formal advanced strokes.

Readiness Skills, Attitudes, and Understandings

Examples of aquatic readiness motor skills (Figure 1.3b) include water entry, water buoyancy and balance, breath control, and arm and leg locomotor action. As discussed later in this text (chapter 4), many of these activities are acquired in predictable developmental sequences. Other motor skills, such as throwing or hopping, develop in similar motor sequences (Halverson & Williams, 1985; Roberton & Halverson, 1984). Knowledge of the order in which these skills appear can assist both the learner and instructor in important ways.

The aquatic readiness attitudes (Figure 1.3c), such as respect for the water, obeying safety principles and adhering to facility rules, and, particularly, appreciation for safe practices around the water, also are important to the development of later specialized aquatic skills. Aquatic readiness understandings (see

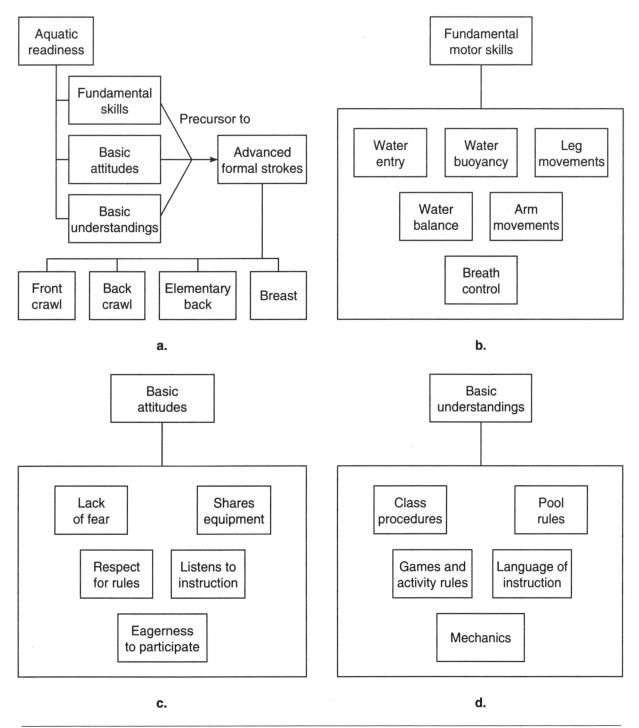

Figure 1.3   The fundamental aquatic skills children should acquire before achieving competence in traditional strokes.

Figure 1.3d) are fundamental to the development of our aquatic skills. We must have basic knowledge about water such as an appreciation for such basic physical and biomechanical concepts as buoyancy, relaxation, and submersion. In fact, the limits to progress in enhancing human aquatic skills probably derive from deficits in our cognitive understanding of the water and aquatic principles.

A child's success in acquiring aquatic skills depends upon the child's fundamental aquatic readiness. As will become apparent to you, the reader, as a teacher, learning facilitator, play leader, or parent, it is necessary for you to develop basic comprehension of the three readiness areas. Such comprehension will permit you to provide developmentally appropriate activities and experiences for your children.

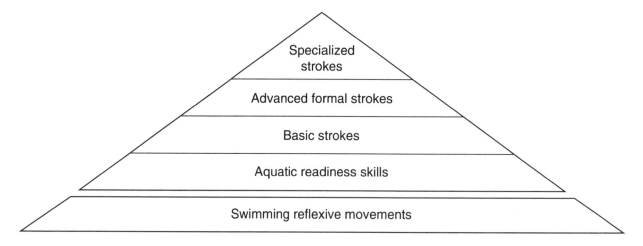

Figure 1.4   Pyramid of aquatic skills leading to specialized strokes, with aquatic readiness skills as the foundation for later development and learning.

A DEVELOPMENTAL PERSPECTIVE: CHANGING STROKES FOR LITTLE FOLKS
CONCEPT 1.4

Aquatic readiness skills are best understood from a developmental perspective.

How well children develop aquatic skills depends on their level of aquatic readiness.

The term *development* has been used in many ways. In this text, we'll use it to mean gradual change in behavior that results in ordered and predictable sequences of skills or movement patterns. For instance, from a developmental perspective, as children improve breath-holding or leg-kicking skills, they not only hold their breath longer and travel farther while kicking but also change the way they hold their breath and move their legs in the water. Examples of how these changes are measured and how they normally occur are presented in chapters 3 and 4.

Characteristics of a Developmental Perspective

From a developmental perspective, skill acquisition involves hierarchical integration, differentiation, and individualization. We will discuss each of these in turn.

To say that qualitative, ordered changes in aquatic behaviors are *hierarchically integrated* means that we build upon previously acquired skills that are interwoven with and fundamental to other, more advanced skills. The whole notion of aquatic readiness implies hierarchical integration because we are sug-

gesting that certain fundamental aquatic skills such as balance, buoyancy, and breath holding are crucial to subsequent aquatic skills such as formal advanced strokes and most other water safety skills. It makes no sense to attempt to teach an advanced formal stroke to a child who is unable to control her or his breathing or to balance and float in a horizontal position.

Differentiation (or *progressive specialization*) in one sense is the opposite of integration: In contrast to integration's interweaving of fundamental skills with later learning, the differentiation developmental principle is that as we improve, we become more specialized. Such specialization is evident to the competitive swimmer. Skill and success in one stroke (e.g., the front crawl) does not necessarily generalize to success in other strokes (e.g., back crawl or breaststroke). As we gain proficiency in a stroke, thereby more clearly differentiating that stroke from other strokes, we become more specialized in the specific demands of that stroke.

Finally, *individualization* is the principle that, despite our having much in common as we gradually

change, integrate, and differentiate aquatic skills, we also are very much influenced by individual differences in our talents and experiences. The developmental perspective for learning and teaching in aquatics suggests that swimming skills develop with a common order and structure in all persons but with many individual differences. For instance, all persons change their leg-kicking skills in a predictable sequence (see chapter 4), but some prefer to learn the whip or frog kick before learning the flutter kick; others prefer to learn the flutter kick first and then move on to other kicking actions.

Contrast the developmental perspective with the more traditional learning perspective. A typical person using the learning perspective usually views skilled performance as the ultimate behavior that results from teaching activity. Any deviation from the characteristics of skilled performance usually is classified as an *error*. Essentially, learning is the elimination of these errors.

In contrast, instructors who use the developmental perspective are more likely to view skill performance as changing in an ordered sequence. The developmentalist sees these changes as progressive skill increments in the way most children develop. Each developmental performance level marks the next naturally occurring step in the overall progress toward advanced or skilled movement. These changes mark progress *toward* skill, not errors *away from* incorrect or inefficient movement (as the learning perspective would dictate). Performance changes represent a less-well-articulated, or less efficient, form but nonetheless a necessary step in the process of acquiring the advanced level of a skill (see Figure 1.5).

Aquatic readiness particularly acknowledges individual differences in learning to swim.

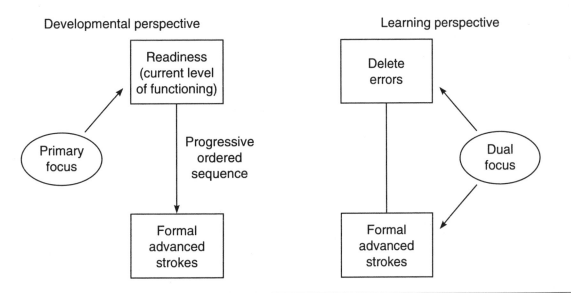

Developmental perspective

Learning perspective

Figure 1.5 The primary focus of the developmental perspective versus the learning perspective.

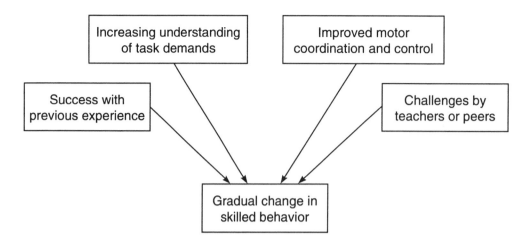

Figure 1.6   Success, challenge, understanding, and coordination effect gradual changes in skilled behavior.

As the swimmer interacts with the environment (e.g., the pool deck, the water), her or his swimming movements change as a result of new experiences, current level of maturation, perceptions, needs, and task demands. For instance, young swimmers gradually and progressively alter the way they enter the water (Reid & Bruya, 1984). Slowly they progress from rudimentary approaches to water (e.g., sitting at the edge of the pool and lowering themselves into the water with assistance) to more aggressive and difficult entries (standing at the pool's edge and jumping or diving in without assistance). When the instructor is using the developmental perspective, these changes are more likely to be viewed as gradual and sequential skill enhancements that mark real progress in performance rather than as various degrees of error in their deviation from an ideal of pool-entry skill.

Instructors who decide to use the developmental perspective view the process of gradual change as a response to the stimuli illustrated in Figure 1.6. In-stead of expecting every child to demonstrate an advanced mode of entry (e.g., jumping or diving with a flight phase) after eliminating *errors* from the child's movement repertoire, they will expect the child to advance gradually, one step at a time.

SUMMARY

You are now acquainted with this book's developmental aquatic readiness perspective. We feel it is important for aquatic professionals like yourself to break the mold of traditional swimming ideas and learn and adapt new and innovative ideas. With this in mind, we welcome you once again to *Aquatic Readiness*. The next chapter begins by trying to separate fact and fiction in infant and preschool aquatics. In debunking the myths and fictions, we hope to challenge you to view the aquatic information you receive with a more critical eye.

Chapter

2

Fact and Fiction in Aquatics for Young Children

Aquatic programs for young children have been controversial for the past 20 years. Doctors, researchers, swimming instructors, aquatic administrators, and parents have voiced strong condemnation of these programs as often as they have voiced strong support for them. The preschool swimming instructor is at the center of the controversy.

Besieged by concerned parents and supervisors for more and better information, swim instructors too often have been reluctant to admit that they don't have adequate resources to answer the questions. Instead, they hazard guesses, which is how rumors get started, as they say! Half-truths and plain falsehoods tend to gain credence merely from being repeated often enough.

SOURCES OF MISINFORMATION
CONCEPT 2.1

Information regarding aquatics for young children contains many claims that range from fact to fiction, and the preschool instructor needs to be able to distinguish between them.

The swimming instructor certainly is not the only source of misinformation. Parents, pediatricians, and even national organizations often cite untruths or half-truths about preschool swim programs. For example, the CNCA, the distinguished consortium of national aquatic organizations, was on record for many years as saying that children under 3 years of age couldn't and shouldn't learn to swim in organized programs. To support this, the CNCA made unsubstantiated claims that children under 3 have "developmental limitations." We have joked that apparently this meant that *disorganized* programs for young children were OK! Seriously, much ground has been lost due to misinformation spread by aquatic organizations and other "experts." The truth is that there are a lot of things about aquatics for young children that we just don't know yet.

This chapter addresses controversial topics in aquatics for young children. Views that appear to be supported by empirical evidence we have labeled *facts*. We contrast these to views that apparently do not have empirical support, which we have labeled *fictions*. Both proswimming and antiswimming fictions have caused a great deal of confusion. Usually fictions are well-intentioned or express deeply felt convictions. Many of the controversies revolve around differences of opinion that currently cannot be resolved empirically. The intent of this chapter is to highlight disagreements, point out what we do know, and indicate what we still need to find out.

There are two ways to confront and debunk misinformation. The first is to develop and distribute an objective body of knowledge for preschool and infant swimming that is integrated with current early childhood educational, developmental, and medical information. The second is to cultivate an informed and critical group of aquatic instructors in our nation's swimming programs. A fundamental aim of this text is to provide a knowledge base and to contribute to the development of such informed aquatic instructors. It is important that instructors and parents of young children have a questioning, critical mind-set and correct information (see Figure 2.1).

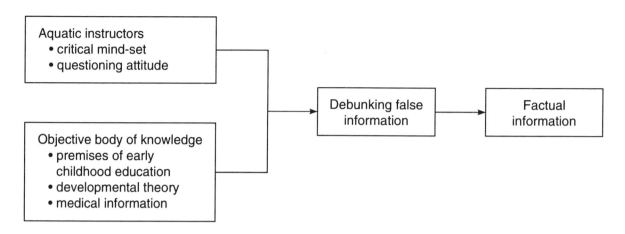

Figure 2.1 Factual information for aquatic readiness programs depends on two factors: an objective body of knowledge and informed aquatic instructors.

DEVELOPMENTAL ISSUES
CONCEPT 2.2

There are fictions about the role of aquatics in the child's overall development.

Most parents want to provide their children with opportunities for achievement. And it seems that many of today's parents believe that if they can get their children involved early in learning experiences, the children will be better equipped to manage in modern society. However, opinion is divided on the effects of exposure to such early learning experiences in aquatics.

Fiction #1: Early Aquatic Experience Leads to Superior Child Development

Parents often ask, "Why should my child take swimming lessons? What difference does it really make?" Unfortunately, the answer is neither simple nor evident.

Fact 1:

There is little concrete evidence to support the view that infant development is accelerated due to early aquatic experiences. In a large, longitudinal study, Diem (1982) observed enhanced social, cognitive, and movement development at school age in children who had early swim-and-gym experience. However, in a smaller study, Langendorfer (1974) was able to demonstrate no short-term enhancements from either early swimming or early movement experiences. The fiction here results from the lack of hard evidence that aquatic experiences benefit other areas of a young child's development.

Fact 2:

The child development literature does provide some possible guidance. McGraw (1935/1975) demonstrated that early enrichment experiences resulted in few profound effects on normal children; early water experiences had very specific enhancement effects only on swimming skill (McGraw, 1939). Other early child development researchers have demonstrated the ability to enhance development for children from deprived environments (Dennis, 1940).

Conclusion:

The bottom line is that for normal children, early experiences have limited but specific enhancement effects. Early experiences for handicapped or deprived children and infants also may have more generalized remedial effects.

Fiction #2: Early Aquatic Experiences Produce No Long-Term Effects, Because Young Children Do Not Have Good Long-Term Memory

This fiction is the "flip side" of the claim that infant and preschool swimming produces superior child development: that early swimming experiences have no effect.

Fact:

Little evidence is available to substantiate these claims except for testimonial accounts. The McGraw twin studies (1935/1975, 1939, 1963) showed definite long-term qualitative improvements in basic swimming (and other) skills as a result of early experiences. Studies on the Head Start Program for poor and underprivileged children in the United States seem to indicate that early cognitive deprivation can be remediated through cognitive programs.

Conclusion:

Early-experience effects seem to be *skill specific*. This means that your baby or child can have enriching experiences, but the enrichment will be specific to a particular area of skill. Early water experiences (including the bath) may enhance the child's later aquatic skills. More study is needed to investigate the relationship between early experience and skill acquisition.

SKILL ACQUISITION ISSUES
CONCEPT 2.3

There are fictions about the acquisition of aquatic skills by young children.

To counteract some of the common fictions dealing with children's acquisition of aquatic skills, it is necessary to understand some basic developmental and physiological information.

Fiction #3: Young Children, Especially Under 3 Years, Cannot Learn to Swim

The definitions of "young child" and "swim" are important to an understanding of whether children under 3 years old can learn to swim. *Young child* here indicates any person from birth to 6 years old. To *swim* means to propel oneself in, through, or under water.

Fact:

It has been suggested as a rule of thumb that children who are creeping, standing, and walking certainly can begin to learn to swim (Langendorfer & Willing, 1985). In fact, the acquisition of land-based locomotor skills may signal the point at which a child is both interested in and capable of mastering locomotion in the water as well as on land. Developmentally, age is a very poor predictor of when a child can learn to swim or perform any motor skill.

The types of strokes a young child will demonstrate are not "traditional strokes" like crawl or elementary backstroke (see chapter 4) but are instead something like a dog paddle or human stroke. However, the movement will involve limb movements (legs and/or arms) and cause movement through the water, and, by our definition, that is all it takes to swim.

Conclusion:

With practice, young children can begin demonstrating rudimentary swimming movements in the water sometime after their first birthday. Some will be able to perform earlier; many will perform only at a later age. The age at which a child first moves in the water probably is not very important!

Fiction #4: Young Children Can and Should Learn Advanced Strokes

Whether young children can learn advanced strokes depends on how these strokes are defined. The term *advanced formal strokes* here means the six traditional forms of swimming strokes (crawl, back crawl, breaststroke, sidestroke, elementary backstroke, and butterfly) plus common variations such as trudgen and inverted breaststroke.

Fact:

The motor development literature suggests that young children develop motor patterns very gradually over time and experience (Roberton & Halverson, 1984). This occurs with such skills as throwing, jumping, hopping, and striking (Halverson & Williams, 1985; Langendorfer, 1987b, 1987c; Roberton, 1977, 1978). The same phenomenon occurs with aquatic motor patterns (Balan & Langendorfer, 1988a, 1988b; Langendorfer, 1984a, 1984b, 1987; Langendorfer, Roberts, & Ropka, 1987; Langendorfer & Willing, 1985; Reid & Bruya, 1984). When the young child first tries the strokes, the quality of his or her aquatic movement is rudimentary, as is that of the toddler who is cruising and stepping awkwardly before learning to walk with a more advanced pattern. We can observe young children performing "dog paddle," or "human stroke," or "beginner stroke." These skills simply are rudimentary ways of moving through the water that eventually serve as the basis for traditional forms of swimming strokes (i.e., advanced formal strokes).

Conclusion:

When young children are observed swimming or moving in the water, they are not swimming at the same developmental level as persons using advanced formal strokes. Instead, they are demonstrating a basic aquatic locomotor pattern that is prerequisite to later advanced formal strokes. These children should be learning the basic aquatic skills and strokes before being introduced to advanced formal strokes.

Fiction #5: The Swimming Reflex Is Really Swimming

Fact:

The swimming reflex is a primitive motor behavior that some young babies demonstrate in the water shortly after birth (McGraw, 1939). It involves alternating arm and leg flexion and extension with some sideward bending of the trunk (see Figure 2.2).

Because this reflex looks somewhat like a dog paddle, many people have supposed that it really is swimming. However, this behavior is really a reflex and not under the infant's conscious control. It does not permit the infant to lift her or his head above the water surface and thus has no survival value to an infant.

Zelazo (1983) has suggested that the swimming reflex represents a preswimming pattern. The claim is that if it is regularly exercised, the reflex can promote early swimming, because the child becomes conditioned in the alternating pattern as in a dog paddle or crawl stroke. Zelazo used few subjects and based his arguments largely on previous research connecting reflexive stepping and early voluntary walking, which also used a small sample. At this point, his research is the only published evidence, so for now it can be concluded that there is little evidence to support this contention.

Conclusion:

The "swimming reflex" has little value for swimming programs for infants and young children, because it occurs at a very young age and is not a voluntary activity. At present, the reflex should not be a reason for starting infants swimming at a young age.

Fiction #6: The Epiglottal, or "Breath-Holding," Reflex Can Prevent Drowning and Water Intoxication in Infants and Young Children

Fact:

The epiglottal reflex, unlike the swimming reflex, does have functional value: It normally permits the infant and young child, as well as adults, to swallow food and drink without choking. This is possible because the epiglottis is a piece of tissue that covers the opening to the lungs during eating or drinking. Unfortunately, although the epiglottis automatically covers the opening to the lungs during breath-holding in swimming, it cannot prevent either drowning or water intoxication.

Drowning is asphyxiation due to submersion in the water. When the brain runs out of oxygen, it and other body tissues die. The epiglottal reflex cannot prevent that. It simply keeps water out of the lungs.

On the other hand, the few rare reported occurrences of water intoxication (or, *hyponatremia*, an electrolyte imbalance in the blood) have resulted from swallowing too much fluid, not from having the water enter the lungs! Thus, the epiglottis cannot prevent that condition, either.

Figure 2.2 According to McGraw (1939), voluntary aquatic locomotion (c) emerges after reflexive swimming behavior (a).

Conclusion:

The epiglottal reflex can prevent young children from choking on the water if they submerge after taking a breath. This is not surprising, because it is no different from what occurs normally during eating and drinking. Obviously, a child who submerges unexpectedly may try to get a quick breath when the mouth is already submerged and may then choke and cough because the epiglottis has not had time to close.

PEDAGOGICAL ISSUES
CONCEPT 2.4

There are fictions about teaching methods and strategies for working with young children in the water.

As most people have observed from their own experiences in school, not all students learn in the same way. Some learn best by seeing things (visual cues), some learn best by hearing things explained (auditory cues), others learn best by touching things or moving (kinesthetic cues). No matter what specific modality an instructor chooses, he or she needs to be aware of certain underlying educational principles. These will help make the instructor immune to misinformation about what teaching methods are appropriate for aquatics.

Fiction #7: Certain Methods of Teaching Swimming to Young Children Are Superior in Efficiency to All Other Methods

Proponents of operant conditioning and behavior modification have claimed that these behavioral methods represent particularly superior means to teach young children to acquire swimming skills.

Fact:

Operant conditioning is a learning approach popularized by many American psychologists. According to operant conditioning theory, actions are learned and repeated based upon reinforcement ("conditioning"). The approach does not recognize the learner as having any innate ability to actively construct her or his own actions. Instead, in this view, specific conditioning experiences with the environment create actions and learning.

Practically speaking, behavior modification in the aquatic setting requires conditioning of a large number of stimulus-response relationships. Obviously, no one can anticipate all types of situations young children may find themselves in, and thus one cannot provide the relevant conditioning for all possible reactions. For instance, one action behavior modification proponents like to reinforce is the child's turning to grasp the side of the pool entering the water (especially after falling in or being pushed in from the pool side). This is conditioned by repeated practice sessions in which the child is rewarded for following the proper sequence of events. Unfortunately, if the child falls into the water from a dock, boat, or steeply sloping shore, the same type of reaction may be ineffective or inappropriate. Certainly young children's deaths by drowning in toilets and bathtubs are not prevented by such fall-and-turn conditioned reactions. In fact, their conditioned ability to fall and turn may put them at greater risk of drowning if parents acquire a sense of security from this skill and fail to supervise them as closely as possible in all aquatic settings.

Conclusion:

Operant conditioning techniques may be effective for teaching specific simple tasks or ordered performances, but there is little published evidence to indicate its superiority over other methods of aquatic instruction. Overall, operant conditioning is less desirable than student-centered learning when the child is capable of actively participating in the learning experience. However, there is little evidence to support the superiority of *any* particular teaching technique over another, especially when used with infants and young children.

Fiction #8: Learning to Swim, for Infants and Young Children, Is Deadly Serious Business and Should Be Structured Work

Although Fiction #8 is stated in the extreme, some programs that stress drownproofing to make children and infants "water safe" have, in fact, stated their philosophy in such extremes.

Fact:

Many early child development experts (Frost & Klein, 1985; White, 1986) have stressed the importance of play for children's early learning. In fact, much of the developmental literature suggests that the "work of childhood is play."

The work of Swiss developmental psychologist Jean Piaget stressed the active role of children during play in constructing their intelligence, movement, and feelings (Roberton & Halverson, 1984). An important aspect of Piaget's theory focused on the different ways in which young children think and move as they construct their world during play. Many times this active construction is very different from the ways in which adults attempt to structure aquatic experiences. Thus, techniques that approach skill and water safety development from the adult perspective of "work" are probably inappropriate for infants and young children.

Conclusion:

Children are motivated to learn through what they perceive to be fun and play. Our aquatic programs should be sensitive to this developmental perspective and not force an adult work ethic upon young children. Preschool aquatic experiences should be fun, playful experiences! (See Figure 2.3.)

Fiction #9: The Child Automatically Learns to Swim Simply by Playing in the Water

There is some truth to this notion. Children playing in the water sometimes do learn to propel themselves in the water. However, it is unlikely that they will learn to perform advanced aquatic skills unless they receive instruction and guidance.

Fact:

The most efficient and rapid learning can occur under the guidance of a trained swimming instructor. As chapters 4, 5, and 6 detail, properly prepared aquatic instructors and play leaders are able to (a) encourage youngsters to improve at their own developmentally appropriate rates of learning, (b) supply appropriate feedback and practice situations, and (c) provide necessary challenges to children. The swimming instructor's role as a *play leader* or *play facilitator* in the aquatic environment needs to be better understood.

Conclusion:

Play is an important learning tool for the young child, but the best learning comes from an environment

in which trained adults arrange playful settings for children. This aquatic environment should encourage playful interaction and exploration by the child while the play facilitator provides adequate challenges, feedback, motivation, and reinforcement.

HEALTH AND SAFETY ISSUES
CONCEPT 2.5

There are fictions about the health and safety of infants and young children in aquatic experiences.

Infants and young children are particularly vulnerable, so fictions concerning their health and safety probably should be expected. Many of these fictions (both pro and con) have originated from a divided medical community. Proponents of aquatics for young children tend to listen to more liberal or permissive medical experts, whereas opponents of aquatics for young children cite the opinions of more conservative and cautious medical experts. Many people automatically assume that medical experts are particularly knowledgeable about children in the water. However, little medical knowledge or research is applicable to the aquatic setting. Doctors often find themselves in the situation of swimming instructors: unwilling to say "I don't know the answer" when asked a question beyond their expertise. Unfortunately, when medical doctors guess at answers or present opinions as facts, their pronouncements are

The aquatic environment should contain objects that encourage interaction and exploration. (Large equipment shown is from the North Texas State Developmental Aquatics Movement Program [DAMP].)

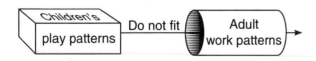

Figure 2.3   Children learn and structure the world differently than adults do.

given credibility because the doctors have medical expertise in other areas. For that reason, it is important that instructors of young children become aware of the health implications of aquatic environments.

Fiction #10: Young Children Are Put at Increased Risk of Disease, Injury, or Other Harmful Health Conditions When Placed in the Water

As with fictions about child development and teaching methods, there is precious little information about children's risk of disease from swimming.

Fact:

When the water supply is well maintained and other participants in the aquatic program are in good health, the risk to a child's health is minimal. Naturally, children in group situations, whether in child care or in extended families, might contract viral and bacterial diseases (Langendorfer, 1989). However, there is nothing inherent in the aquatic environment that makes it either more or less healthy than other environments for infants and young children.

Conclusion:

Any young child showing signs of disease (runny nose, fever, cough) should not participate in group activities, aquatic or otherwise. Swimming instructors, aquatic administrators, and maintenance personnel must strive to achieve safe and clean aquatic conditions for everyone.

Fiction #11: Swimming-Pool Water Acts as a "Culture" for Bacteria and Other Harmful Parasites That Cannot Be Killed by the Chlorine

Stories have been rife in the aquatic community about epidemics of giardosis and other diseases closing pools from coast to coast. People have even asked if AIDS can be contracted in swimming pools. It may be instructive to recall the panic of the 1950s, when people feared, mistakenly, that polio could be spread through swimming pools.

Fact:

Polio was not spread in the past, nor are giardia or AIDS being spread today, through swimming pools.

Aquatics activities can be safe and healthful if common sense is used.

Properly maintained public swimming pools (and this stipulation is crucial) are safe for everyone to enjoy (D'Alesio et al., 1981). Home and motel pools, hot tubs, beaches, and open water facilities, on the other hand, might not be so safe (Greensmith et al., 1988; Harter et al., 1984; Hopkins et al., 1981; Ratnam et al., 1986). Public pools must keep chlorine or bromine, pH, and bacterial, viral, and fungal levels to state minimums. Oftentimes open water and home facilities are not properly controlled or maintained and can be contaminated.

Conclusion:

Swimming pools are no more (and likely less) prone to spreading disease than any other environment. Chlorine or bromine is usually an effective agent for preventing the spread of disease *through* the water. However, physical contact in the water and pool environment can transmit disease just as it does in daycare and family settings.

Fiction #12: *Hyponatremia* Is a Common Malady Associated With Aquatics for Infants and Young Children

From all the publicity given *hyponatremia* (often called water intoxication) in newspapers, parents' magazines, and even Burton White's newest edition of *The First Three Years of Life*, it would appear that hyponatremia is epidemic in our infant and preschool swimming programs. Nothing could be farther from the truth.

Fact:

Only three cases of swimming-related infant hyponatremia have been reported in the medical literature (Bennett, Wagner, & Fields, 1983; Goldberg, Lightner, Morgan, & Kemberling, 1982; Kropp & Schwartz, 1982). All of these have been of a case-study or single-individual nature. Apparently hyponatremia is induced mainly in persons with a predisposition to kidney malfunction (i.e., whose kidneys do not filter out the excessive fluid rapidly enough). None of the reported cases have resulted in death or a permanent problem.

Conclusion:

Despite its high profile in the media, hyponatremia appears to be a rare condition that should concern only persons who are submerging relatively small and young infants a number of times over an extended period of time (e.g., during a long lesson period; see Figure 2.4). As a precaution, the CNCA has taken the moderate position of urging that there be no more than 6 submersions per child, per lesson, and that lessons be conducted in warm water and limited to 30 minutes or less (see CNCA Guidelines in appendix). Such precautions should prevent swimming-related incidence of hyponatremia.

Fiction #13: Forced Submersion Is the Cause of Hyponatremia and Other, Psychological Traumas to Young Infants

The CNCA and YMCA guidelines for preschool swimming both refer to "forced" submersion as a particular evil. This is a classic case of fiction. Because it conjures up the image of a parent or instructor repeatedly shoving a struggling and crying child underwater, no one has questioned the assumptions underlying it.

Fact:

A child may swallow various quantities of water whether submerged or not. The submerged child may swallow water whether the submersion is initiated by themselves or forcefully by an adult. A child may be scared by the water environment whether

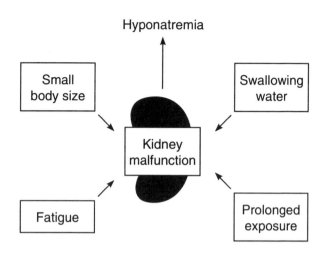

Figure 2.4 Water intoxication (hyponatremia) may result from numerous submersions, small body size, and a prolonged lesson period.

submerged or not and whether forced or not. Because the terms *force* and *submersion* have been used together, they have become powerfully associated. *Force* is a relative term. Any parent who submerges her or his child underwater is "forcing" the child under in the sense of overcoming the body's natural tendency to float, but this can be done gently and lovingly. Even a child's crying is not always a good index for evaluating the situation. Some children cry as a manipulation technique, and others cry from fatigue, chill, or the unexpected. And some terrified children might not even whimper!

Conclusion:

The aquatic environment for young children should be one of love, play, and fun. It certainly should not involve force, except in extreme cases where a child's immediate health or safety is at risk. Submersion itself may or may not be part of the fun, depending upon the parent, the child, and the situation. Submersions should have educational value and be controlled and limited.

Fiction #14: Swimming Increases Middle-Ear Infections in Young Children

One of the most frequent health-related conditions in early childhood is ear infections. For some reason, swimming and water have shared a great deal of the blame for the high incidence of early childhood ear infections.

Fact:

Young children, whether exposed to the water or not, have lots of middle-ear infections. The small size of the eustachian tube prevents adequate air exchange and drainage within the ear and results in bacterial infections in the middle-ear cavity. Doctors are divided as to the treatment. Many seem to believe that, with age-related growth, the eustachian tube will elongate and widen, and the condition will remediate. In the meantime, antibacterial medication or ear tubes are often prescribed (Arcand et al., 1984; El Silimy & Bradley, 1986). Some doctors even permit swimming, although usually not deep submersion, with ear tubes in place (Becker, Eckberg, & Goldware, 1987; Chapman, 1980). Several recent studies of large groups of children found that *outer*-ear infections are related to swimming in lakes and rivers but not to swimming in properly chlorinated pools (Osment, 1976). Five studies demonstrated conclusively that swimming with ear tubes, followed by antibacterial ear drops, did not cause further or more frequent infection (Arcand et al., 1984; Becker et al., 1987; Desterbeck et al., 1986; Siegel, 1987; Wight et al., 1987).

Conclusion:

Existing medical studies of young children's being in swimming pools supports allowing young children to swim. It is doubtful that swimming causes or even contributes to middle-ear infections, and it is equally doubtful that water exposure during an infection aggravates the condition.

THE NEED FOR INFORMATION!
CONCEPT 2.6

There is a strong need for concerted research efforts in aquatics for young children to provide additional definitive separation of *facts* from *fictions*.

A common characteristic among researchers is that they are never easily convinced that enough information has been gathered to conclusively prove any hypothesis. We are no exception. Until there is sufficient documentation to debunk fictions and support facts about aquatic readiness for young children, the gathering of information must continue.

Fiction #15: We Know Enough About Infant and Preschool Swimming and Should Not Clutter Our Minds With More Conflicting Information

Actually, we don't know any swimming instructor or parent who really believes that we don't need more information on this topic. However, all of us sometimes cling to our old beliefs as if we did believe Fiction #15.

Fact:

As demonstrated throughout this chapter, in many areas we simply have too little information about what we should be doing when teaching children to swim. We don't know much about *how*, *when*, *why*, or even *whether*. There appears to be no evidence that young children and infants can't or shouldn't have water experiences. However, we haven't established why we should recommend this experience or what constraints we should put on it.

Conclusion:

Until more studies have been conducted and replicated, we suggest following the CNCA *Guidelines for Aquatic Programs for Children Under Three Years of Age* (CNCA, 1985). As instructors, we should refrain from venturing guesses and half-truths about swimming for young children. As parents and instructors, we must cast a critical eye toward myths and fictions and be able to separate them from facts.

SUMMARY

We have presented information in this chapter that has, we hope, helped dispel some of the misinformation prevalent in the areas of child development, skill acquisition, teaching methods, and health and safety as they pertain to aquatic readiness. Throughout we have sought to convince you of the importance of relying on sound evidence instead of hearsay and tradition.

The next chapter points out the current poverty of our measurement instruments (i.e., tests) for swimming, especially for young children. It also highlights some important concerns for instructors who wish to use currently existing tests or formulate their own.

Chapter

3

Assessing Aquatic Behavior in Young Children

The number of preschool aquatic programs has increased dramatically over the past 2 decades. However, advances in assessing and testing swimming behavior in young children have not kept pace. In fact, until recently, no new swimming tests had been published in the past 3 decades. In addition, teaching ideas, techniques, games, and stunts have been surprisingly static for the past 50 years. The presence of a few traditional assessment instruments apparently has distracted both researchers and instructors from thinking about or working on new testing instruments.

Preschool aquatic programs generally have "piggy-backed" on preexisting agency learn-to-swim programs (e.g., American Red Cross, YMCA of the USA), and as a result they have used relatively traditional assessment approaches. A traditional approach to teaching and testing swimming essentially (a) uses a predetermined list of water skills to be learned; (b) incorporates a single teaching progression of those skill items; and (c) uses a posttest checklist for indicating their accomplishment. The completion of all selected skill items, often accompanied by a "combined test" that requires the swimmer to demonstrate several skills in sequence or combination, typically is required for certification by an agency program (see Figure 3.1).

NEW APPROACHES TO AQUATIC ASSESSMENT
CONCEPT 3.1

Many valuable things can result from taking an alternative approach to testing young children.

New approaches to aquatic assessment more directly aligned with a water competence model and an aquatic readiness curriculum can achieve each of the results shown in Figure 3.2. Improvements in aquatic readiness programming can be the overall result.

Increased Variety of Experiences

Adopting the water competence model and aquatic readiness approach for aquatic testing procedures can improve your teaching in many ways. First, it can dramatically increase the range of experiences your testing fosters. Instead of teaching for, and testing, a narrow selection of skills, such as specific skill combinations or advanced formal strokes, by attending to a wide variety of aquatic behaviors, you

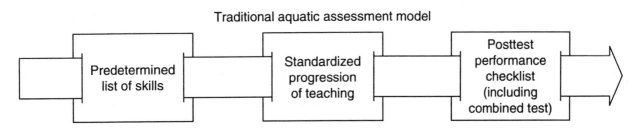

Figure 3.1 The traditional approach to teaching and testing swimming uses a fixed set of skills and a standardized teaching progression leading up to a posttest of skills.

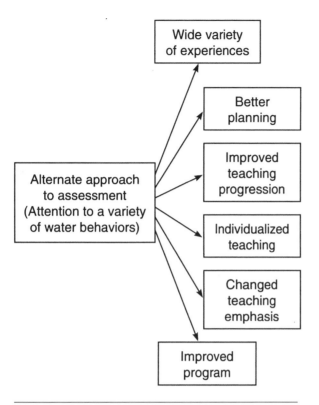

Figure 3.2 Deviating from traditional assessment procedures can have several important consequences.

can encourage children to develop a broad range of aquatic readiness skills, such as

- water entry,
- submersion,
- buoyancy,
- arm patterns,
- leg patterns,
- glides,
- twists and turns,
- directed splashing, and
- breath control.

Enhanced Program Planning

Second, assessment instruments can enhance the efficacy of your program planning. Better and more broadly conceived tests provide you with more pretest information about your swimmers' skills, which in turn can help you select or create better drills, activities, and games for class. With a better understanding of the great variety of possible skills, you can plan and implement broader learning experiences.

Improved Teaching Progressions

Third, the use of information about aquatic developmental sequences in your assessments can increase the validity of your teaching progressions. By keying your teaching progressions and activities to match actual student preferences for changing movement patterns, you can be more effective in helping children improve their swimming skills. More effective teaching progressions evolve from close approximation to naturally occurring developmental sequences (see the Aquatic Readiness Guide in chapter 4).

Improved Individualized Prescriptive Teaching

Fourth, alternative developmental assessment instruments that anticipate changes in form (movement patterns) as well as results (movement products) can provide important prescriptive information to help you individualize your teaching. Pretesting is particularly useful for individualizing instruction in swimming and water skills.

Shifted Teaching Emphasis

Fifth, improved testing can shift your focus away from mass instruction to individualized teaching. Swimming and water skills are enhanced faster and more effectively when individual needs are considered than under normalized techniques of mass instruction, so an important goal for preschool swimming instructors is to individualize their teaching methods.

Improved Measurement— Improved Programs

Finally, assessment instruments with good reliability and developmental validity improve the overall swimming program. When the tests are consistent and measure what they are intended to measure (i.e., changing swimming patterns), you can more successfully meet your program goals and participant needs, serving your children better and enhancing aquatic learning.

A SIMPLE INSTRUCTIONAL MODEL FOR AQUATIC ASSESSMENT AND TEACHING
CONCEPT 3.2

Assessment is intimately related to program planning and teaching procedures within a simple instructional model.

Often instructional models are complicated and unworkable. In this text, we propose a simple, easy-to-use model for integrating *testing*, *planning*, and *presenting* aquatic motor skills to young children. The components of the 4-P's model (Figure 3.3) are *assessment* (pretesting) and *evaluation* (posttesting), *planning*, and *presenting* (teaching). Pre- and posttesting occur at intervals, perhaps even daily, throughout the program as ongoing, formative evaluation. Posttesting also occurs formally at the end of a program session as individual summative evaluation or to evaluate the program. The components of the 4-P's curricular model can be arranged in simple linear order, or circularly, as in Figure 3.3, to indicate the dynamic interaction among components.

Integrating the 4 P's

Each phase or component of the program is an integral part of the program but also independent. Neither planning nor presenting can be effective before some type of assessment has been done. Testing, planning, and teaching for subsequent programs should wait until after posttest evaluation of the current program. The 4-P's model can be used not only as an overall program guide but also as an effective daily guide. For instance, according to the model as a program guide, pretesting should occur during the first program lessons. This initial prescriptive needs assessment is followed by long-range curricular planning (using an individualized education plan and an aquatic readiness guide—see chapter 4) and general program presentation. The final lesson periods should include some type of posttest or summative evaluation (Baumgartner & Jackson, 1991; Johnson & Nelson, 1986; Safrit, 1986), which may also serve as a program evaluation.

The 4-P's instructional model
for aquatic readiness

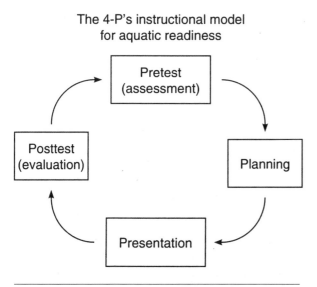

Figure 3.3 The 4-P's curricular model can be used to demonstrate the integration of testing and implementation of aquatic readiness activities.

4 P's for Organizing the Daily Lesson Plan

All presentation periods or lessons should have the same general organization: (a) testing participants for their proficiency in the particular skills for that day; (b) basing daily activity planning on those results; (c) presenting activities that will lead to desired behaviors; and (d) posttesting to determine if the behaviors were changed. Figure 3.4 shows a sample planning sheet using this model. Daily assessment and evaluation, as described, provide formative evaluation data that permit the instructor to maintain concern for student progress and to obtain information needed for long-term activity planning (Baumgartner & Jackson, 1991; Johnson & Nelson, 1986; Safrit, 1986).

DESIRABLE QUALITIES FOR AQUATIC MEASUREMENT INSTRUMENTS
CONCEPT 3.3

Aquatic assessment instruments must conform to measurement and evaluation standards, including adequate levels of validity, reliability, and objectivity.

To be accurate and useful, aquatic assessment instruments must possess certain important measurement qualities. The most important test characteristic is validity. The validity of a test is defined as how well it measures what it is intended to measure (Baumgartner & Jackson, 1991; Johnson & Nelson, 1986; Safrit, 1986). Therefore, to be valid, a test for infant and preschool aquatics must accurately measure all the basic components of aquatics and swimming. It also must do so in a developmentally appropriate way. A test also must report information consistently, or *reliably*, from child to child and from one test situation to another. Additionally, the test must be able to be used *objectively* by swimming instructors from one time to the next and from one swimming instructor to the next. Finally, the test should be able to be easily and concisely *administered* by aquatic instructors. All of these concepts are discussed in the following sections.

Validity of Preschool Swimming Tests

The most important quality of a preschool aquatic test is its validity. Before you use any test, determine the degree to which it actually measures the type of aquatic skill it is intended to measure. Validity is

---

Daily Activity Presentation Schedule

Student: __Jessie Thomas Agagale-ak__   Date: __Nov 19, 1992__

Targeted aquatic motor skill: __Level 3 - entry feet first__

Pretesting:

1) Position the child on the side of the pool and say, "Jump into the water" (repeat 4 times).

2) Classify each behavior as level 1, or level 2, or in transition.

Planning:

1) Present five requests for a level 2 jump from two different places on the side of the pool (practice variability).

2) Present five requests for a level 2 jump from different places on the equipment.

3) Present five requests for a level 3 jump from the side of the pool.

4) Present five requests for a level 3 jump from the equipment.

Presentation:

Use the sentence stem format for presenting requests:

1) "Can you jump into the water while I hold onto you?"

2) "Show me another way to jump in while I hold onto you."

3) "Can you jump in without my holding on?"

4) "Find a different way to jump in."

Record the performances on the table below

Record keeping	10 poolside jumps	10 equipment jumps
Level 2	|||	||||
Level 3	~~||||~~ ||	~~||||~~ |||

Posttesting: (Formative evaluation)

1) From the side of the pool, "Jump into the water." (repeat 10 times).

2) Record level 2 entries. Record level 3 entries.

Conclusion: In transition, additional L 2 & L 3 work needed.

Figure 3.4   A planning sheet for daily activities that is based on the 4-P's curricular model.

---

situation-specific. One test usually cannot fit all situations. For instance, a test of advanced formal strokes is probably not valid for testing young children. Young children are unlikely to have achieved such strokes, and such a test would fail to measure their actual aquatic or swimming skills.

The validity of a swimming test can be established in several ways. The most common, but also weakest, method is to establish content validity (also called "logical" or "face" validity). A swimming test with *content validity* for preschool aquatics is one that appears to measure preschool swimming. For instance, a preschool swimming test with content validity might include items such as water adjustment, buoyancy, propulsion, and entry, because these are commonly accepted beginner swimming skills (American Red Cross, 1981). Content validity is considered a weak type of validity because opinions about what comprise appropriate preschool swimming skills can vary from instructor to instructor.

Other, more robust forms of validity include criterion-related and construct validity. Establishing these requires some comparison to an existing test or to a set of constructs. For example, an aquatic test with *criterion-related validity* would be a test that compares favorably to an existing criterion or standard test recognized as the ultimate measure of the swimming skill being tested. Types of criterion-related validity include *predictive validity*, which is a test that accurately indicates future behavior or success, and *concurrent validity*, which measures the same or similar concept or value to another test. On the other hand, a test that is *construct valid* is a test that accurately measures some established concept or value. For example, water adjustment and buoyancy and breath control are proposed, but not validated, as instructional aquatic constructs within the 1992 American Red Cross Learn to Swim program (American Red Cross, 1992). The "catch-22" for establishing criterion-related or construct validity for a swimming test is the lack of established levels of validity among current tests. At this writing, no established criterion swim test or aquatic standard exists against which to compare a new swim test.

One method for establishing the construct validity of an aquatic test would be to use a group differences method in which it can be shown that children instructed in swimming score significantly higher on an aquatic test than a group of children who have not had swimming lessons (Safrit, 1986). Another possible statistical technique, factor analysis, compares scores on a number of different swimming items all administered to a group of children. A construct, or factor, is identified when certain grouped items all correlate relatively highly. For example, if a factor such as water adjustment (one of the skill requirement areas within the 1992 American Red Cross Learn To Swim Program) is a valid one, the water adjustment skill items in Levels 1 and 2 such as fully submerging the face, holding the breath for 3 seconds, or retrieving objects in chest-deep water all should be performed similarly (i.e., correlate fairly highly) among inexperienced swimmers.

A different type of construct validity for developmental skills, *developmental validity*, has been suggested by Roberton (1977; 1978; Roberton & Langendorfer, 1980). This is a hybrid form of concurrent and construct validity that uses criteria from Piagetian stage theory. A valid developmental sequence instrument is one in which different developmental levels of any skill demonstrate a regular order of change across all persons as well as stable forms of the behavior at any point in time (see Figure 3.5). For instance, a developmentally valid sequence for swimming skills may include changing forms of leg kicking or arm pulling (see chapter 4). Developmental

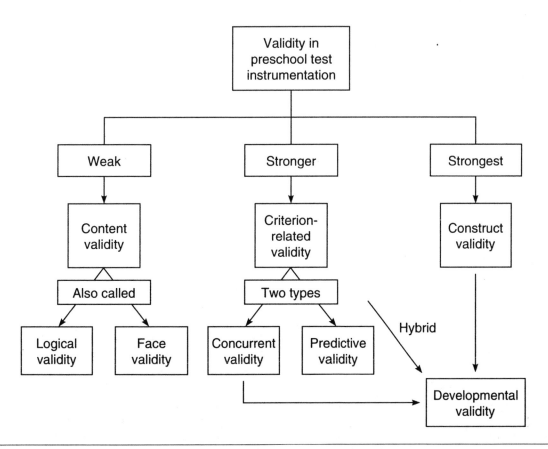

Figure 3.5 Developmental validity is a hybrid of two of the strongest types of validity.

validity is crucial to the developmental aquatic readiness perspective used throughout this text.

Reliability of Preschool Swimming Tests

The *reliability* of a swimming test refers to its consistency in measuring a swimming behavior, or how likely a child is to score similarly on a skill item if tested more than once. A swimming instructor can determine a preschool test's reliability in several ways (see Figure 3.6). The most common is to administer the test instrument more than once to the same children and examine the agreement among the scores for all the trials. The testing trials can be administered on different days or simply by having the students repeat the same test more than once on the same day ("multiple trials"). Another means of assessing the reliability of a test is by comparing it with one, two, or more similar versions of the test at one time, a variation of the concurrent validity technique. For example, the Red Cross Infant/Preschool Aquatic instrument and the YMCA *Y Skipper* instrument could both be given to a group of young children and the results on both compared to determine if both tests classify the children similarly. Finally, the reliability of the test can be determined by using the standard error of measurement, derived from the standard deviation (Safrit, 1986). One advantage of the standard error of measurement is that it uses only a single trial for each item, but it does require a scoring system that assigns a numerical rating to swimming behavior

rather than the more common pass-fail rating system.

For practical purposes, reliability in instructional aquatics probably should be assessed using either more than one trial of each test item or similar, redundant test items. Several items in the 1992 American Red Cross Learn to Swim Program make use of multiple trials (such as 3-second breath holding with face submersion vs. total head submersion) to assure that the child can actually perform the task (American Red Cross, 1992c). Level 2, Primary Skills, also uses several skills across components such as 3-second breath holding and 5-second prone floating (with face submerged) as a type of redundant test item to be assured that breath holding is mastered on a consistent basis (see Table 3.1). In traditional practice, passing a test has boiled down to performing a single skill on a single occasion. It is small wonder that instructors often remark that children seem to "forget" what they had learned in previous courses—they may never have learned it in the first place! A single trial is probably not a reliable measure of whether the child has learned to perform a skill.

Objectivity of Preschool Aquatic Tests and Testers

The degree to which different testers at different times can obtain similar scores for a given test is a measure of the *objectivity* of a swimming test's administration and testers. A swimming test may be both reliable and valid but fail to be accurate if different instructors are administering the test and

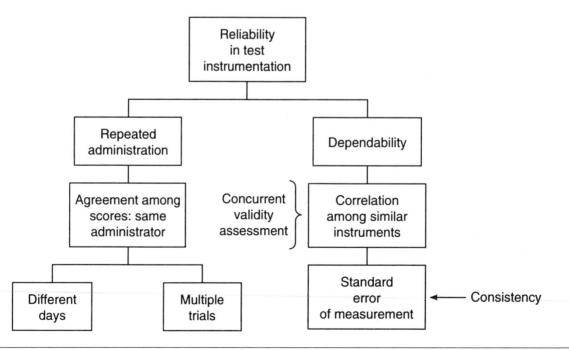

Figure 3.6   Several possibilities exist for determining the reliability of an assessment instrument.

Table 3.1 1992 American Red Cross Learn to Swim Program, Levels 1-3

Level 1: Water Exploration

| | Required skills | |
Component	Skill	Completion requirement
Water adjustment	Fully submerge face	Hold for 3 seconds
Buoyancy/breath control	Experience buoyancy	10 bounces—chest deep *or* 10 bobs with support
	Support float-front	Demonstrate
	Support float-back	Demonstrate
	Bubble blowing	Demonstrate
Water entry/exit	Independent enter and exit from pool w/ladder, ramp, steps	Demonstrate
Locomotion	Move through the water comfortably	Walk 5 yds in chest-deep water *or* walk 5 yds along side of pool with contact
	Supported kicking-front	Demonstrate
	Supported kicking-back	Demonstrate
	Introduction to alternating arm action	Walk 5 yds in chest-deep water, alternate arms *or* demonstrate alternating arms for 10 seconds holding overthrow trough
Personal safety and rescue	Learn basic water safety rules	Discuss importance of following rules
	Familiarity of getting help	Discuss safety persons and EMS
	Reaching assists—no equipment	Demonstrate
	Cramp release	Demonstrate
	Wear lifejacket on deck and enter shallow water	Demonstrate

Level 2: Primary Skills

| | Required skills | |
Component	Skill	Completion requirement
Water adjustment	Hold breath and fully submerge head	3 seconds
	Retrieve objects	Submerge and retrieve object—chest-deep water *or* submerge and retrieve object submerged at appropriate depth
	Orientation to deep water	Explore deep water with support
Buoyancy/breath control	Prone float or glide, unsupported, recovery	5 seconds
	Supine float or glide, unsupported, recovery	5 seconds
	Leveling off from a vertical position	Demonstrate
	Rhythmic breathing, with or without support	Bob 10 times, support optional
Water entry and exit	Step from side into chest deep water and recover from vertical	Demonstrate
	Get out over pool side	Demonstrate
Locomotion	Flutter kick on front	Demonstrate, support optional
	Flutter kick on back	Demonstrate, support optional
	Finning on back	Demonstrate
	Back crawl arm action	Demonstrate

(continued)

Table 3.1 *(continued)*

Level 2: Primary Skills

	Required skills	
Component	Skill	Completion requirement
	Combined stroke front, kick and alternate arms	5 yds
	Combined stroke back, kick and alternate arms	5 yds
Turns	Turning over, front to back	Demonstrate
	Turning over, back to front	Demonstrate
Personal safety and rescue	Float in life jacket with face out of water	Put on life jacket in shallow water and float for 1 minute face up *or* put on life jacket, enter water and float for 1 minute face up
	Perform reaching and extension assist from deck	Demonstrate
	Assist nonswimmer to feet	Demonstrate
	Become familiar with rescue breathing	Video or demonstration

Level 3: Stroke Readiness Skills

	Required skills	
Component	Skill	Completion requirement
Water adjustment	Retrieve object, eyes open, no support	Retrieve object from bottom in chest-deep water *or* retrieve object suspended at appropriate depth
Buoyancy/breath control	Bob submerging head completely	15 times in chest-deep water *or* 10 times with support
Water entry and exit	Bob in water slightly over head to travel to safety	Bob while moving to standing depth *or* bob to side of pool
Water entry and exit	Jump into deep water from side of pool	Demonstrate
	Dive from side of pool from kneeling or compact position	Dive from either position
Locomotion	Prone glide with push-off	Demonstrate 2 bodylength
	Supine glide with push-off	Demonstrate 2 bodylength
	Coordinate arm stroke for front crawl with breathing to side	Swim front crawl, breathe front or side, 10 yards
	Coordinate back crawl	Swim back crawl, 10 yards
	Elementary backstroke	Elementary backstroke kick for 10 yards
Turns	Reverse direction while swimming on front	Demonstrate
	Reverse direction while swimming on back	Demonstrate
Personal Safety and Rescues	Learn safe diving rules	Discussion
	Tread water	Demonstrate
	Jump into deep water with lifejacket on	Demonstrate
	HELP position	Demonstrate, 1 minute
	HUDDLE position	Demonstrate, group of three for 1 minute
	Learn how to open airway	Demonstrate correct technique

Note. Adapted from *Water Safety Instructor Manual* (pp. 91-101) by American Red Cross, 1992, St. Louis: Mosby.

getting different results. Alternatively, if an instructor is not consistent in how she or he administers the same test from time to time, the objectivity of the test scores also is flawed.

You should check your objectivity on a regular basis. In a clinical or research setting, objectivity is usually measured through various sophisticated correlational techniques. In a practical setting, two instructors should independently test several children and compare their scores. They can come up with a simple percentage of agreement to judge how objectively they scored the results. If a videotape of the children is made during testing, each instructor can view the tape and rate the children a second time to determine how consistent she or he is with herself or himself. Ideally, a preschool aquatic instructor should be consistent with other instructors (interrater objectivity) and with themselves at another time (intrarater objectivity).

Test Administration for Preschool Swimming Tests

A final measurement consideration for swimming tests is the set of *administrative* criteria. Such things as amount of time, expense, type of equipment, and amount of specialized training needed by instructors all must be considered regarding a preschool swimming test. Tests should be concise and economical in terms of time and expense. Most practical field tests limit the amount and type of equipment needed as well as the extent of specialized training required by instructors. Because most aquatic instructors receive special testing experience as part of their training, they normally have a good background for administering traditional tests. They may not be familiar with developmental sequence and motor pattern tests.

Too often, instructors choose tests on the basis of administrative concerns. Preference is given to short tests requiring no special equipment or training by the instructor. This is unfortunate. Validity, reliability, and objectivity are much more important criteria than administrative concerns.

Swimming instructors developing or using swimming tests must evaluate them for *validity*, *reliability*, *objectivity*, and *administrability*. Aquatic tests that lack these characteristics have little value as assessment instruments and therefore are not useful for the purposes of planning, presenting, and evaluating as suggested in the 4-P's curricular model.

HOW DO CURRENT TESTS MEASURE UP?
CONCEPT 3.4

Traditional aquatic assessment procedures often fail to consider basic measurement concepts of validity, reliability, and objectivity.

This section considers several aquatic instruments used nationally in the United States, including the American Red Cross Beginner and Infant/Preschool Aquatic programs and YMCA Progressive, Tadpole, and Y Skippers programs. We will evaluate them according to the measurement criteria discussed in the previous section.

Aquatic swimming instruments rarely have been constructed to have the important measurement characteristics of validity, reliability, or objectivity. In fact, the creators of preschool or beginning swimming tests have failed even to address any of these measurement issues (American Red Cross, 1981; Baumgartner & Jackson, 1991). They seem to put a premium on ease of administration and similarity of the test routine to the skills taught.

Are Tests Valid?

Most aquatic programs apparently rely on the face, or content, validity of their instruments, even though validity is not usually even mentioned by name. This means that the proposed swimming tests are taken to measure what they are intended to measure simply because they appear to measure it. The tests are usually developed by groups of experienced aquatic instructors and administrators who serve as the expert panel for established content validity. To the extent that this panel of experts does a thorough job, levels of validity may be adequate. Because this form of validity is the weakest, however, many biasing influences can pervade the tests and lower their validity. At present most preschool and beginner aquatic instruments have equal, but potentially low, levels of validity.

Are Tests Reliable?

In addition, beginning swimming tests seldom mention or employ any means for determining reliability. Neither the American Red Cross's *Swimming and Aquatic Safety* (1981) nor *Water Safety Instructors' Manual* (1992) refer to reliability for the former

Beginner swimming tests nor the 1992 Learn to Swim program requirements. There is mention in *Swimming and Aquatics Safety* to retesting, but its purpose is "to pass deserving students" (p. 18), which only indirectly addresses the notion that a single trial test may not produce reliable measurement. The Red Cross's *Water Safety Guide for Training Instructors* has an appendix for videotaping swimming skills, but its purpose is to enhance student learning by providing knowledge of performance feedback rather than to assist instructors with improving reliability.

Baumgartner and Jackson do mention validity and reliability for a Jackson and Pettinger (1969) "swimming achievement for intermediate swimmers," a more advanced stroke evaluation instrument. Safrit (1986) mentions validity and reliability for only the Jackson, Jackson, and Frankiewicz (1979) crawl swimming endurance test. She makes no mention of other tests, especially for young children. This apparent lack of instrument reliability casts doubt upon both the validity and the consistency of our measurements of children's swimming behavior.

Are Instructors Objective?

No traditional aquatic tests we surveyed cited levels of objectivity. The potential seriousness of this omission can be highlighted by reference to the annual reports of the American Red Cross. From 1982 to 1985, authorizations for ARC water safety instructors ranged from 181,241 to 188,990 annually. These authorized instructors conducted from 305,873 to 340,337 water safety courses and awarded over 2.1 million swimming certificates each year (ARC, 1985). That just one national agency contacts this large number of instructors and swimmers each year suggests the potential magnitude of the objectivity problem. Without information regarding how accurately and efficiently these instructors are administering the tests and awarding the certificates, there could be extreme problems with quality control and instructional effectiveness.

Are Swimming Progressions Developmentally Valid?

Finally and not surprisingly, traditional aquatic instruments have failed to consider the developmental validity of their progressive (i.e., sequential) programs (Harrod & Langendorfer, 1990; Reid, Bruya, & Langendorfer, 1985; Roberton, 1977, 1978). As explained previously, *developmental validity* is the degree to which proposed sequences follow the actual developmental order of changes. Tradi-

tional swimming instruments rarely have considered developmental changes, even though they have presented both their skills and their program levels in a "progressive," or sequential, format. For instance, the ARC has long used a participation certificate indicating that face submersion precedes prone floating, which in turn precedes back floating. The YMCA Tadpole program, on the other hand, suggests that leg kicking should occur before arm movements (paddling) and that face submersion follows those activities (see Table 3.2). Both the ARC and the YMCA programs suggest that water entry progresses from climbing into the water to jumping to forward diving. Even though all these progressions are proposed throughout the materials, nowhere is the developmental validity of these progressions mentioned or tested. In fact, the Red Cross (1981) suggests that "the order in which [beginner swimming skills] are taught can vary. Instructors may elect to teach all skills in the prone position first, or they may teach them as listed. The manner in which they are taught and learned will also vary according to the teaching approach used" (p. 133). Such admission of variability suggests a lack of developmental validity, despite the impression given that skills are progressive.

In a seminal research study, Harrod (Harrod, 1991; Harrod & Langendorfer, 1990) demonstrated that in fact the Red Cross Beginner skill order was far from developmentally valid. Using a scalogram technique to test the order of beginner skill acquisition, she found that beginner swimmers preferred to learn beginning aquatic skills in an order that deviated widely from the suggested Red Cross progression. This research demonstrated a relatively simple but comprehensive way to determine if future proposed teaching progressions match children's preferred order of acquisition.

TESTING INDEPENDENT OF PROGRAM CONTENT
CONCEPT 3.5

Aquatic programs should use assessments that are independent of instructional procedures.

Most swimming instructors undoubtedly are familiar with aspects of typical swimming programs offered by such national agencies as the American Red Cross and YMCA (American Red Cross, 1981, 1988, 1992c; deBarbadillo & Murphy, 1973; YMCA, 1987). The ARC and YMCA swimming programs present swimming skills as traditional motor performance or sport skill tests mentioned previously (Johnson & Nelson, 1986). They either fail to include any assessment instrument at all, as with the YMCA

Tadpole and Y Skippers programs (see Tables 3.2 and 3.3), or they use standard product or result scores, as the ARC Beginner course does, requiring, for example, a prone float for 5 seconds or underwater breath holding for 3 seconds (see Table 3.1) as scores of swimming skill. With these types of product scores, little or no emphasis is given to the form with which the skill is performed. Also, there is no developmental information regarding how the skills should change in form as they are acquired. Instead,

Table 3.2   YMCA Tadpole Program

Teaching techniques and procedures

---

1. Holding the child for towing (p. 25)—description of what the teacher does to tow the child through the water

2. Leg movement on front (p. 26)—description of the teacher's actions and several forms of flutter kicking that may be observed

3. Arm movement for dog paddle (p. 28)—description of how the instructor should move the child's hand to promote arm movement

4. Swimming the dog paddle (p. 30)—description of how to release support of the child to form independent locomotion using dog paddle

5. Arm and leg movement for crawl (p. 31)—describes the crawl as being the next "step" beyond dog paddle in swimming evolution

6. Leg movement on back (p. 32)—stresses the similarity between back and front flutter kicking

7. Floating and gliding (p. 33)—describes the importance of floating and gliding, but no description of the skill itself

8. Learning to breathe while swimming (p. 35)—description of a teaching progression from momentary breath holding to rhythmic breathing used during stroking

9. Developing rhythm of movement (p. 36)—stresses the prerequisites for developing smooth, skilled swimming stroking

10. Treading water (p. 37)—describes treading action and its role as a "relaxer" and change of pace

11. Water entries—jumping, sitting, and standing dives (p. 37)—describes some activities that can encourage these forms of water entry

12. Rescue methods (p. 40)—examples of basic reaching, extension, and throwing rescues for preschoolers

---

Note. Adapted from *Teaching the Very Young to Swim* (pp. 24-42) by J. deBarbadillo and M.M. Murphy, 1972, New York: Association Press.

Table 3.3   YMCA Y Skippers Program

Goals for the Under-3 Program

Level 1 Shrimps
• To introduce infants and parents to an aquatic environment
• To encourage appropriate expectations by parents
• To introduce basic aquatic safety
• To provide positive parent-child experiences and relationships

Level 2 Kippers
• To provide a positive aquatic environment for infants
• To introduce infants to basic water skills such as kicking, breath control, and body control
• To introduce and emphasize basic aquatic safety
• To have fun in the water using toys and flotation devices

Level 3 Inias
• To encourage the child's independence in the water
• To encourage purposeful movements in the water and in response to visual or verbal cues
• To introduce or enhance basic aquatic safety
• To provide parent and child with shared experiences, socialization, and interaction

Level 4 Perch
• To encourage the child's exploration of the aquatic environment
• To encourage children to propel themselves through the water
• To teach basic aquatic and boating safety, emphasizing parental responsibility
• To begin transition to aquatics for children 3 to 5 years of age

---

Goals for the 3-Through-5 Program

Level 1 Pike
• To explore the environment
• To adjust to a group situation
• To move through the water independent of adult support, with a flotation device
• To learn basic water and boating safety

Level 2 Eels
• To move toward independence
• To learn basic swimming techniques
• To introduce PFDs and boating safety

Level 3 Rays
• To voyage into confidence
• To increase endurance
• To be introduced to boating and water safety

Level 4 Starfish
• To be creatively challenged
• To develop water competence

(continued)

Table 3.3 *(continued)*

Goals for the 3-Through-5 Program

- To learn more about basic assists, boating, and water safety
- To prepare to move to the YMCA Progressive Swimming Program

---

Skills for parents and children

Entering and exiting the pool
Front towing
Knee cradle
Arm and leg movements
Back cradle
Use of PFDs
Getting wet
Back towing
Launch
Climbing out of the pool

Skills for children

Towing
Leg movement on front
Arm movement for the paddle stroke
Doing the paddle stroke
Arm and leg movement for the crawl stroke
Leg movement on the back
Finning
Floating and float gliding
Survival float
Elementary backstroke
Breathing while swimming
Rotary breathing
Developing rhythm of movement
Treading water
Jumping into the pool
Sitting dive
Surface dive
Swimming underwater
Somersaults
Teaching rescue methods

Note. Adapted from *Y Skippers* (pp. 23, 30-34, 121, 125-138) by YMCA of the USA, 1987, Champaign, IL: Human Kinetics.

all skill changes are assumed to result from the teacher's intervention and teaching practices and not the learner's own sequences of change (see chapter 4).

A major deficit in current swimming skills tests is the lack of an assessment instrument that is independent from the presentation methods and progres-

Table 3.4 YMCA Progressive Swimming Skills

Polliwog (beginner) level skills

1. Endurance swim (jump into shallow water, swim 60-75 ft with flotation or 20 ft without flotation)
2. Survival float (stay afloat for 1 min with flotation)
3. Lifesaving skills (elementary nonswimming throwing assists)
4. Personal safety skills (use of a PFD)

Minnow (advanced beginner) level skills

1. Combination swim (front dive, swim 60-75 ft front crawl with rotary breathing and return 60-75 ft with back crawl)
2. Survival float (3 min on front)
3. Nonswimming assists (reaching and extension rescues)
4. Mouth-to-mouth resuscitation
5. Safety swim (jump into deep water, swim 30 ft on front, tread and scull 10 s, return to starting point, return flutter back scull)

Note. From *Progressive Swimming and Springboard Diving Program* (pp. 39-41) by L.C. Arnold and R.W. Freeman (Eds.), 1972, New York: National YMCA Program Materials.

sions. The teaching materials and the tests of current preschool aquatic programs are virtually one and the same. For example, both the YMCA Polliwog and Minnow combined tests (see Table 3.4) within the Progressive Swimming Program and the Red Cross's Water Exploration and Primary Skills levels merely reflect the skills taught in their teaching progressions. The lack of separation of assessment and presentation of activities probably explains the failure to examine the measurement elements mentioned previously, because the original developers never considered their programs to be "tests" and therefore ignored test construction.

The 4-P's curricular model stresses the integration, but independence, of assessment, planning, and teaching activities. Nevertheless, failure to maintain each component's independence obscures the unique purposes and functions of each. By confounding what is taught with what is tested, the instructor does not adequately focus on either component. Combining testing and teaching also reveals a lack of planning and individualizing of instruction. Failure to adequately plan for individual differences among students results in a standardized teaching approach that ignores the uniquenesses and developmental differences of each student. For example, the recently published Infant/Preschool Aquatic Program from the American Red Cross presents a fairly standardized set of skills that cross three age levels. No attempt is made to separate assessment/evaluation from teaching (see Table 3.5).

Table 3.5   American Red Cross Infant/Preschool Aquatic Program Progressions

Infant/parent level

Water adjustment
Water entry
Front kick
Bubble blowing
Front (prone) glide
Underwater exploration
Back float
Arm movement, prone position
Combined skills, prone position
Safety skills (rolling over, parent safety-reaching assists)
Water exit

Toddler/parent level

Water adjustment
Water entry (jumping in, assisted to unassisted)
Front kick with flotation support
Bubble blowing
Prone glide
Underwater exploration
Back float
Back glide
Arm movement, back position
Combined skills, back position
Safety skills (PFDs, changing positions, parent safety)
Water exit (unassisted)

Preschool level

Water adjustment
Water entry (jumping in, assisted to unassisted)
Front kick
Breath control (rhythmic bobbing, rotary breathing)
Front glide
Front float
Underwater exploration
Back float
Back glide
Combined skills, back position
Safety skills (changing directions, bobbing to safety,
    treading water, PFDs, combined safety skills, rescues,
    rescue breathing)

Note. Adapted from *Infant and Preschool Aquatic Program: Instructor's Manual* (pp. 58-96) by the American Red Cross, 1988, Washington, DC: Author.

As we proposed in this chapter's introductory remarks about the 4-P's model (see Figures 3.3 and 3.4), each component of the curriculum has unique emphases and functions. Assessment must go on throughout the instructional process but ideally should be separate from it. Instruction must rely upon the assessment information but must involve much more than simply testing. The process of planning uniquely links assessment to instruction, whereas evaluation provides information from the instructional process for further assessment, planning, and presentation.

RECENT RESEARCH IN AQUATIC ASSESSMENT
CONCEPT 3.6

Recent aquatic research provides a basis for revising aquatic assessment practices.

Aquatic researchers have begun to investigate aquatic motor skill behaviors in young children. Recent observations indicate that children acquire aquatic motor skills in ways that can be measured both validly and reliably. They also demonstrate that with sufficient practice and collaboration, instructors can be highly objective in their assessments. These new studies promise to alter and improve current aquatic assessment practices for young children. Ultimately, knowledge of the unique way that aquatic skills can change over time can enhance swimming instruction in programs for young children.

Linking Motor Development and Preschool Aquatics

The motor developmental literature provides ample evidence that motor skills change over time in both pattern and product scores (Roberton & Halverson, 1984). A number of studies have identified robust motor sequences for such skills as throwing (Roberton, 1977, 1978; Roberton & Langendorfer, 1980), striking (Harper & Struna, 1973; Langendorfer, 1987c), hopping (Halverson & Williams, 1985; Roberton & Halverson, 1984), and rolling (Roberton & Halverson, 1984; Williams, 1980). There is growing evidence that aquatic skills progress similarly through ordered motor sequences (Erbaugh, 1978, 1980; Langendorfer, 1984a; Langendorfer et al., 1987; McGraw, 1939; Oka, Okamoto, Yoshizawa, Tokuyama, & Kumamoto, 1978; Reid, Bruya, & Langendorfer, 1985; Wielki & Houben, 1983). Figure 3.7 illustrates some of these theories, which are described in the following paragraphs.

The McGraw Swimming Sequence

McGraw (1935/1975, 1939) provided the first evidence for regular ordered changes in infant aquatic behaviors (see Figure 3.7a). She demonstrated a shift from stereotypic "reflexive" swimming of the newborn to the "disorganized or struggling behavior" of the 1st-year infant and another shift to the intentional or deliberate kicking and paddling motions of

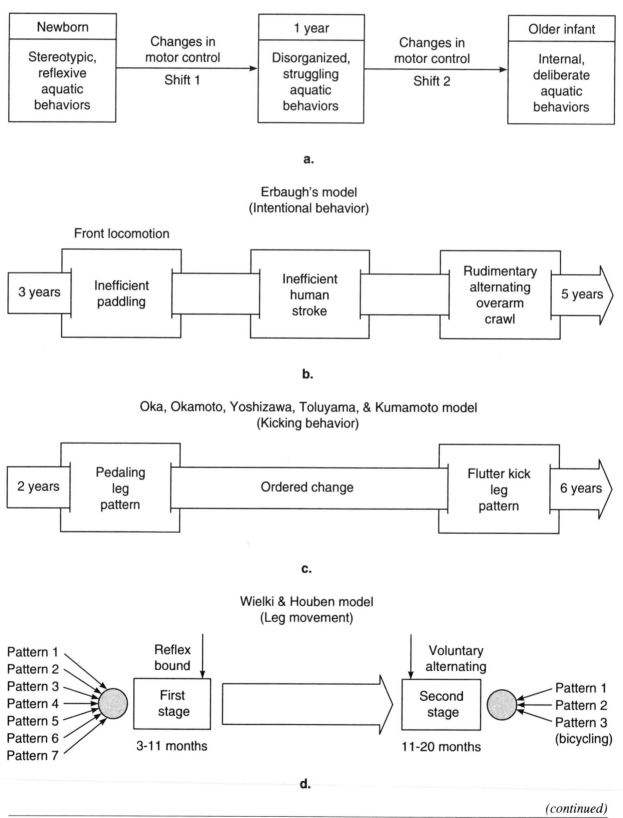

Figure 3.7 Models of regular, ordered changes in aquatic motor behavior.

(continued)

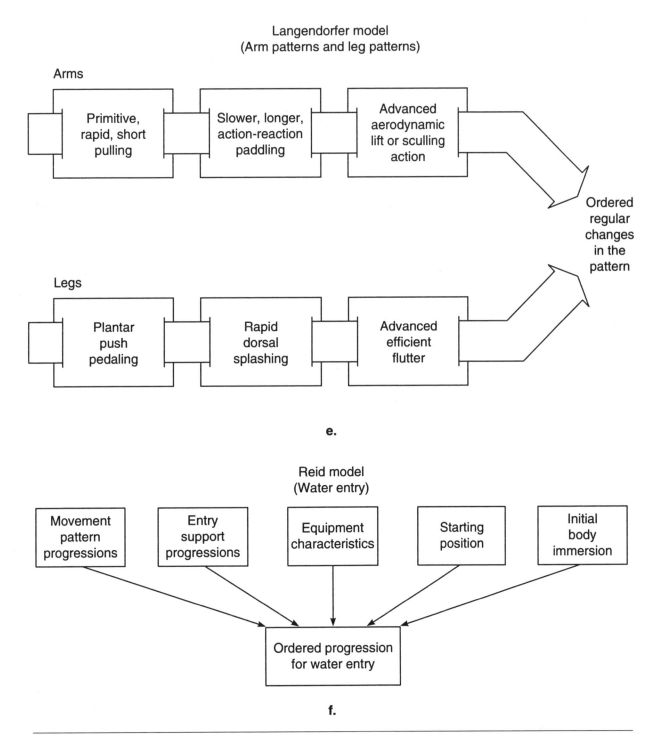

Figure 3.7 *(continued)*

the older, water-experienced infant (McGraw, 1939). McGraw hypothesized that these aquatic changes reflected alterations in neural control structures. She claimed that shifting neural control sites could be generalized to explain changes in other motor activities such as prone and erect locomotion, rolling, and sitting behaviors (McGraw, 1945/1963). Because she was not primarily interested in aquatic behavior,

McGraw did not attempt to observe further changes in the intentional phase of swimming.

Erbaugh's Developmental Aquatic Instrument

Recently, Erbaugh (1978, 1980, 1981, 1986a) extended McGraw's sequence by demonstrating sequential changes in intentional aquatic skills in preschool children. She developed an aquatic assessment instrument for preschoolers in which aquatic skills could be measured validly, reliably, and objectively (Erbaugh, 1978, 1980). Using this instrument, she noted a series of differences in aquatic motor patterns and accomplishments across age groups (see Figure 3.7b). For example, in the front locomotion category, the typical arm pattern of "inefficient paddling" action for the 3-year-olds differed from the "efficient human stroke" and rudimentary attempts at "alternating overarm crawl" arm actions in 5-year-olds. Similar kinds of differences were observed in other aquatic categories (Erbaugh, 1978, 1980).

Erbaugh (1981, 1986a) subsequently observed that her hypothesized changes in aquatic movement patterns for young children were verified longitudinally between the ages of 3 and 5 years. In addition to changes in product scores such as distance able to swim and amount of independence from teachers in water, she observed developmental changes in arm and leg patterns and body and head positions. Importantly, Erbaugh observed that some of these aquatic changes were sequential in nature (Erbaugh, 1981, 1986a). The younger and less experienced 3-year-olds predominantly moved through the water with a "leg-dominated" pattern, whereas the older and more experienced 5-year-olds used arm patterns, particularly with an "overarm crawl" pattern.

Sequential Changes in Kicking (Japanese Model)

In a developmental vein similar to that of Erbaugh, a Japanese group (Oka et al., 1978) identified regular age-related shifts in the muscular organization and qualitative patterns of leg "kicking" motions as well as increased distance of locomotion across the preschool years. In particular, they noted a pattern shift from the "pedaling" swimming action of 2-year-olds to a "flutter kick" action used predominantly by 6-year-olds (see Figure 3.7c).

Sequential Changes in Leg Movement (Wielki and Houben Model)

Wielki and Houben (1983) observed 40 infants kicking in the water over a period of 4 years and described seven patterns of aquatic leg movements within two stages (see Figure 3.7d). Movements in the first stage (four separate action patterns) demonstrated by infants 3 to 11 months old were considered reflexbound, similar to McGraw's reflexive phase. They

were described as "violent and random in nature" (p. 67) and were relatively stereotypic and repetitive. All types disappeared over the period from 5 to 10 months. The three types of movements in the second stage were voluntary and alternating. They emerged in infants aged 11 to 20 months and were more efficient than the reflexive types in propelling the infant in a prone position. The most advanced type was described as a "bicycling" motion (pp. 67-68).

Developmental Aquatic Sequence Changes (Langendorfer Model)

Langendorfer (1984a, 1987d; Balan & Langendorfer, 1988a, 1988b; Langendorfer et al., 1987) has hypothesized changes in movement components (arm action, leg action, body position) for supine and prone aquatic locomotion. These observations appear remarkably consistent with both the Erbaugh and the Japanese observations. The arm action sequence was hypothesized to shift from primitive rapid, short, pulling motions to slower, but longer, "action-reaction" paddling movements to an advanced aerodynamic "lift" or "sculling" action. Similarly, leg actions were hypothesized to change from "plantar push" (i.e., pedaling) to "rapid dorsal splashing" to an advanced "efficient fluttering." Finally, he hypothesized decreases in horizontal body position angle in the water in both prone and supine locomotion actions (see Figure 3.7e).

Changes in Aquatic Entry (Reid Model)

Most recently, in a continuing longitudinal study, Reid and Bruya (1984; Reid et al., 1985) proposed and then identified sequences in water entry skills (see Figure 3.7f). Categories in entry behaviors included movement pattern progressions, entry support progressions, equipment characteristics, starting positions, and degree of initial body part immersion. Frequency of occurrences based on 100 videotaped trials suggested that feetfirst entries, supported either directly by large equipment or by teachers, were the easiest methods for young children to use for initial entry into the aquatic environment. The data also suggested that the young children in the sample were more likely to enter after some body part was already wet or immersed in the water. The hypothesis from the data is that these frequently occurring behaviors are developmentally most primitive. Age and skill differences, however, have not yet been identified to confirm any developmental trends.

SUMMARY

This chapter has proposed a unique new curricular model for aquatic readiness. We also have reviewed the basic concepts of assessment and measurement that should be applied when testing young children's aquatic skills. These basic measurement concepts of validity, reliability, objectivity, and administrability were then used to evaluate the adequacy of existing traditional and more recent developmental aquatic tests for young children. The traditional tests used by the Red Cross and YCMA either lack assessment instruments per se or link them directly to the teaching progression. The more recent developmental instruments were found to have attended to and achieved more satisfactory levels of validity, reliability, and objectivity.

In conclusion, assessing changes in movement patterns and aquatic behaviors provides a better understanding of the way aquatic movements naturally emerge and develop. This understanding can be used to improve the quality of aquatic assessment for young children and enhance the young child's aquatic learning environment.

The next chapter operationalizes some of the developmental assessment ideas proposed in this chapter. It presents a battery of developmental changes in fundamental aquatic motor patterns that serve as assessment instruments for young children. In addition, an aquatic readiness guide is provided to help you or the parent in planning appropriate presentation experiences for young children based on their assessed developmental levels and needs. Subsequent chapters focus on how you can use this understanding of changing aquatic movements to improve the aquatic learning environment.

Chapter

4

Aquatic Readiness Assessment: Developmental Changes in Aquatic Motor Patterns

To adequately instruct young children in aquatic readiness, you need to know the information we have discussed in earlier chapters: the water competence model and a developmental perspective on teaching aquatics (chapter 1); various facts and fictions of infant and preschool swimming (chapter 2); and the 4-P's instructional model along with important measurement principles for use in aquatic assessment (chapter 3). This chapter supplements chapter 3 with concrete examples of changes in the components of aquatic movement patterns in the form of a new assessment instrument: the Aquatic Readiness Assessment (ARA). This chapter also provides checklists and illustrations to insure that you assess aquatic skill changes objectively. Finally, to encourage you to use the developmental assessment information obtained through the ARA, we present a novel "readiness guide" for planning and selecting appropriate activities and games.

The Aquatic Readiness Assessment outlines a battery of developmental aquatic tests that instructors can use to assess young children's beginning skills (pretest), their progress (formative evaluation), and the outcomes of their learning (summative evaluation, or posttest). Some components of the ARA have established levels of validity, reliability, and objectivity. Others are hypothesized and are currently being tested and evaluated to establish these measurement characteristics. We will indicate the state of each instrument to assure you have accurate information.

DEVELOPMENTAL AQUATIC MOTOR SEQUENCES
CONCEPT 4.1

Developmental aquatic motor sequences provide crucial programming information for aquatic readiness.

Motor developmental researchers have demonstrated that motor skills change in regular ordered progressions over time, with or without formal instruction. These "motor sequences" have been demonstrated for a number of skills, including throwing, striking, jumping, hopping, catching, kicking, and rolling (Halverson & Williams, 1985; Langendorfer, 1987b, 1987c; Roberton, 1978; Roberton & Halverson, 1984; Roberton & Langendorfer, 1980; Seefeldt, 1980; Williams, 1980). In chapter 3 we illustrated examples of aquatic motor skills that progress through motor sequences in a manner similar to fundamental motor skills (Balan & Langendorfer, 1988a, 1988b; Erbaugh, 1978, 1980, 1981, 1986a; Langendorfer, 1984a, 1987d; Langendorfer et al., 1987; Reid & Bruya, 1984; Wielki & Houben, 1983).

Motor Sequences as Individualized Educational Plans

Motor sequences provide an important type of assessment instrument. Because motor sequences are hierarchically ordered changes in movement patterns, knowledge of how a child is currently moving tells the instructor both what behaviors the child has already accomplished and what he or she has yet to accomplish (Roberton, 1990). Langendorfer (1984a) has suggested that in this way motor sequences are like Individualized Educational Plans (IEPs), which instructors use to prepare prescriptive programming for children with handicapping conditions. Instead of limiting IEPs to adapted aquatics, however, we are suggesting that they are useful in preparing lesson plans for *all* children.

Motor Sequences in Prescriptive Teaching

In chapter 3 we suggested that traditional aquatic programs and their assessment instruments fail to consider *change*. Usually aquatic tests have set a particular criterion for achievement, and to "pass" a particular course, children have to achieve that criterion. A *motor sequence* test sets sequential criteria that a child progressively achieves. Not only is this a more developmentally valid approach and a more realistic testing approach, but the graded steps also provide progressive teaching information to the instructor.

The basic rule of thumb for programming using motor sequences is to provide instruction to any child at one level (stage, phase, or step) above their current level of functioning. Instead of using the most advanced or elite level of behavior as the expected criterion, the instructor progressively draws the child to it, one step at a time. For example, instead of teaching young children the bent-arm overwater recovery version of the competitive crawl stroke, one ought to start out with the dog paddle, progress to a human or beginner stroke, and finally to a rudimentary crawl stroke (Erbaugh, 1978; Langendorfer, 1984a). This progressive approach permits the child's own natural tendencies, as demonstrated by research, to be augmented by the instructor and the aquatic environment.

COMPONENTS OF THE AQUATIC READINESS ASSESSMENT INSTRUMENT
CONCEPT 4.2

The basic motor components of aquatic readiness include water entry, breath control, buoyancy and body position, arm actions, leg actions, and combined movements.

Developmental researchers have suggested that, to be valid, developmental assessment instruments (i.e., motor sequences) must be *inclusive* and *comprehensive* (Halverson & Williams, 1985; Langendorfer, 1987b; Roberton, 1977). This means that any testing instrument must be able to detect and measure *all* important behaviors, and that *all* behaviors listed within the instrument are both *important* and *regularly observed in children*. This suggests that no behaviors are left out, nor are extraneous behaviors included.

In addition, developmentally valid sequences also must show a robust order of change over time, but at any one point in time they also must be relatively stable and consistent. In other words, in a valid sequence, most children will show the same progression of change (e.g., from dog paddle to human stroke to rudimentary crawl, etc.). Each child, however, will mainly show only one or two types of behavior from that sequence across a number of trials at any time. For example, in a valid sequence a child would only be able to do a dog paddle or human stroke and not more advanced forms of crawl.

The behaviors listed in Concept 4.2 and explained in the paragraphs that follow have been identified and included from several existing aquatic programs or instruments. As a result, we both assume *content validity* and have established *developmental (construct) validity* where appropriate.

WATER ORIENTATION AND ADJUSTMENT
CONCEPT 4.3

A child's orientation and adjustment to the water can change in a regular ordered sequence from strong, debilitating fear to no reluctance or fear.

As we discussed in chapter 1, water and movement in the water present a markedly different environment to naive individuals than does land. Most swimming instruments and programs of instruction acknowledge the importance of water orientation and adjustment (American Red Cross, 1981, 1992a; Murray, 1981; YMCA, 1987). None, however, have addressed water orientation and adjustment directly as assessment items. The importance of orientation and adjustment to the water lies in the fact that it is likely that none of the other components of aquatic performance will be achieved until an intermediate or advanced level of adjustment is reached by a swimmer.

We have hypothesized a developmental sequence for water orientation and adjustment based on our own experiences and by using the way that water orientation and adjustment is most commonly used in the literature (American Red Cross, 1981, 1992c). Most of the citations use either water entry or submersion skill items as indication for having achieved adjustment and orientation to the aquatic environment. As you can discern from the decision rules in Table 4.1, we have relied on the person's reaction to initial entry into the water as our criterion for assessing water orientation and adjustment. Someone too fearful to even enter is categorized as level 1 while the person lacking reluctance or fear receives the advanced level 3 rating (see Table 4.1).

Validity—None has been established; content validity cited.
Reliability—None has been established.
Objectivity—None has been established.

Table 4.1   Water Orientation and Adjustment Component of the Aquatic Readiness Assessment

Step/level	Decision rule
1. No voluntary entry; demonstrates fear of the water	Obvious expressions of fear including crying or refusal to enter water.
2. Voluntary entry with hesitancy but minimum fear of the water	Expressions of reluctance to enter water, but can be coaxed; interferes with movement, entry, and submersion activities.
3. Voluntary entry with no fear of the water	No overt expressions of fear or reluctance and no interference with performance of any aquatic skills.

WATER ENTRY
CONCEPT 4.4

Water entry patterns change in a regular ordered sequence from no entry without assistance to entry with sustained flight.

Water entry skills are important components of aquatics. Unfortunately, water entry items are often either not included within an instrument (Murray, 1981) or assessed by items with poor discriminability (American Red Cross, 1981; deBarbadillo & Murphy, 1972). As a result, assessment instruments and instructors sometimes have ignored a child's inability to enter, or fear of entering, the water. This means that too often the most rudimentary level of water entry tested is jumping into the water from the side of a pool. This type of entry is too advanced for many young children because it may mean that the child must be able to hold her or his breath and even to swim somewhat. Erbaugh (1978) was the first to publish a sequence of 18 tasks for entering the water. More recently, Reid and Bruya (1984; Reid, Bruya, & Langendorfer, 1985) have identified a robust entry sequence, which will be discussed in this chapter.

Reid and Bruya (1984; Reid et al., 1985) identified a motor sequence for entering the water (see Table 4.2 and Figure 4.1). The prerequisite skill for this sequence is the ability to stand independently. Thus, this checklist is inappropriate for measuring the pre-walking infant. The checklist for water entry is primarily designed for pool entry but can be expanded to include entry from beaches and docks and in other water environments.

Reid and Bruya (1984) observed that the patterns of children entering the water varied both with age and experience. Initially, children will not enter the water voluntarily. As they progress in both skill and confidence, they begin to expand their levels of entry until they can enter using a flight phase in which the center of gravity actually travels upward and outward over the water (see Table 4.2 and Figure 4.1).

Validity—Developmental, using cross-sectional sample and across-trials prelongitudinal screening technique (Roberton, 1977) using N = 60 children in the test sample.
Reliability—Exceeds 90% across-trials consistency within individual.
Objectivity—Exceeds 80% exact agreement for both intra- and interobserver objectivity.

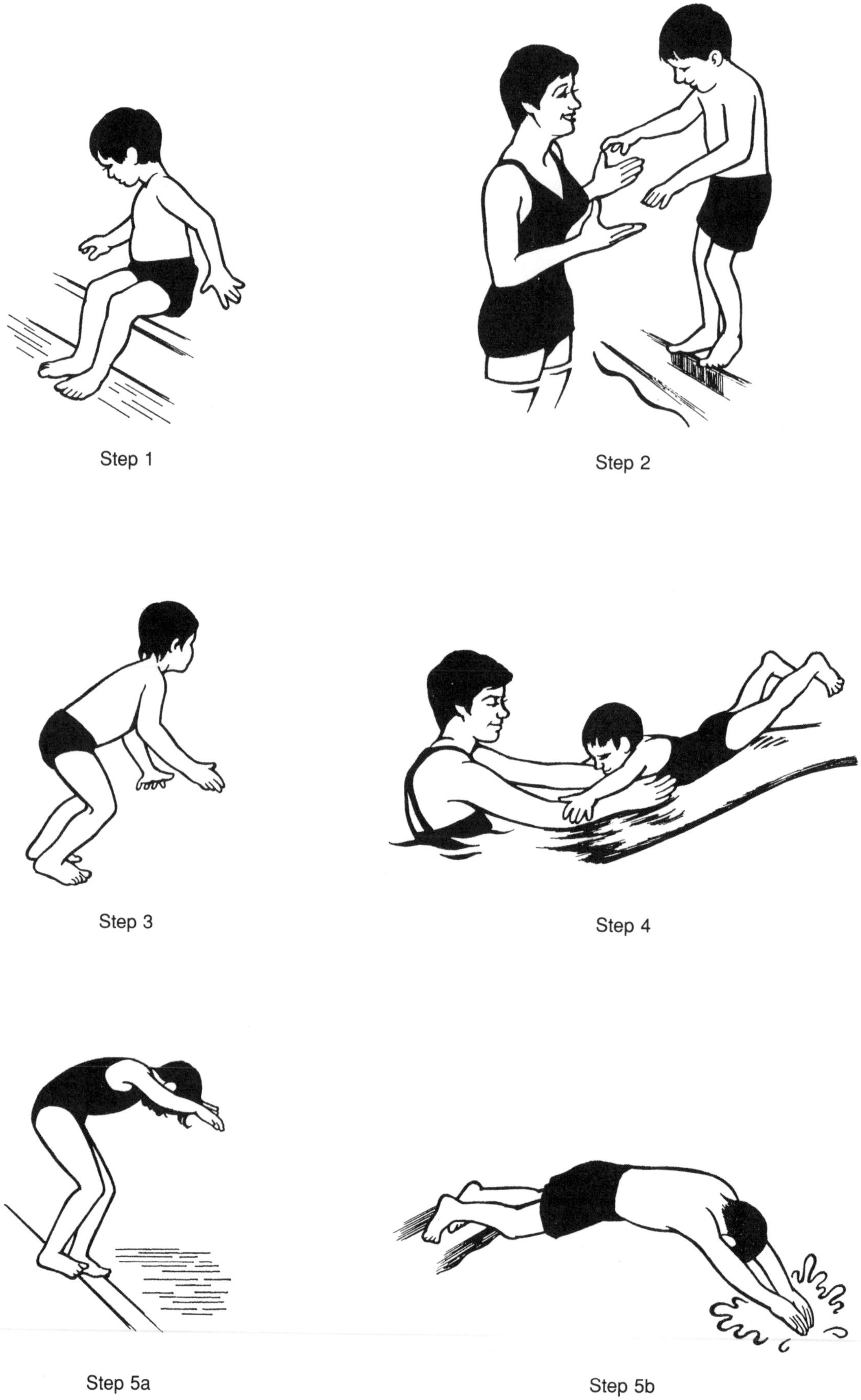

Step 1

Step 2

Step 3

Step 4

Step 5a

Step 5b

Figure 4.1   Water entry sequence.

Table 4.2 Water Entry Component of the Aquatic Readiness Assessment

Step/level	Decision rule
1. No voluntary entry	Child either refuses to enter or cannot enter the water without assistance.
2. Assisted feetfirst entry	Child enters water using support of another person to climb, slide, or jump into water, with feet the first body part that enters the water.
3. Unassisted feet-first entry	Child enters water with feet contacting first with no visible physical support by adult.
4. Assisted headfirst entry	Child enters water touching hand, arms, head, or chest to water first, while an adult maintains physical support or contact.
5. Unassisted head-first entry	Child enters water without support and makes initial water contact with hands, arms, head, or chest.

Note. Adapted from Reid and Bruya (1984, November).

BREATH CONTROL
CONCEPT 4.5

Breath control patterns change in a regular ordered sequence from reflexive breath holding to repeated rhythmic breaths during stroking.

All infant and preschool programs and instruments deal with some type of breath control component. As you may recall from chapter 2, the practice of submersion of young children has been particularly controversial. The component of *breath control* deals with ability to submerge as well as hold the breath and repeatedly get a new breath in a timely manner. Like water entry, breath control has often been measured by items too difficult for young children to initially accomplish. A set of items modified from Erbaugh's (1978) original 15 tasks is presented in Table 4.3 (see Figure 4.2).

Breath control, like primitive arm and leg action, is basically a reflexive, or automatic, action for very young infants, so there is no prerequisite skill or age level for this checklist. The first level of this checklist begins when the child's epiglottis automatically closes when the face is submerged, whether this submersion is controlled voluntarily by the child or by a parent's or instructor's action. Skills in breath control progress to enable the young child to tolerate and control water in and around the mouth, nose, and

face. The most advanced stage in this sequence is represented by the child's ability to repeatedly get a breath while moving through the water doing an advanced stroke or other skill.

Validity of sequence—Content validity.
Reliability—None established so far.
Objectivity—None established so far. (Desired criterion: 80% agreement within and across testers.)

Table 4.3 Breath Control Component of Aquatic Readiness Assessment

Step/level	Decision rule
1. Reflexive breath holding	Child holds breath ''automatically'' when face is covered by water.
2. Spitting or shipping	Child voluntarily takes water into mouth and can expel it.
3. Voluntary face submersion	Child permits part of face to get wet by either splashing or partial submersion and holds breath briefly (1-4 seconds).
4. Repeated breath holding	Child can repeat submersion and breath holding while in water.
5. Extended breath holding and/or rhythmic breathing with stroke	Child can submerge and hold breath for 5 or more seconds *or* Child combines breathing with stroking in a rhythmical manner for 5 or more breaths.

BUOYANCY
CONCEPT 4.6

Buoyancy patterns change in a regular ordered sequence from supported buoyancy to sustained relaxed float with no movement in prone or supine position.

Another often overlooked and poorly measured water adjustment skill is buoyancy. The American Red Cross Beginner course includes items labeled as *buoyancy and body position*, but it fails to address adequately the child's changing skills in staying afloat, maintaining a particular posture in the water, and shifting from that body position to different ones. The buoyancy checklist presented in this chapter (see Table 4.4 and Figure 4.3) is adapted from the Wielki & Houben (1983) and Langendorfer (1984a; Langendorfer et al., 1987) instruments. Several different sequences are identified within this component to measure the variety of changing dimensions included.

Step 1

Step 2

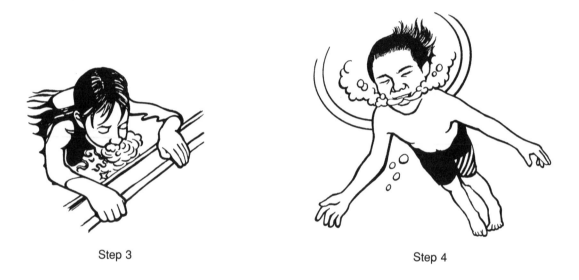

Step 3

Step 4

Step 5

Figure 4.2 Breath control sequence.

Buoyancy differs from breath control and primitive arm and leg movements in that it is not organized as a reflex at primitive levels. Instead, observation reveals that initial levels of buoyancy are usually aided by some type of support such as a parent, an instructor, or a flotation device. Initial independent buoyant support is attained only through vigorous limb movements. It is not until the child's skill is relatively advanced that the child permits the water to support the body while he or she maintains a relaxed or resting position.

Validity—Content validity.
Reliability—None established so far.
Objectivity—None established so far. (Desired criterion: 80% exact agreement both within and across raters.)

Table 4.4 Buoyancy Flotation Checklist

Step/level	Decision rule
1. No flotation	Child does not permit water to buoy body up; shows fear.
2. Flotation with assistance	Child will maneuver in water with direct support of adult or facility.
3. Flotation with support	Child floats in water while supported by flotation device or minimal adult assistance.
4. Unsupported flotation	Child maintains flotation using water support only.

BODY POSITION
CONCEPT 4.7

Body position patterns change in a regular ordered sequence from vertical (90° to 45° from horizontal) to horizontal in both prone and supine positions (0° to 10° from horizontal).

Body position in the water appears to rely on righting reactions that develop sometime during the 1st year of life. Righting reactions normally interact with gravitational stimuli. In the water, balance is confounded by the spatial difference between the body's center of buoyancy and the center of gravity. A young child gradually learns to shift body positions from one that is approximately vertical (90° from the surface of the water) to one that is horizontal (0° to 10° from the water surface; see Table 4.5 and Figure 4.4).

Validity—Developmental validity and construct validity based upon Langendorfer (1984a), Langendorfer et al. (1987), and Balan and Langendorfer (1988a, 1988b).
Reliability—Exceeds 90% across-trials consistency.
Objectivity—Exceeds 85% exact agreement between two or more raters.

Table 4.5 Body Position Checklist

Step/level	Decision rule
1. Vertical	Trunk 90° to 45° from horizontal surface
2. Inclined	Trunk 44° to 20° from horizontal
3. Level	Trunk 19° to 10° from horizontal
4. Horizontal	Trunk maintained less than 10° from horizontal

Note. Adapted from Langendorfer et al. (1987) and Wielki and Houben (1983).

ARM ACTIONS
CONCEPT 4.8

Arm action patterns change in two regular ordered sequences: The first focuses on the change in propulsion patterns from no action to using the arms like paddles to using the arms to produce lift like a propellor or airfoil. The second sequence focuses on the shifts in recovery patterns from no action to underwater recovery to straight- and bent-elbow overarm recovery patterns.

The arm action component is an important and novel way of viewing the mechanics of progressing through the water. All other assessment instruments and programs for young children assume that the child is simply taught the overarm crawl mechanics and that, with proper instruction and practice, errors are expunged. Two developmental sequences for arm action have been identified by filming and taping underwater stroking actions of both children and adults in much the same way as swim coaches have identified the arm mechanics characteristics of elite swimmers. The first sequence, arm propulsion actions, is probably the most important and simultaneously the most difficult arm action to identify accurately because the action all occurs under water. The second sequence focuses on the recovery patterns used in prone swimming; for intermediate and advanced swimmers these actions occur above the surface of the water and are more easily identifiable.

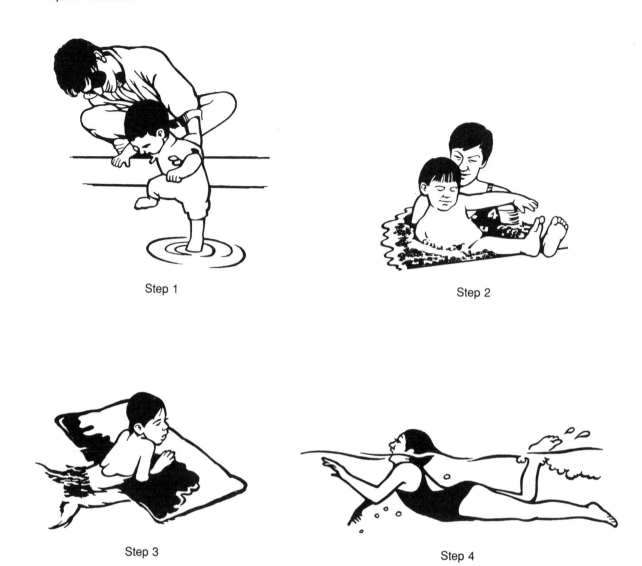

Step 1

Step 2

Step 3

Step 4

Figure 4.3 Buoyancy and body position sequence.

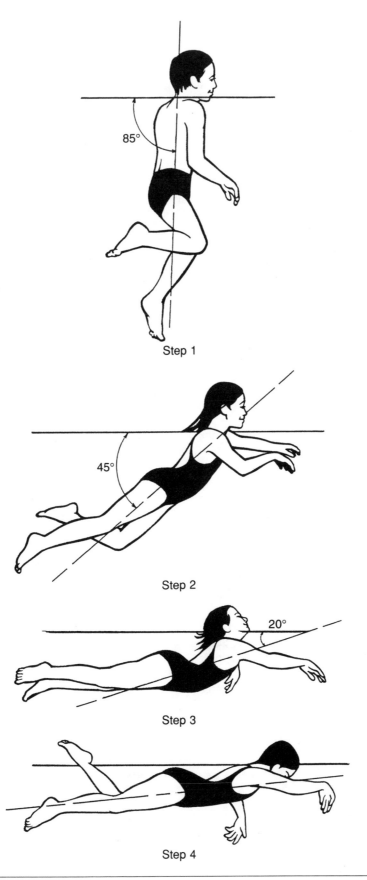

Figure 4.4 Changing body position patterns.

Understanding both shifts in arm patterns is crucial to effective progressive instruction.

Initial levels of aquatic arm propulsion may be based upon reflexive arm motions. However, observations have revealed that many very young children simply do not move their arms. Therefore, this lack of action is described as the most rudimentary level. The first voluntary arm propulsive actions of young children in the water appear to begin with the rapid flexion-extension pushing pattern described in Table 4.6. Gradually the child gains the skill to expand the range of motion, acceleration patterns, and change to "lift" propulsion associated with more advanced arm patterns (see Table 4.6 and Figure 4.5).

Validity—Developmental (construct) validity (Langendorfer, 1984a; Langendorfer et al., 1987; Balan & Langendorfer, 1988a, 1988b) using children and adults. Sequence levels appear to be stable and vary only to adjacent levels across trials (i.e., robust order of change over time is predicted).

Reliability—Behavior across trials is greater than 90% consistent and reliable.

Objectivity—Interobserver agreement exceeded 80% at all levels.

The second arm action sequence identifies the changing arm recovery patterns observed in both children and beginning adults. Like the arm propulsion action sequence, the initial level deals with the presence of no propulsive or recovery arm action. The second level is actually the first active level in which recovery of the arms occurs under the surface of the water. Gradually the pattern shifts from rather feeble overwater attempts to efficient attempts with the arms bent approximately 90° to 135° at the elbow throughout the recovery (see Table 4.7 and Figure 4.5).

Validity—Developmental (construct) validity (Langendorfer et al., 1987; Cool, 1992) using children and twins. Sequence levels appear to be stable and vary only to adjacent levels across trials (i.e., robust order of change over time is predicted) as well to follow the predicted order longitudinally across the twins.

Reliability—Behavior across trials is greater than 90% consistent and reliable.

Objectivity—Interobserver agreement exceeded 80% at all levels.

Table 4.6 Arm Propulsion Action Checklist

Step/level	Decision rule
1. No arm action	Arms not used in a propulsive action; they either hang at the side or extend forward.
2. Short downward push	Arm pushes downward rapidly with virtually no backward pulling action; action is short and rapid with little forward propulsive action.
3. Long push-pull paddle	Arm action initially is downward push, followed by backward pull with arm extension.
4. Lift propulsion	Arm enters water by driving forward, catching and pulling backward with an "S" pull action, "high" elbow, and rapid backward acceleration; main propulsion is lift rather than paddle action.

Note. Adapted from Langendorfer et al. (1987) and Cool (1992).

Table 4.7 Arm Recovery Action Checklist

Step/level	Decision rule
1. No arm action	Arms show no recovery motions during swimming.
2. No overwater recovery	Arms make all recovery actions under the surface of the water; may be either alternate or bilateral actions between arms.
3. Rudimentary overarm	Arms come above the water surface either only briefly or part way through the recovery.
4. Straight overarm	Arms are fully or mostly extended at the elbow throughout the overwater recovery beyond 150°. Palm of hand strikes water first.
5. Bent-elbow overarm	Elbow recovers out of water first and is highest arm point throughout much of recovery with flexion ranging from 90° to 130°. Thumb side of hand and fingers enter water first.

Note. Adapted from Langendorfer et al. (1987) and Cool (1992).

Arm propulsion

Arm recovery

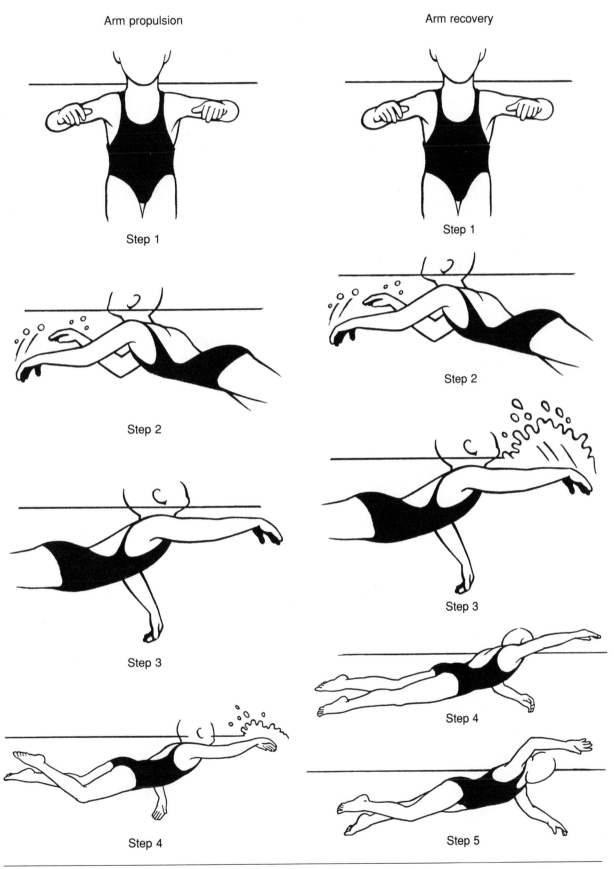

Figure 4.5   Changing arm action patterns.

LEG ACTIONS
CONCEPT 4.9

Leg action patterns change in a regular ordered sequence from reflexive "cigarette lighter" movements to advanced formal stroke leg actions such as straight-leg flutter kick, whip kick, scissors kick, or dolphin kick.

The changes in the leg action component parallel the motor sequence for arm action described in the previous section. The checklist is drawn from the combined work of Erbaugh (1978, 1980, 1981, 1986a), the Japanese research group (Oka et al., 1978), Langendorfer (1984a, 1987c; Langendorfer et al., 1987), Balan and Langendorfer (1988a, 1988b), and Wielki and Houben (1983). The changes in leg action are particularly important because they appear to naturally precede the development of arm action in most infants and young children. Wielki and Houben observed that body position and the age at which a child is first exposed to the water are critical factors in how this component develops.

The most rudimentary aquatic leg actions have been described in a variety of ways. The ARA chooses to use the Wielki and Houben (1978) observation called the "cigarette lighter" movement in which the legs simply cross while flexing and extending. Gradually children substitute a more pronounced "pedaling" action, called "plantar push" by Langendorfer (1984a). More advanced sequence levels result in more stylized aquatic leg-kicking movements as described in Table 4.8 and illustrated in Figure 4.6.

Validity—Balan and Langendorfer (1988a, 1988b) demonstrated that changes in these leg patterns were generally stable within time (i.e., consistent) as well as varying only to predicted adjacent levels. This suggests a robust sequence order.

Reliability—Trials are 90% consistent within subjects.

Objectivity—Observers agree 90% or more of the time in categorization.

Table 4.8   Leg Action Checklist

Step/level	Decision rule
1. No leg action	No leg motion is apparent.
2. Plantar-push "bicycling"	Alternating flexion-extension of hips and knees with flexed ankles—sole of foot is propulsive surface against water.
3. Rudimentary flutter	Alternating flexion-extension at knee with toes pointed and some hip flexion. Knee flexion exceeds 90° maximum flexion.
4. Bent-knee flutter	Alternating flexion-extension of legs with knee flexion less than 90°.
5. Straight-leg flutter	Alternating flexion-extension of legs with knee flexion less than 30°.

Note. Adapted from Balan and Langendorfer (1988a, 1988b), Erbaugh (1978, 1981), Langendorfer (1984), Oka et al. (1978), and Wielki and Houben (1983).

Step 1

Step 2

Step 3

Step 4

Step 5

Figure 4.6   Changing leg action patterns.

COMBINED MOVEMENT
CONCEPT 4.10

Combined swimming movement patterns change in a regular ordered sequence from rudimentary dog paddle to advanced formal strokes.

Finally, a *combined movement* category attempts to describe the combined interactive effect of body position, arm actions, leg action, and breath control. The checklist presented draws heavily on the work of Erbaugh (1978) and Langendorfer (1984a; Langendorfer et al., 1987). Note that this checklist predicts that a number of rudimentary styles of stroking naturally will be used by the young child prior to the onset of advanced formal strokes. This suggests that instructors should delay introducing advanced formal strokes until earlier forms of stroking (e.g., dog paddle or human stroke) are well established. This suggestion unfortunately is contrary to traditional methods of instruction, in which advanced formal strokes such as front crawl are normally introduced early. This component of swimming stroke readiness suggests that formal strokes traditionally are introduced much too early for optimal aquatic learning.

In some senses, the combined movement component is a composite of arm, leg, breath control, and body position components. However, because these components can vary independently from one another, the combined stroke composite profile produces a simple means for describing the holistic aspects of prone aquatic locomotion. The motor sequence begins with the inability to independently move through the water and progresses to more refined levels of locomoting through the water (see Table 4.9 and Figure 4.7).

Validity—Developmental and construct validity established by Langendorfer et al. (1987) and Balan and Langendorfer (1988a).
Reliability—Categorizations exceed 90% consistency across trials.
Objectivity—Raters agree 90%.

ADMINISTERING THE AQUATIC READINESS ASSESSMENT
CONCEPT 4.11

Administration of the ARA involves observing multiple trials and in varying conditions to achieve satisfactory results.

Table 4.9   Combined Movement Checklist

Step/level	Decision rule
1. No locomotor behavior	Child is unable to locomote independently in water.
2. Dog paddle	Front stroke is characterized by plantar push or rudimentary flutter kick, circle downward arms, and vertical or inclined body position.
3. Beginner or human stroke	Front stroke is characterized by bent-knee flutter kick, pull-push arms, and inclined body position. Rotary breathing optional.
4. Rudimentary crawl	Front stroke is characterized by rudimentary alternating arms with flutter kicking. Breathing pattern may vary.
5. Advanced crawl or other advanced formal stroke	Front stroke with defined arm, leg, and breathing patterns, usually with horizontal body position.

Note. Adapted from Erbaugh (1978), Langendorfer (1984a), and Langendorfer et al. (1987).

There are several things you can do to prepare for using the ARA effectively, including establishing adequate levels of observer objectivity, acquiring necessary test administration equipment, preparing the child for testing, and actually administering the test. The following sections provide some detail on these recommended preparations.

Establishing Objectivity

To use the ARA, you must establish an adequate level of objectivity in observing the sequential movements described within the components of the instrument. As we suggested in chapter 3, objectivity means general agreement both with other instructors and with oneself on different occasions. Operationally, we suggest being able to agree 80% or better on each component with another observer and with oneself on separate occasions. Make copies of Table 4.10, the ARA checklist, and use them for establishing both inter- and intraobserver objectivity.

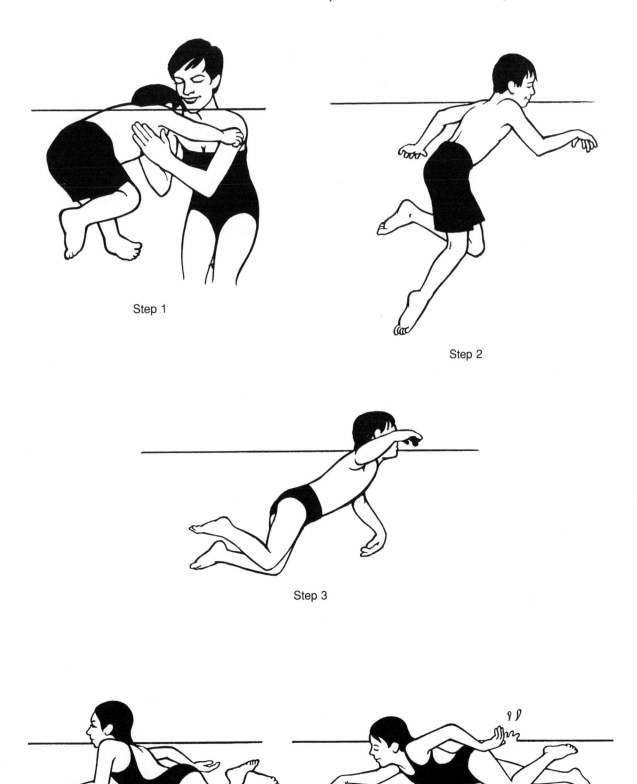

Step 1

Step 2

Step 3

Step 4

Step 5

Figure 4.7 Changing combined movement patterns.

Table 4.10   Aquatic Readiness Assessment Checklist

Water orientation and adjustment component (Place check or date of accomplishment)

Level		Level name
_____	1.	No voluntary entry, demonstrates fear of the water
_____	2.	Voluntary entry with hesitancy but minimum fear
_____	3.	Voluntary entry with no fear of the water

Water entry component (Place check or date of accomplishment)

Level		Level name
_____	1.	No voluntary entry
_____	2.	Assisted feetfirst entry
_____	3.	Unassisted feetfirst entry
_____	4.	Assisted headfirst entry
_____	5.	Unassisted headfirst entry

Breath control component (Place check or date of accomplishment)

Level		Level name
_____	1.	Reflexive breath holding
_____	2.	Spitting or shipping
_____	3.	Voluntary face submersion
_____	4.	Repeated breath holding
_____	5a.	Extended breath holding and/or
_____		Rhythmic breathing with stroke

Buoyancy/flotation checklist (Place check or date of accomplishment)

Level		Level name
_____	1.	No flotation
_____	2.	Flotation with assistance
_____	3.	Flotation with support
_____	4.	Unsupported flotation

Body position checklist (Place check or date of accomplishment)

Level		Level name
_____	1.	Vertical (90° to 45°)
_____	2.	Inclined (44° to 20°)
_____	3.	Level (19° to 10°)
_____	4.	Horizontal (less than 10°)

Arm propulsion action checklist (Place check or date of accomplishment)

Level		Level name
_____	1.	No arm action
_____	2.	Short downward push
_____	3.	Long push-pull
_____	4.	Lift propulsion

Arm recovery action checklist (Place check or date of accomplishment)

Level		Level name
_____	1.	No arm action
_____	2.	No overwater recovery
_____	3.	Rudimentary overarm
_____	4.	Straight overarm
_____	5.	Bent-elbow overarm

Leg action checklist (Place check or date of accomplishment)

Level		Level name
_____	1.	No leg action
_____	2.	Plantar push "bicycling"
_____	3.	Rudimentary flutter
_____	4.	Bent knee flutter
_____	5.	Straight leg flutter

Combined movement checklist (Place check or date of accomplishment)

Level		Level name
_____	1.	No locomotor behavior
_____	2.	Dog paddle
_____	3.	Beginner or human stroke
_____	4.	Rudimentary crawl
_____	5.	Advanced crawl or other advanced formal stroke

HOW TO USE THE ARA CHECKLIST TO IMPROVE OBJECTIVITY

1. Familiarize yourself with the decision rules for each level within the components of the ARA. Ask yourself what is the critical feature that categorizes that behavior according to the decision rule.
2. Study Figures 4.1 through 4.7 to get a visual image of what the decision rule is describing. Focus *only* on one component and sequence level at a time.
3. Observe several children of different abilities actually swimming. For arm, leg, and body position components, it is helpful to do this underwater with goggles or a mask or through an underwater window if one is available.
4. Ask a coinstructor to repeat Steps 1 to 3. Then both of you should *again* observe the same children from Step 3, either live or on videotape.
5. Compare both instructors' observations on both occasions on the checklist. Take the total number of agreements between instructors and divide it by the total possible observations and multiply by 100. This figure should be 80% or greater. If not, repeat Steps 1 to 4 until you can agree 80% of the time or more. It may be helpful to go over the decision rules from Step 2 above together.
6. Compare each instructor's first and second observations in Steps 3 and 4. Again divide the agreements by the total observations and multiply by 100. If this value does not meet or exceed 80%, further training is still needed by the instructor who is not consistent.

Required Equipment

You need very little equipment to administer the ARA. Basically, a writing implement (a pencil is best), copies of the ARA checklist, a clipboard, and perhaps a copy of the text with the decision rules and figures are all that are necessary. If possible, it is helpful to have a chair, small table, or lectern on which to set materials while writing on them and to keep them dry and out of the way. If you expect the materials to get wet, it is a good idea to have one copy of the checklist copied onto a piece of waterproof paper (which can be obtained from a drafting store) or laminated. An inexpensive lamination procedure is to put clear "Contac" paper on both sides of the paper.

As previously mentioned, a videocamera is ideal for later analysis, but it is not necessary. If you use a videocamera, position it on a tripod a safe distance away from the pool edge. Avoid filming into windows or other sources of glare on the water surface. It is best if a person other than the test administrator does the actual taping, because giving the test requires the instructor's full attention. If an underwater window or filming periscope is available, the swimmer should be positioned to obtain a sideview picture.

Setting the Stage for the Child

An important and often overlooked step in testing is preparing the child to be tested. This at first may seem to be an unimportant procedure, but an evaluative situation to a child can be very stressful. The social facilitation literature suggests that low-skilled children's performance may be affected negatively in such a situation. The best thing is usually to describe the administration of the ARA as "playing some games" or "doing some fun things." If the child appears to be anxious, especially if he or she scores Level 1 or 2 on the water orientation and adjustment component (which you should always administer first), it may be appropriate to delay testing until she or he feels more relaxed. Sometimes letting a child sit on the side and watch a classmate being tested can reduce anxiety significantly. For some children it is helpful to get them involved by letting them look through the camera lens, use a stopwatch, or hold the clipboard. The purpose of the testing is to elicit the most advanced behavior from a child possible. Anything that assists that effort can be beneficial.

Testing the Components

Testing each of the components can be accomplished by organizing your observational strategies to match the child's actions:

- Restrict observations to one component at a time.
- Observe the water orientation and adjustment component first.
- If they score at least Level 2, observe water entry as the child enters the water.

- Next, request that the child show how she or he can swim, or put his or her face in the water, or move independently away from the wall (depending upon the child's apparent skill level).
- Observe slow-moving components such as breath control and buoyancy while the child is warming up.
- Use several repetitions to observe, one at a time, the arm and leg actions, composite stroke, and body position.
- Where possible, try to get an underwater side and front view of the stroking components using a periscope or goggles.

The ARA has been validated in several situations. Students have been requested to swim both short distances (5 to 10 feet) and long distances (45 to 75 feet). The child just starting to stroke, slowing down, or reaching for a wall or object often alters her or his stroke to a more primitive level. It appears that stroke observations obtained when the child is "up-to-speed" with her or his stroke present the tester with the most accurate description of the child's "best" pattern.

HELPFUL HINTS FOR USING THE ARA
CONCEPT 4.12

There are several "tricks of the trade," such as observing multiple trials and in varying conditions, that can enhance use of the ARA.

Administration of any developmental sequence instrument presupposes that the most advanced level of behavior of which the person is capable can be elicited in a reliable manner. Often the use of a goal requiring rapid or forceful movement helps (Roberton, 1977, 1978). Other times a number of trials and varying conditions may need to be employed to ensure that the most advanced behavior level is observed. Nevertheless, there are times when a fearful, fatigued, or otherwise distressed child will not provide valid, reliable aquatic behaviors. At such a point, it is best to postpone assessment until a later period.

Record the Movement on Videotape

In testing the ARA, several things can be useful. First, record the swimming behaviors on videotape. It is ideal if the videotape can be recorded underwater for the arm, leg, and body position assessments. Some pools have underwater windows; others may have an underwater camera housing available. We have used periscopes in which the video is recorded through a submerged mirror as the child swims. Even if underwater views are impossible, certain behaviors captured on tape from above water are easier to categorize at a later date under slow motion and repeated observations.

Use More Than One Trial

Another important factor in obtaining reliable data is to observe or tape several trials of each behavior. As we suggested in chapter 3, behavior that can only be elicited once should be suspect and may not indicate valid, reliable performance. It may be helpful to ask a child to simply repeat a performance "once more" or "a couple more times." Alternatively, it might be helpful to ask a child to go through a number of skills and then repeat them again later. This may be less boring for both the child and yourself.

Use a Second Pair of Eyes

It is important to have another instructor verify your observations. It is very easy for one person to misinterpret a particular skill or movement, especially if the limbs are moving rapidly or if there is a great deal of water movement or splashing. This is where the videotape can be especially helpful. A second instructor can view the tapes after class and verify or question your classifications. When a disagreement is not resolvable, a second assessment observation is probably in order.

Getting the Best From the Child

When you cannot elicit what you believe is the most advanced behavior the child is capable of, several "tricks" may be tried. The first is to test several children simultaneously and try to encourage a "social facilitation" phenomenon to occur. Often when children see another child perform, they do so also, in a mild form of competition with their peer. Another technique is to switch places with the child and let them test you first. Then switch places again and say, "OK, now your turn." Another technique is to try a different water depth or a second pool if one is readily available. We have even had success testing young and inexperienced swimmers on water adjustment and breath control skills in a warm water plastic pool placed on the deck. Often a simple change of venue or reduction in water depth can alleviate a child's fears.

AN AQUATIC READINESS GUIDE FOR INSTRUCTORS AND PARENTS
CONCEPT 4.13

Implementation of developmental aquatic assessment can be enhanced through the use of a readiness guide.

It still may not be apparent to many instructors or parents why it is important to pretest as well as posttest. It also may not be obvious why or how a developmental instrument can assist the teacher in planning or presenting individualized activities and lessons. The traditional format of having 10 prearranged lessons still seems the easiest and best means for structuring the curriculum. This section presents the instructor or parent with an individualized alternative to the inflexible set of lesson plans.

Developmental Readiness

In chapter 1 we presented some of the qualities of a developmental perspective. From that perspective, motor skills, including swimming skills, are acquired through a complex interaction of the child's actions and the environment's effects. Developmentally, skills are acquired sequentially in a relatively fixed order. The acquisition process is characterized by dynamic hierarchical, or pyramid, organization combined with increasing integration and specialization. As a result of the developmental perspective, skill acquisition takes on a pattern that is useful to instructors and others involved in the learning process.

When a child shows a certain level of developmental behavior, that behavior locates the child at a definite place on a developmental continuum. It suggests the skills that the child has already acquired as well as other skills that the child has yet to master. Knowledge of present skills can indicate which skills are next to be learned. We call this phenomenon, which predicts the likelihood of change, *developmental readiness*. Based on your knowledge of developmental sequences and the child's present level of functioning, it tells you what behaviors the child is "ready" to learn. When you know the skills the child is ready for, you can predict what kind of activities and experiences will best assist the child in acquiring those next skills.

Developmentally Appropriate Practices

Recently, early childhood and physical educators have given a great deal of attention to the concept of *developmentally appropriate practices* (DAP) in their respective areas. Unfortunately, from a developmental perspective, the discussion has largely been void of an operational definition for what constitutes appropriate and inappropriate practices. The National Association for the Education of Young Children (Bredekamp, 1987) put forth two "definitions" that identified "age appropriate" and "individually appropriate" practices for early childhood education. Age appropriate practices are those that rely on similarities in growth and development within a population group based on age constraints. Individually appropriate practices address the actual needs of specific children.

The need for an acceptable definition for developmentally appropriate practices arises directly from the concept of developmental readiness, or the likelihood that individuals will change their performance. As we pointed out in chapter 1, because age is simply a marker for other causes of change, all readiness is ultimately individually based. Therefore, developmentally appropriate practices are those that are most likely to promote and foster change within an individual, which is to say, developmentally appropriate practices are those that address a child's developmental readiness.

Aquatic Readiness

Aquatic readiness is simply the concept of "developmental readiness" applied to aquatic skills. It suggests that children have a natural tendency to acquire aquatic skills in a preferred order despite environmental interventions. It also predicts that experiences and practice will be most successful in changing aquatic skills when they match the child's natural tendencies and readiness. We are advocating that a child should be taught skills when the child's behavior indicates that he or she is ready to learn them.

The Aquatic Readiness Assessment was developed with this concept of developmental readiness in mind. Skills have been ordered as a result of observing children and their changing swimming patterns. Skills are grouped in homogeneous components that appear to have fairly well-established orders of acquisition across most swimmers. When a child demonstrates Level 2, for example, you can be confident that the child already can perform Level 1 and probably is ready to progress toward learning Level 3.

Aquatic Readiness Guide

This readiness guide evolved from the recognition that not all instructors, particularly those with traditional training, would understand the rationale for pretesting and using the ARA for preparing appropriate individualized lesson plans. The guide is organized according to the Aquatic Readiness Assessment components discussed in this chapter. To use the guide, determine which component you are concerned with (these can be found in the first column). Next read the descriptions under the third column (''If the child uses'') to determine the present skill level of the child. Finally, read the information under the fourth column (''Then she or he is ready for'') that corresponds to the appropriate skill level to discover what activities it would be appropriate to present to the child next. For example, assume you're interested in working on breath control with a child and you know that the child can hold his or her breath for a short time while going under the water voluntarily. By looking under the breath control component on the

Aquatic Readiness Guide, you would find out that the child is at Level 3. You would also find that some activities you could introduce to the child to help him or her progress to the next level are games like Magic Candle and London Bridge. The advantages of using games to enhance aquatic readiness are discussed in chapter 8, and the games referred to in the Aquatic Readiness Guide can be found in the appendix at the end of the book.

As you become more familiar with the readiness concept and process, you will begin creating your own activities and games that fit the process. Our experience suggests that some of the most effective learning activities are developed on the spur of the moment and in concert with the child's aquatic readiness. These use a ''a teachable moment'' to full advantage.

AQUATIC READINESS GUIDE

Component	Level	If the child uses . . .	Then she or he is ready for . . .
Water orientation and adjustment	1	No voluntary entry, demonstrates immense fear of the water	Water orientation activities such as *Pool Exploration*, water play games such as *Sink or Float?* and *Washcloth Activities*
	2	Voluntary entry with hesitancy but minimum fear	Reassurance and positive experiences in the water; water orientation activities such as *It's Raining, It's Pouring* and *Name Game*
	3	Voluntary entry with no fear of the water	Water orientation activities such as *Trick/Stunt Tag* and *Salmon Says*

Component	Level	If the child uses . . .	Then she or he is ready for . . .
Water entry	1	No voluntary entry	Pool exploration activities; games and activities at poolside; gentle coaxing and encouragement; water orientation activities
	2	Assisted feetfirst entry	Water orientation games; beginning water entry games such as *Humpty Dumpty* or *Jump Into My Circle*
	3	Unassisted feetfirst entry	Water entry games such as *Jack Be Nimble*, *Parachute Jump*, or *Easter Egg Coloring*
	4	Assisted headfirst entry	Water entry and diving lead-ups such as *Alligator* or *Rocket Booster*
	5	Unassisted headfirst entry	Advanced forms of diving and diving games such as *Rocket Booster*
Breath control	1	Reflexive breath holding	Water on his or her face, and water orientation games such as *Washcloth Activities* and *Sink Play*
	2	Spitting or shipping	Having water in and around his or her mouth and breath control activities such as *Ping Pong Push* and *Whale Spitting*
	3	Voluntary face submersion	Playful splashing and breath control activities such as *Magic Candle* and *London Bridge*
	4	Repeated breath holding	Breath control activities such as *Flower Garden*, *Sunken Treasure*, and *Teeter Totter*
	5	Extended breath holding and/or rhythmic breathing	Breath control activities such as *Charlie Over the Water*, *Obstacle Course*, and *Water Croquet*

(continued)

Aquatic Readiness Guide (*continued*)

Component	Level	If the child uses . . .	Then she or he is ready for . . .
Buoyancy/flotation	1	No flotation	An adult to hold her or him closely in the water; flotation activities such as *Sink or Float?*
	2	Flotation with assistance	An adult to hold her or him in the water with lessening support and flotation activities such as *Push Against the Wall* and *Gingerbread Cookie*
	3	Flotation with support	Activities in the water with minimum or no outside support; flotation activities such as *Airplane* and *Ride 'Em Cowboys*
	4	Unsupported flotation	Flotation activities without any support besides the water, such as *Float Tag, Glide and Slide,* and *Timber!*
Body position	1	Vertical body position	Body position activities such as *Head, Shoulders, Knees, and Toes*
	2	Inclined body position	Body position activities such as *Immunity Tag* and *Pancakes*
	3	Level body position	Flotation and buoyancy activities such as *Float Tag* and *Print*
	4	Horizontal body position	Flotation and buoyance activities such as *Log Tag* and *Rocket Ship*
Arm propulsion action	1	No arm action	Arm propulsion activities such as *Alligator Swim* and water orientation activities
	2	Short downward push	Arm propulsion activities such as *Cork Scramble*
	3	Long push-pull paddle	Arm propulsion activities such as *Wave to the "Fishies"*
	4	Lift propulsion	Arm propulsion activities such as *Water Wheelbarrow*

Component	Level	If the child uses . . .	Then she or he is ready for . . .
Arm recovery action	1	No arm action	Arm propulsion activities such as *Alligator Swim* and water orientation activities
	2	Underwater recovery	Arm activities such as *Wave to the ''Fishies''*
	3	Rudimentary overarm	Arm propulsion activities such as *Twenty Ways*
	4	Straight overarm	Arm propulsion activities such as *One Arm Swim*
	5	Bent-elbow overarm	Arm propulsion activities such as *Water Wheelbarrow*
Leg action	1	No leg action	Leg propulsion activities such as *Airplane* and water orientation activities
	2	Plantar push ''bicycling''	Leg propulsion activities such as *Musical Kickboards*
	3	Rudimentary flutter	Leg propulsion activities such as *Kickboard Killer*
	4	Bent-knee flutter	Leg Propulsion activities such as *Hot and Cold*
	5	Straight-leg flutter	Leg propulsion activities such as *Kickboard Tug of War* and *Newspaper Relay*
Combined strokes	1	No locomotor behavior	Arm/leg propulsion activities such as *Spider Swimming* and water orientation activities
	2	Dog paddle	Arm/leg propulsion activities such as *Who Can . . . ?*
	3	Beginner's or human stroke	Arm/leg propulsion activities such as *Carp and Cranes* and *Handicapped Tag*
	4	Rudimentary crawl	Arm/leg propulsion activities such as *Sharks and Minnows II* and *Water Wheelbarrow*
	5	Advanced crawl or other advanced formal stroke	Advanced stroke games such as *Stroke Switch* and *T-Shirt Relay*

SUMMARY

The ARA is an individualized, developmental assessment instrument that was constructed to provide instructors or parents with information about how well the child is performing in comparison with his or her previous performances as well as possible future performances. In concert with the Aquatic Readiness Guide, it provides a unique and valuable pretest and planning method for aquatic skills for young children.

The ARA is not intended to have age norms. Norms often have been misused to compare children with other children their own age, resulting in the static lesson plans of traditional swimming programs. The ARA primarily is meant to be used not to compare children with other children but to assess an individual child's progress and to help plan effective and timely learning activities. It also is intended to be used with a variety of different teaching techniques, such as the ones described in the following chapters, to facilitate individualized teaching.

5

Educational Aquatics: A Movement Education Approach for Aquatic Readiness

As part of the aquatic readiness concept, we have proposed a broad, new outlook on aquatics for young children—water competence—in which an important outcome of swimming instruction is the acquisition of a broad set of aquatic skills, understandings, and knowledges that span a number of aquatic areas (chapter 1). We followed with the 4-P's instructional model, which places a priority on preassessment and individualized planning before teaching (chapter 3), and a new developmental assessment instrument, the ARA (chapter 4). In this chapter, we present a novel approach for structuring the aquatic skill acquisition process.

EDUCATIONAL AQUATICS: MOVEMENT EDUCATION IN THE WATER
CONCEPT 5.1

Educational aquatics proposes a movement education approach for organizing the acquisition of aquatic skills into conceptual areas and for presenting that movement content to young children in a water environment.

The traditional swimming instructor, like the traditional physical educator, commonly uses a teacher-centered approach in talking, telling, commanding, or in some other way verbally instructing the swim-

mer to pursue a very narrow set of skills. *Educational aquatics* encourages children to learn to move in the water through a unique exploratory process.

Barrett (1984a) suggested that a movement education scheme provides a thorough and comprehensive way to classify, observe, structure, and evaluate movement in all forms and environments. *Movement education* has been described as ''a lifelong process of change'' (Logsdon, 1984, p. 12) and the content of the physical education curriculum. It also has been seen as an approach for teaching physical skills. Rejecting the traditional teacher-centered approach, movement education advocates encourage children to use their natural creativity and sense of expression to explore and expand their movement capabilities.

UNIQUENESS OF A WATER ENVIRONMENT FOR MOVEMENT
CONCEPT 5.2

Educational aquatics uses the uniqueness of a water environment in structuring aquatic movement and learning.

Water is certainly a unique environment for human movement. As a result, human aquatic movement differs greatly from our locomotion and movement on land. The following sections discuss the main reasons for these differences.

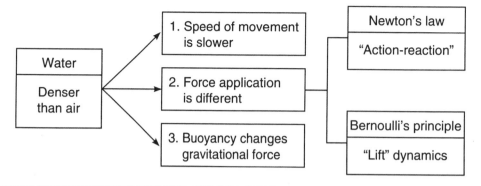

Figure 5.1   The demands of moving in the water are very different from the demands of moving on land.

Water Density and Locomotion

Because water is much denser than air, it provides greater resistance than air does to human movement, so movement in the water environment occurs at a much slower speed than movement in the air. Also, the production of force in the water results from a different type of muscular effort than in the air. Humans moving in the water propel themselves using not only Newton's action-reaction principle but also Bernoulli's principle of fluid dynamics, which is a variation on the "lift" that makes airplanes fly in the air (see Figure 5.1). However, the human swimmer must generate lift under much slower velocities than an airplane is capable of. Because all of this is different from how we move on land, unique learning experiences, and unique methods for presenting these experiences, are required. These are explained later in this chapter.

Breath Control

Human life cannot be supported in the water without oxygen to breathe. In swimming, this means that we must regularly contact and breathe in the air above the water (or have an underwater supply of air, as from a scuba-diving tank). Regulating breathing is the most crucial and limiting factor associated with aquatic experiences.

Streamlined Movement

Water density places different demands on the aquatic mover than land-based activities do. To move through the water efficiently and quickly, we must propel ourselves horizontally along the axial plane of the body. In contrast, most land locomotion skills are performed in an upright posture. The horizontal body position and need for streamlining in the water inter-

act with the means to create force and to balance around the center of buoyancy.

Buoyancy

Being denser (heavier) than the human body, water promotes buoyancy in the human body. This means that the effect of gravity on body parts in water is different from its effect in air. Essentially the density of the water and the buoyancy of the body counteract the effect of gravity. As a result, the body balances around a different point in the water than in the air (see Figure 5.2), making body positioning and movement in the water radically different from that on land. Adapting to these differences requires special learning experiences.

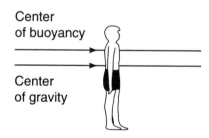

Figure 5.2   Because of water's density and the body's buoyancy, the body balances around a different point in the water (center of buoyancy) than in the air (center of gravity).

Temperature Regulation

Water conducts heat from the body more rapidly than air does. As a consequence, in water the body chills much more rapidly and cools more efficiently during rigorous exercise. There is a definite limit to the length of time a person can remain in a water environment. In addition, the cooling effect of water slows the heart rate and stimulates the micturition (urination) reflex. In modern pools, temperatures are regulated between 78 degrees and 85 degrees. Hypothermia is less of a restrictive factor than in ambient water temperatures in lakes, rivers, or oceans, but still must be considered when structuring the child's learning environment.

CONCEPTUAL FRAMEWORK FOR EDUCATIONAL AQUATICS
CONCEPT 5.3

Educational aquatics provides a novel means for structuring aquatic learning by using a conceptual framework that organizes the body, space, effort, and relationship aspects to water movement.

Logsdon and Barrett (1984) described how Rudolph Laban's movement description system provides an important and comprehensive means for structuring human movement. The four aspects of all movement, according to this system, are (a) what the *body* is doing, (b) where or in what *spaces* the body is moving, (c) how much *effort* or force the body is exerting to perform the movement, and (d) what *relationships* occur as the body moves (see Figure 5.3). These characteristics of movement are useful for conceptually organizing all human movement in a variety of environments, including in the water. We will now discuss each aspect in turn from a movement education perspective.

Body Aspects

Chapter 4 demonstrated how the changing components of aquatic movement could be described and assessed. In a similar way, this first aspect of movement, the *body*, is organized within movement education as having four dimensions: (a) body actions, (b)

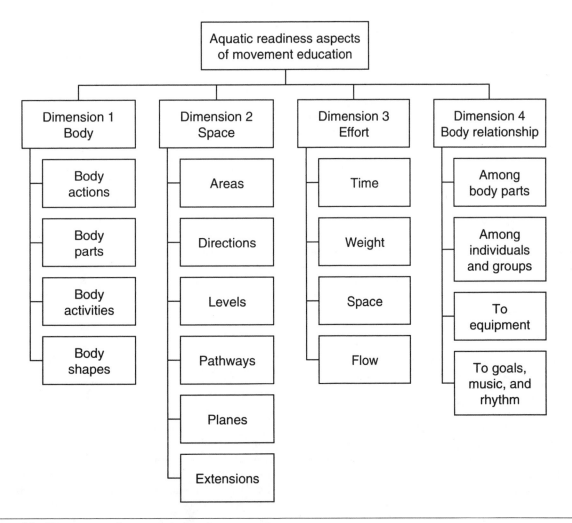

Figure 5.3   Four aspects of movement education.

interrelations among body parts, (c) body activities, and (d) shapes of the body. The manner in which the body and its parts move alone and in relationship to one another in the water describes the body aspect of movement from an educational aquatics perspective.

In traditional aquatics, the body aspect of the human swimmer is given a limited description as the 6-10 advanced formal strokes. These strokes prescribe in very exact, but limiting, terms the acceptable body actions, activities, and shapes of a swimming person. For example, a ''correct'' front crawl stroke, which is the stroke most commonly taught first in the United States, is prescribed as an alternating pulling of the arms with an overwater recovery accompanied by a six-beat flutter kick and rotary, rhythmic breathing.

In contrast, from an aquatic readiness perspective and from an educational aquatic approach to teaching, the body aspects of aquatic movement are much broader and more varied. The individual child explores and determines for him- or herself different actions, shapes, relationships, and activities that are appropriate to his or her own needs and skills. For example, in chapter 4 the ARA depicts the beginning levels of several rudimentary styles of swimming in the water, such as dog paddle or human stroke, as possible body aspect configurations. When choices are presented to young swimmers, the emphasis is on exploring the body in the water rather than on prescribing some predetermined stroke or style of swimming.

Space Aspects

The second aspect, *space*, is where the body is moving. The dimensions of space include areas, directions, levels, pathways, planes, and extensions (Logsdon & Barrett, 1984). As applied to water and to educational aquatics, these dimensions refer particularly to body positioning, body streamlining, and buoyant balance, each of which is different from space aspects of movement on land.

For example, on land, the developmentally most advanced posture for body movement is vertical, or at an angle approximately 90° from the floor surface. Except in very windy conditions or at high speeds, streamlining is relatively unimportant and does not seriously impede forward progress. However, in the water the developmentally most advanced posture for locomotion is in a horizontal plane parallel to the surface of the water (see the body position component of the ARA in chapter 4). In addition, streamlining the body to reduce resistance is crucial to efficient aquatic locomotion. For this reason all sprinting strokes use an overwater recovery to avoid unnecessary resistance during recovery. These dramatic differences in use of space often offer imposing challenges to novice swimmers of any age.

Effort Aspects

The *effort* aspect is how the human body and its parts are used to perform a movement. The four factors of movement effort are time, weight, space, and flow (Logsdon & Barrett, 1984). In educational aquatics, these factors refer to the unique ways humans must move their bodies to create effective propulsive force in the water while minimizing water resistance, which relates to the body's buoyant forces and streamlining as it moves through the water.

On land, the most important effort, or force, aspect of movement involves Newton's law of action-reaction. To accomplish a movement in one direction, a mover must push against a solid surface or gain resistance due to friction in the opposite direction. For applying force or effort in the fluid medium of water, the most efficient movement is achieved by use of lift according to Bernoulli's principle of hydrodynamics. In other words, a swimmer's hands, arms, legs, and feet produce forward momentum most efficiently when they create a pressure differential by passing the curved body part rapidly through the water in much the same way that a wing, propellor, or sail produces forward momentum. This is perhaps the most difficult aspect of movement for a swimmer to accomplish and requires extensive practice and guidance for most persons.

Relationship Aspects

The *relationship* aspect is how body parts and persons interact. Specific dimensions of the relationship aspect include relationships among body parts; relationships among individuals and groups; relationships of persons to apparatus and equipment; and relationships to goals, music, rhythms, and other factors (Logsdon & Barrett, 1984). In educational aquatics, this aspect includes how the body parts work together in the water to produce strokes; how persons can work alone or together in the water, especially related to water safety; how persons can use small and large equipment to assist aquatic movement; and how persons create water movements to music or other external constraints.

In human terrestrial locomotion, most locomotor skills involve alternating actions by the arms and legs using the natural dynamics of the limb masses swinging like pendula through gravitational space. In the water, locomotor activities such as advanced strokes involve either alternating or simultaneous actions of the arms and/or the legs. Depending on the type of stroke and its dynamics, the limbs are required to move in relations dramatically different from those of terrestrial locomotion under gravitational influence. The water slows the speed of movement while negating gravity's tendency to produce pendular actions.

Educational aquatics uses the special characteristics of the water and the particular aspects of movement education to create a unique conceptual content for the acquisition of aquatic skills. The next pages outline special aspects of how children can gain broad experiences in the water from a movement education approach.

CONTENT AREAS WITHIN EDUCATIONAL AQUATICS
CONCEPT 5.4

Educational aquatics is organized into seven content areas: entry, buoyancy and floating, pushing off and gliding, breath control, arm motions, leg motions, and combined locomotor skills.

From the educational aquatics perspective, young children need to have a variety of experiences ranging across the broad concepts related to the water environment. These content areas are organized in a broader framework than the similar concepts of traditional aquatic learning, and they are introduced in ways uniquely different from how aquatic skills are traditionally taught. Refer to Table 5.1 as you read about the content areas in the following paragraphs.

Water Entry and Exit

The first content area, *water entry and exit*, concerns the variety of ways a young child can get into and out of the water. Table 4.1 introduced a five-step water entry checklist. As we mentioned previously, water entry is a set of skills that typically is neglected in most aquatic programs but that can radically change how young swimmers adapt to the water environment. This content area was developed to explain how to introduce young children to the water and how to increase their skill in the wide variety of ways they can get into and leave the water.

Buoyancy and Floating

The second content area, *buoyancy and floating*, concerns how the body acts and reacts in a buoyant and liquid environment. The movement skills and

Table 5.1 Educational Aquatic Content Areas

Content area	Description
1. Water entry and exit	Movements associated with getting into and out of the water
2. Buoyancy and floating	Movements and tasks involved in suspending the body in the water, both on stomach and on back
3. Pushing off and gliding	Movements and tasks that permit the child to use a solid object or surface to move through the water
4. Breath control	Skills dealing with being able to breathe while moving in and through the water
5. Arm actions	Movements of the arms with the purpose of supporting or propelling the body through the water
6. Leg actions	Movements of the legs with the purpose of supporting or propelling the body through the water
7. Combined aquatic locomotion	Movements and actions taken together that permit a person to move through the water

experiences surrounding buoyancy and floating have to do with the young child's ability to balance around a center of buoyancy and to maintain a posture supported only by the water itself. Because young children and novices obtain a breath of air differently in the water than on land, this content is another important one for aquatic experiences.

Pushing Off and Gliding

Pushing off and gliding is the content area in which young children and novices begin to learn how to move through the water using Newton's action-reaction principle, which they previously learned for on-land movements. By acting against various stable surfaces in the water, such as the pool bottom or wall, children can learn how to initially propel their bodies. Then they learn to become more streamlined and to maintain a horizontal posture in the water.

Breath Control

The content area of *breath control* is an obvious and traditional skill area at all levels of aquatics. In educational aquatics, however, the scope of this content area has expanded beyond simply bubble blowing, breath holding, and rhythmic breathing with defined strokes. All kinds of ways of breathing and dealing with water in and around the mouth and nose are explored and experienced, providing young children with more options for structuring their breath control in a variety of aquatic activities.

Limb Actions

The *arm action* and *leg action* content areas traditionally have been limited to a few types of arm and leg movements associated with formal advanced strokes. In educational aquatics, a broad range of aquatic arm and leg movements are explored and informally rated by the children for their efficacy in propelling the body through the water. Such breadth of experience should be related to improved skill in mastering all the advanced formal strokes as well as other modes of aquatic movement (e.g., paddling boats, sculling, underwater swimming).

Combined Aquatic Locomotion

The content area of *combined aquatic locomotion* encourages child and novice to explore all the possible ways of moving her or his body through the water. This content area combines the use of several other content areas including floating, gliding, breathing, arm actions, and leg actions. A method designed to increase exploration of the variety of ways to move in the water also will eventually carry over to increase the child's efficiency in formal advanced strokes, because this method increases the child's cognitive understanding and experiential base in the water.

PRESENTING THE CONTENT OF EDUCATIONAL AQUATICS
CONCEPT 5.5

Educational aquatics presents the content areas using skill themes and alternative content structuring techniques.

An educational aquatics approach to aquatic skill acquisition employs an indirect method of teaching. Through the use of *skill themes* (Gabbard et al., 1987; Graham, Holt/Hale, & Parker, 1987; Holt/Hale, 1988), all of the content areas are explored and contrasted in as wide a variety of ways as possible. We feel that such a breadth of experience dramatically improves and enhances the quality of learning by broadening the experience foundation.

Skill Themes

Problem-solving and exploratory teaching approaches are used with skill themes. Request the children to try a variety of different movements within the area covered by the particular skill theme. For example, if you want to cover the skill theme for *entry into the water*, you might ask a child to show ways of putting his or her face in the water, emphasizing the skill theme of *breath control*. At the end of a typical educational aquatic lesson, any child will have practiced and explored a wide variety of movements related to the designated skill themes.

The use of skill themes starkly contrasts with traditional teacher-centered methods. Traditionally an aquatic instructor identifies a specific aquatic skill and requests children to learn and practice that skill. For instance, to encourage water entry, the traditional swimming instructor shows the child exactly how to turn and climb backward into the water. To learn breath control, the instructor demonstrates and then asks the child to submerge or blow bubbles exactly as demonstrated. At the end of the traditional lesson, a child has practiced only the set of teacher-defined skills.

Problem Statements in Developing Skill Themes

To elicit movements related to a particular skill theme, the instructor (or parent, in the case of small children in the water with a parent) asks children to show how many different ways they can enter the water. This verbal statement is referred to as a *problem statement*. The problem statement is composed of two parts: the sentence stem and the content. The sentence stem can be a command or a question. We will discuss the sentence stem in more detail a bit later. First we will explain the content.

Content-Structuring Techniques

Indirect teaching or presentation methods rely on structuring movement environments (in the present case, aquatic movement environments) to elicit various forms of movement. In the current chapter, we are presenting a verbal form of elicitation that poses questions to young swimmers and requests them to solve the problems posed by the question. It assumes that the child possesses an innate ability to produce satisfactory modes of movement, in this case swimming movements, without direct instruction by an instructor. The instructor's role becomes one of using insight into the aquatic learning process to ask the correct questions of young children.

The content of the problem statement can be structured verbally in three ways: (a) direct, (b) indirect, and (c) limited structuring (Kirchner, Cunningham, & Warrell, 1977). The following sections describe these content-structuring techniques (see also Table 5.2).

Direct Content Structuring

The method of direct content structuring is very much like the traditional command style method described by Mossten (1966, 1972) and is commonly used by traditional swimming instructors when working with children and novices. Basically, to use this technique is to make a straightforward statement that tells the child what to do (e.g., "OK, let's start by climbing down the ladder backward, taking one step at a time, and getting into the water"). The statement implies a teacher-defined correct response; the child is told what to do and how to do it. Frequently, in this technique, the content is signaled by statement stems such as "I want you to . . ." or "OK, next we will . . . ."

Indirect Content Structuring

The indirect problem statement is the most expansive of the three techniques. Using this technique, the instructor allows a wide range of responses. Examples include "Can you figure out other ways to climb into the water?" and "Show me as many ways as you can think of to climb into the water" and "How many different ways can you climb into the water?"

Expansive questions and statements, however, are difficult for some children to interpret. If children are having a hard time, using short prompts after an expansive question or statement can help the child

to understand and initiate activity. "How about a knee in first . . . ?" or "Maybe use your arms first to enter . . . ?" are examples of short prompts.

This technique is usually best employed with children who are already fairly secure in the water and who are in the process of expanding their base of experience. Later in this chapter we will explain the Greene-Horne expansion, a technique which is one simple way to systematically introduce practice variability into the setting using indirect questions or statements.

Limited Content Structuring

The method of limited content structuring requires an expansive question or statement usually with multiple alternatives. The content can be presented either directly or indirectly. The limited content-structuring technique is most easily understood when used as a transition between the direct and indirect content-structuring techniques. For example, "Now try to use your feet so they make less splash" (transition from direct) or "How can you use your feet so they make less splash?" (transition to indirect).

Employing a more direct style with the limited structure technique provides a transition from the direct technique to the limited content-structuring technique. For instance, suppose the child is faced with the challenge of figuring out what to do next. The task is to solve the movement problem by selecting more than one, but a limited number of, movement solutions (e.g., "Now use three different ways to climb down the ladder to get into the water"). This example sentence is direct in its style, because the introduction to the movement problem or challenge still implies that the task is to be completed at the request of the instructor and with solutions she or he finds appropriate. A more indirect style of presentation for the limited movement problem or

Table 5.2   Content-Structuring Approaches

Type of content structuring	Range of appropriate responses	Sample
Direct (command)	Teacher-defined correct response	"Let's climb down the ladder into the water."
Limited-direct (statement)	Wider range of teacher-defined correct responses	"Show me three ways you can climb down the ladder into the water."
Limited-indirect (question)	Wider range. Student-defined correct responses	"Can you show me three ways to get into the water?"
Indirect (question)	Widest range	"How many different ways can you climb into the water?"

challenge begins the transition to the indirect content-structuring technique.

Sentences for the limited content-structuring technique may also include challenges of a less direct style and still limit the number of solutions (e.g., "Can you show me three ways to climb down the ladder to get into the water?"). This technique, with the structure of the content changed very little, encompasses a different attitude or context that is usually interpreted by listeners as being less structured and providing more choices for the child.

The basic difference between this style of limited-content question and the direct style of limited-content statement is that this style uses a question stem rather than a statement stem. The nature of the stem is less demanding of a correct response by the child, because it is usually expressed as "Can you . . . ?" rather than "Now use . . . ." The statement or question stem technique will be explained in more detail later in this chapter.

The advantage of the question over the statement is that usually the question appears to provide the child with more choices. This can be important to the fearful or uncertain child. The direct style of limited statement may be viewed by young aquatic readiness children as making demands of them that they are either unable or unwilling to meet. When they respond to a demanding statement with inactivity, they are indicating their lack of readiness.

In addition, the use of the more indirect style of limited question stem and the implied choices in "Can you . . . ?" are often more successful in eliciting responses. Apparently, giving children some latitude for making their own decisions reduces anxiety and increases their motivation and willingness to try. When they choose not to perform a skill under multiple alternative conditions, then you can take this as an indication that the child views the request as too difficult or fails to comprehend.

The advantage gained through using the indirect style within the limited technique is that the child has not come in direct conflict with you in spite of not having performed as requested, so nothing has been lost from your rapport with the child, and you have gained new information about the child's perceived competence. Your task changes at this point. Instead of forcing the child into an activity through implied threats or your authority, you can evaluate the content of the movement problem with the intention of making the request less difficult.

Note that problem statements or questions should usually be accompanied by demonstrations and affirming verbal comments (see chapter 6 on the use of feedback and reinforcement). The combination of your modeling technique, the accepting nature of your incidental comments and planned reinforce-

ment, and the choices implied by the question stem provide a setting in which the child's needs become more obvious and acknowledged. By using this information about the child's needs, you can adopt content activities more appropriate to the individual child.

Question Stems in Developing Skill Themes

A crucial component in developing a skill theme is the use of a question stem in the problem statement. Each of the three content-structuring techniques briefly described earlier can be introduced using a similar form of beginning. The beginning words are the sentence or statement stem (Kiemele & Bruya, 1978) or question stem. We advocate that the question stem be used in place of the statement stem commonly used by traditional teachers. We believe the command statement often has the unfortunate effect of narrowing or limiting the child's choices and movements, whereas the question stem actually increases the range of movement options.

Through making movement choices, the child begins to understand cognitively and perceive motorically which motor patterns are most efficient. Thus the process of narrowing choices or options to the most efficient pattern is one in which the child actively participates. The premises upon which this reasoning is based include the belief that children best retain what they learn if they make decisions about their learning while they learn. In effect, this reasoning seems to replicate, in a simple manner, the complex interaction between reasoning and sensorimotor activity that Piaget (1963; Roberton & Halverson, 1984) discusses.

Shaffer's Technique

This system was first introduced in the United States by Shaffer (1969), although it had been used previously as the topic for at least two European books on the subject (Diem, 1957; Hackett-Layne & Jenson, 1966). Basically, the system as proposed by Shaffer can be broken into two parts. The first part, the question stem, signals the second part (the content), which is a problem statement or verbal challenge. These question stems are open-ended questions that pose a simple but direct challenge to the young child. They take the form of "Who can . . . ?" or "How many ways can you . . . ?" The teacher then inserts appropriate kinds of movement options from within a particular content area. Each question elaborates on previous questions and on the solutions achieved by the children. Obviously, the questions stems are verbally dependent and must be stated simply and directly, especially for very young children. This approach probably will not work well for prelingual children under 12 months to 18 months.

Greene-Horne Variability Technique

The content aspect of a structuring procedure can be used systematically to include variations in practice. These variations are used to expand the child's understanding of the demands of the situation and the performance of a particular movement in the water environment. The Greene-Horne system (Greene & Horne, 1969) presents a list of concepts that can be used to build variations for practicing movement, including *speed*, *intensity*, and *direction*.

Suppose that you are trying to systematically expand water entry options that use the ladder. For instance, assume that you have presented the following indirect content-structuring question: "How many different ways can you climb into the water?" Further assume that the child has tried several possibilities, but you want to continue expanding the demands on the entry activities. By using one of the concepts of the Greene-Horne variability technique (Greene & Horne, 1969), you can elicit further solution variations.

"How many different ways can you climb into the water?" can be expanded using the speed concept: "Can you use three of those different ways and climb into the water sometimes very quickly and sometimes very slowly?" Using the direction concept to expand the entry question, the instructor can ask, "Can you use one of those ways to climb into the water frontward, backward, left, or right safely?" Each concept proposed by Greene and Horne encourages the exploration of several movement variations. Put in combination (e.g., speed plus direction; direction plus intensity), the concepts provide an almost unlimited set of aquatic movement variations.

The Greene-Horne variations are not presented simply at random. You need to expand options gradually and only in response to the child's success. If a child is hesitant to attempt any option, you can return to a previous option that is less challenging. Further options offered to a hesitant child should be geared to that child's willingness to participate and ability to accomplish the task (see Figure 5.4).

PRESENTATION PHASES IN EDUCATIONAL AQUATICS
CONCEPT 5.6

Educational aquatics encourages instructors to use problem solving and guided discovery statements to help children explore the aquatic content areas in learning Phase 1 skill themes and also encourages learning at Phase 2 by integrating the separately learned Phase 1 skill themes using another series of problem statements.

In educational aquatics, young children are encouraged to experiment with skills in a wide variety of situations and conditions. The previous section described how you can structure problem and question stems to promote experimentation and to increase practice variability. Initially, the aquatic skill themes should be explored singularly. That means that children should be encouraged to explore each content area, such as entry, floating, gliding, or arms, as a single unit. This in-depth exploration of aquatic content areas occurs as part of Phase 1 in educational aquatics. Integration and refinement of skill themes are the focus of Phase 2. In each phase, these objectives are accomplished through problem solving and guided discovery. Table 5.3 shows examples of how different question stems can be used for problem solving and guided discovery in both phases of aquatic education.

Phase 1: Guided Discovery and Problem Solving

The main thrust of Phase 1 is a thorough and creative exploration of each skill theme at each child's own

Practice variability and feelings of success

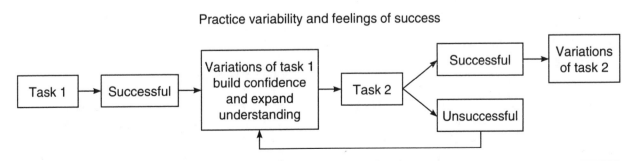

Figure 5.4   Variations can be used to increase confidence before undertaking the next level of difficulty.

Table 5.3 Examples of Phase 1 and Phase 2 in an Educational Aquatics Movement Education Approach

Phase 1

Sample activities from each content area: Problem solving

How many different ways can you get into the pool?
Which ways can you float while holding on to the wall?
Show me how you push off from the wall.
Who can get their face wet with water a different way?
How many ways can you make your arms move through the water?
Who can make the biggest splash with their legs?
How many ways can you move through the water? Show me!

Sample activities for each content area: Guided discovery

Which way gets you into the water without getting your face wet?
Which is the easiest way to float with your face in the water?
Who can push off the wall and go the farthest?
How many times can you bob your face and make bubbles?
Which arm movement makes you go backward?
Which leg movement makes you go forward easiest?
How far can you swim without touching the side?

Phase 2

Combined sample activities from two content areas: Problem solving

Who can jump in and come up floating on their back?
Who can push off, glide, and then roll over and float?
Who can hold their breath and glide underwater?
How can you move your arms and keep your head up?
Who can kick their feet without splashing while they glide?
Who can jump in and swim to the other side without touching?

Sample activities for each content area: Guided discovery

Which jump lets you start swimming sooner?
Which body position lets you kick with less splash?
Which arms and legs are easiest to use together?
Which arm movement lets you breathe easiest?
Which kick lets you glide farthest and easiest?
How many breaths can you take while you float on your back?

level of readiness. For instance, a young toddler might explore ways to get into the water (e.g., climb over the gutter, climb down the ladder, slide in on a mat, climb or jump to her or his parent). An older preschooler might explore getting into the water by jumping (feetfirst, kneefirst, cannonball, twisting) as well as by headfirst diving (sliding, kneeling, sitting, standing). Whatever the skill, each child is encouraged to explore as thoroughly as possible all alternatives at his or her own level of readiness.

Your role in the exploratory process at Phase 1 is to provide the initial challenge using a broad *question stem* (e.g., "Who can . . . ?" or "How many ways can you . . . ?"). This should be done in reference to the Shaffer technique as described earlier. As the children begin to demonstrate their ideas, you might present more specific challenges or prompts (e.g.,

"What if you tried . . . ?" or "Suppose you . . . ?"). You also might select a performance by one child as a demonstration and suggest, "Who else can try it like Jane?" Move from a teaching technique of movement exploration and problem solving (broadly stated question stem) to guided discovery (more specific suggestions and narrower choices) selected from the exploration process solutions. In this way you use your knowledge and expertise both in aquatics and with children to shape a unique and broad-based learning experience. Within each lesson at Phase 1, you should explore each of the major skill themes. Each subsequent lesson builds upon previous lessons for a thorough exploration of each skill theme.

There also is a natural progression in skill themes across lessons. Initially, you will do a great deal of exploration of entry, breath control, and arm and leg actions. After the children gain experience and are comfortable with these content areas, lessons can begin to explore more difficult areas such as gliding, floating, and combined strokes. However, even when the children have achieved more advanced levels of aquatic readiness, there is a continuing need to practice all content areas.

The traditional instructor who has relied on command style teaching and direct progression of skills may feel uncomfortable at first with educational aquatics. This approach requires exchanging a teacher-centered approach and curriculum for a child-centered one. The traditional instructor may feel that he or she is relinquishing control of the class. And in fact, control of learning is shifted to the child. However, effectively using educational aquatics requires more knowledge, experience, and planning from the instructor than does traditional aquatics. It certainly draws more from the teacher's own creativity and ability to generate new problem sentences. The initial problem-solving approach seems very simple, but it can be a challenge to adapt unsuccessful question stems to ones that young children can understand and react to. You will become successful at using guided discovery to produce skilled movement only through study and experience, but you will find it to be meaningful and well worth your effort to become skilled at selecting variations that foster children's learning and enjoyment.

Phase 2: Refining and Integrating Skill Themes

Phase 2 of educational aquatics is an important extension of Phase 1 skill themes. As in Phase 1, you pose a series of problem statements with question stems. However, in this phase, the problem statements require the child to both (a) refine movements and (b) integrate two or more content areas previously explored. For example, you might use the familiar ''Who can . . . ?'' question stem and specify a refined skill (e.g., ''Who can enter the deep water without getting your head wet?'') This would be followed by an entry and a breath control theme (e.g., ''Who can jump into the pool and get three breaths in a row?'').

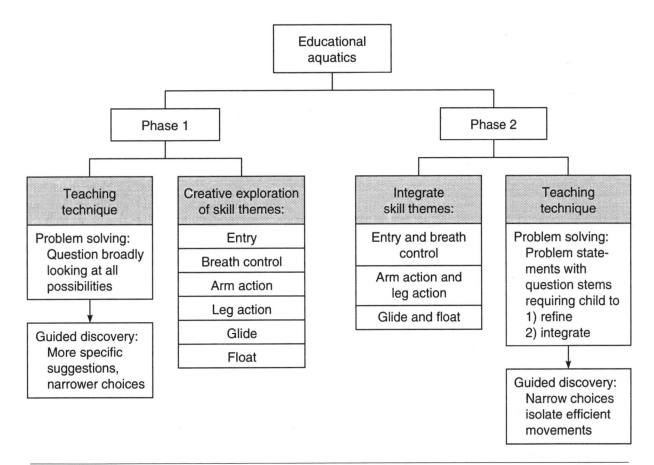

Figure 5.5   In educational aquatics, the instructor solicits the broadest exploration of all movements and then eventually leads the student to narrow the choices for a skilled movement. As the children progress in their understanding and performance of skill theme activities, they are asked to consider more advanced or integrated (combined) skill themes.

Obviously, for you the challenge is to keep such problem statements simple enough that the child's limited language and vocabulary do not prevent her or him from understanding and attempting the problem solution.

Another challenge for you at Phase 2 is to attempt to present, in combinations, as wide a diversity of skill themes as possible to enhance practice variability. The typical swimming instructor introduces a flutter kick and uses one or two drills (kicking at the gutter, kicking with a kickboard) and then adds alternating crawl arm movements (perhaps first on the deck, then in shallow water, and then unassisted) and finally launches the child into a crawl stroke. In contrast, instructors who use educational aquatics from an aquatic readiness perspective would spend several lessons exploring all the possible arm movements that the children could think of to use in the water and then explore the effectiveness of all those patterns. Finally, the unsuccessful or inefficient arm movements would be discarded. The instructor also should simultaneously present problem sentences to explore all possible ways to move the feet and encourage the selection of a small set of efficient leg kicks. Then, and only then, would Phase 2, arm and leg movements in different combinations, be attempted. If three types of arm movements and three types of leg kicks are discovered to effectively move a child forward in the water, then there are nine possible arm-and-leg combinations to explore. Figure 5.5 summarizes the presentation phases.

Some instructors may feel this approach is inefficient and wastes time. The literature on movement education and motor learning schema strongly suggests that nothing could be farther from the truth. Educational aquatics may appear to take more time initially, but the lengthy presentation and practice time is needed by the children to adjust to the water and organize their movement, both cognitively and motorically. To promote a child's water competence, aquatic readiness, and overall aquatic learning in the most effective way, a strong foundation of time and experience is needed. The technique we describe is the most successful way to provide that foundation. Any shortcut in time robs children of important prerequisites and fundamentals in their aquatic education.

SUMMARY

This chapter discusses a radically nontraditional way to present aquatic readiness skills to young children. A child-centered teaching approach that uses a movement education technique called educational aquatics has been described in detail. You must understand the uniqueness of the aquatic environment and be able to integrate the four aspects of movement (body, space, effort, and relationships) into aquatic learning. Educational aquatics uses seven concept areas (paralleling the ARA assessment areas) that serve as skill themes for introducing young children to movement in the water.

A particularly important uniqueness of educational aquatics is the method of presenting aquatic readiness. You will use problem statements, with either command or question stems, to elicit a variety of movement experiences. You can deliver these problem statements using direct, limited, or indirect content structuring. Finally, skill themes are explored in two phases. In Phase 1, problem solving and guided discovery teaching methods are used to thoroughly explore variations within each individual skill theme. In Phase 2, the emphasis is on further skill refinement and on combination of skill themes to promote a wider range of water competence skills.

The educational aquatics approach to presenting aquatic readiness is based on learning and pedagogical principles common to movement education and physical education. It is proposed as an alternative to traditional aquatic teaching methodology. A number of well-established learning principles are involved in educational aquatics, and these are described in more detail in chapter 6.

Chapter

6

Setting the Aquatic Learning Environment for Readiness

This chapter presents several traditional motor learning concepts with which any instructor of young children should be familiar. Such concepts can be used with a variety of teaching techniques, including movement education (see chapter 5) and play theory as well as more traditional instructional styles.

This chapter will familiarize you with the importance of

- setting goals for learning,
- variability and specificity of practice,
- stages of learning,
- feedback and reinforcement,
- motivational techniques, and
- learning styles individualized to enrich the aquatic learning environment.

GOAL-DIRECTED AQUATIC SKILL LEARNING
CONCEPT 6.1

Learning for aquatic readiness is purposeful and goal directed and can be enhanced when the child understands the purpose of the targeted skill.

One of the basic differences between voluntary swimming and the infant swimming reflex is that voluntary swimming skills are goal-directed. The swimming reflex has been variously described as stereotyped, obligatory, and primitive, because the young infant is not cognitively in control of this movement and cannot adapt it (see chapter 2). In contrast, aquatic movements that develop later in the

first year of life and after are flexible, adaptive, and purposeful to varying degrees. The motor skills in this chapter are of the second variety: voluntary aquatic motor skills.

Goals and Purposes for Learning

A basic feature of teaching voluntary movement is the need to help children understand, at least in rudimentary ways, the goal and purpose for learning any task or movement that they are asked to perform. Only when children are moving purposefully can they develop a movement plan that permits adaptive and flexible movement. When young children are asked merely to react to a single, unvarying stimulus, their responses usually are primitive. However, if they understand, even in a limited way, the goal toward which they are striving, they can vary their responses to see what works best for them (see Table 6.1).

A Goal-Setting Example: Breath Control

Suppose you want a young child or infant to hold his or her breath before going underwater. The child needs to understand in a basic way what holding the breath means and how he or she can accomplish it. One common technique for getting young children to hold their breath has been to blow in their faces to stimulate a breath-holding or gasping response. The problem with such a technique is that what it stimulates is a reflex; the child does not learn anything, he or she simply reacts. A reflex or reaction,

Table 6.1 Differences Between Reflexive Movement and Voluntary, Goal-Directed Movement Skills

Movement	Characteristics
Reflexive	Standard stimulus → automatic stereo-typed reaction (Result = little active learning by the child)
Voluntary	Understand goal → select appropriate behavior (Result = active and adaptive learning by the child)

by definition, is nonadaptive and does not involve learning.

A better alternative is the "1-2-3" or "ready-set-go" technique before submerging. When this is presented to the child progressively, the child learns that the "1-2-3" signal given by the parent or instructor means to hold her or his breath in expectation of going underwater. In other words, the signal encourages the child to develop a simple movement plan anticipating submersion.

Setting a Basic Goal

Of course, a basic learning problem still must be solved. How does the young child *learn* the "1-2-3" or "ready-set-go" signal? One technique has been simply to count "1-2-3" and submerge the child the first time. This can be rather traumatic for some children, and it relies on trial-and-error learning. It does not permit the child to develop a plan.

An alternative, *goal-setting* method can be suggested. Consider other situations, outside of swimming, in which a child must learn breath control. Eating, drinking, blowing through a straw, and blowing out a candle are all examples. By having the child pretend to be blowing bubbles through a straw or blowing out an imaginary candle, you can elicit voluntary breath control from the child (see the game Magic Candle in the appendix). By pretending, yourself, to be blowing through a straw and then going underwater, you can demonstrate the goal of breath control to even a young child. The child learns the goal while actively controlling his or her own learning. The child also can induce you to produce variations of your own example (e.g., with and without a real straw, with and without an imaginary candle, after bubble blowing or making a motor boat sound) that enhance learning (see "Presenting the Content" in chapter 5).

Indirect Goal Setting

An interesting characteristic of goal setting with young children is the paradox of *indirect goal setting*. The adult caretaker often wishes to promote a *primary goal* such as breath control. A child who cannot cognitively understand the adult's goal might understand a *secondary goal* of blowing out a candle on a birthday cake. Since the child finds the secondary goal interesting and motivating, the adult can use it to indirectly promote and develop the primary goal. Indirect teaching techniques (see chapter 5) using indirect goal setting are extremely effective ways of helping young children develop specific skills. They also can work well in conjunction with our next concept, practice variability.

PRACTICE VARIABILITY
CONCEPT 6.2

Learning for aquatic readiness is best developed through broad variability of practice conditions.

A persistent characteristic of traditional swimming instruction has been the restricted ways skills are taught and practiced. All too often, programs call for, and instructors use, only one or two methods to introduce, practice, and learn aquatic skills. As we will demonstrate later in this chapter, such monotony can reduce even a small child's motivation levels. Furthermore, there is evidence that such limited practice situations can handicap later learning.

Theoretical Support for Variability

Schmidt (1975, 1977, 1991) proposed in his "schema theory of motor learning" that people who practice motor skills in a "variable" setting learn faster and more accurately than those who practice in a "constant" setting. Similarly, Gentile (1972) predicted that learning "open" skills under "diversified" conditions would produce superior learning.

These theories suggest that, when people learn a skill, a movement *plan* or *schema* is formed in their memories so that they can repeat the skill whenever they need to. Under *constant* practice conditions of learning, the same stimulus is presented repeatedly to elicit a skill (e.g., "blowing in the face" as the only stimulus used to elicit breath control). Under *variable* practice conditions, a variety of stimuli are presented to elicit the same skill (e.g., "blowing through a straw," "blowing out candles," and so on, to elicit breath control). Children who learn the skill as a response to a wide variety of stimuli will be able in the future to respond with the skill in a great variety of situations. That is, they have broad "plans" or "schemata" for action in their memories. Children who learn skills in response to a very limited range of stimuli will have narrower "plans" for action—they will respond with the skill in the future to fewer kinds of situations. Clearly, children who learn under variable conditions will be more versatile in responding to future situations and able to perform their skills in a variety of circumstances. In this sense their learning is *stronger* than learning acquired under constant conditions. This concept is shown in Table 6.2.

A Variable Practice Example: Kicking

A prime illustration of the lack of variability in traditional beginning swimming programs is the teaching of kicking skills. American swimming programs teach almost exclusively the flutter kick to children. The predominance of this practice is so great that "kick" is usually synonymous with flutter kick to most teachers and children. In addition, children usually learn and practice the flutter kick in a static position at pool side or on a kickboard. As a result, American children as a whole are much poorer in scissors- and breaststroke kicking skills than their counterparts in nations where the flutter kick and crawl stroke are not emphasized as much as in American programs.

The leg action sequences we introduced in chapter 4 include rudimentary examples of kicking styles other than flutter kick. These are included for two reasons. First, children naturally develop a variety of kicking styles when encouraged through exploratory

and play techniques as in educational aquatics (see chapter 5). Second, when children are encouraged to develop different kicking styles under varied conditions, they will develop stronger kicking schemata due to this variability of practice (see Figure 6.1).

Encouraging Variable Practice

We encourage you to develop and use a wide variety of teaching styles and practice situations, drills, and games for all the aquatic skills in the program. Chapter 8 lists a number of such games and activities, organized by skill concept and developmental level, to help you introduce the desired variability. All aquatic skills are enhanced by practicing the skill under variable conditions—even advanced formal strokes.

PRACTICE SPECIFICITY
CONCEPT 6.3

Learning aquatic motor skills requires sufficient specific practice experiences.

One major tenet of motor learning is that learners require sufficient specific practice experiences to adequately learn motor skills. Too many aquatic instructors assume that a child needs only to be shown a swimming skill and then to try it once or twice for the child to have learned that skill. This is not consistent with the motor learning research literature.

Repetition

Young children need to actively repeat aquatic skills many times over to really learn them. It is a common complaint of aquatic instructors of children that after children have missed some lessons or a whole session they have "forgotten" everything when they come back. The instructors often blame forgetting or inconsistency in movement on the young child's poor memory or short attention span. Actually, it probably indicates that the child never really learned the skill in the first place. Children must practice a skill over and over before they can repeat it upon request or need.

Inconsistent behavior is often characteristic of an intermediate stage of learning (see Concept 6.4). Improvement in performance is usually very rapid in the beginning and begins to slow after the first dozen or more practice trials. However, often after years of practice, persons are still improving their skills in terms of speed, accuracy, and adaptability (Schmidt,

Table 6.2 Differences Between Variable Practice and Constant Practice

Kind of practice	Characteristics of practice	Result
Variable	Many games, drills, activities, and practice situations	Strong memory, broad skill plan of action, easy adaptation to novel situations
Constant	Limited or no games, drills, activities, and practice situations	Weaker memory, restricted, narrow plan of action, limited adaptability

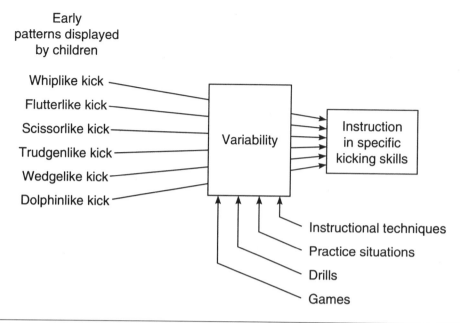

Figure 6.1 Early exposure to a variety of kicking skills enhances learning.

1991). Adult competitive swimmers often continue to improve swimming performance times throughout Masters age-group participation, in spite of aging effects, because they continue to correctly practice specific skills.

Practice Intentions

The adage "Practice makes perfect" should not be taken to mean that mere *repetition* improves performance. Repetition alone does not yield high-level skills. Other factors influence practice, learning, and performance. One important factor, *practice intentions*, is often misunderstood. Instead of stubbornly repeating established movement patterns, the learner must both desire to improve and receive corrective information to help eliminate mistakes and errors. To desire to improve, a child must be enjoying the experience; in children, smiles and laughter are the true marks of positive practice intentions (see Figure 6.2). The crying, reluctant young child lacks positive practice intentions and will not progress in confidence or skills. Older children who drop out of competitive swimming because they are not improving often lack these positive practice intentions. Because they are perpetuating mistakes, they don't improve and often become discouraged. Two things can help to nurture a child's positive practice intentions: corrective input and distributed practice.

Corrective Input

To help a child maintain positive practice intentions, provide corrective input to the child about her or his

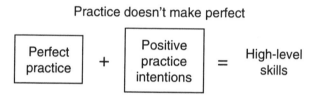

Figure 6.2 Only perfect practice with positive intentions makes perfect.

movement. For our main discussion of corrective input (feedback), see Concept 6.5 later in this chapter. Using guided discovery techniques (see chapter 5), you can provide the child with information about correct techniques and efficient movement patterns. Without corrective input, the child may become habituated to inappropriate or inefficient movements. When a child perpetuates mistakes, he or she will inevitably fail to improve and may even get worse and become discouraged. Such discouragement can defeat the child's positive practice intentions, so you clearly have a responsibility to provide your young swimmers with corrective input that will help them to improve with practice.

Distributed Practice

Another important factor is the practice-to-rest ratio under which aquatic skills are practiced and learned. A practice schedule for motor skills that has short or infrequent rest intervals is called *massed practice*. Practicing with more frequent or longer rest intervals between practice sessions is termed *distributed practice*. Research comparing the efficiency of these types of practice-to-rest ratios has yielded mixed results. Several generalizations, however, may be made. Distributed practice yields superior immediate performance and seems to provide better long-term learning. Also, for complex and fatiguing tasks such as most swimming skills, distributed practice is recommended. Finally, distributed practice appears to be superior for young and inexperienced children (Sage, 1984). Table 6.3 gives a more complete summary of the benefits of distributed practice.

It follows from these findings about practice schedules that aquatic programs for preschoolers and novices need to provide relatively short daily sessions, to include lots of rest between skill practices during any session, and to mix a variety of different skills during any one lesson. One way to provide distributed rest intervals within a lesson is to plan on using a wide variety of skill themes each session (see chapter 5); each skill theme can include practice of several different tasks. Also, interspersing games, songs, and other activities between more monotonous drills can provide rest intervals for the young child, in effect, as well as provide more and varied practice. Having a variety of games and activities (see chapter 8) obviously also improves the child's motivation (see Concept 6.6) and learning schema (see Concept 6.2).

Distributed practice produces superior performance and learning for aquatic readiness.

consistent while moving with more ease and smoothness and less attention to the task (Sage, 1984; Schmidt, 1991). These changes in skill often are characterized as qualitative shifts in style called *phases* or *stages* of learning.

LEARNING STAGES
CONCEPT 6.4

Learning aquatic readiness skills occurs in qualitative learning stages.

Motor skills (including aquatic skills) are learned differently as the learner gains experience. During the learning process, the learner's proficiency increases. The learner becomes faster, more accurate, and more

Definitions of the Learning Stages

The three stages of motor learning are called (a) initial, or cognitive; (b) associative, or intermediate; and (c) motor, or autonomous, respectively. Each has specific characteristics that distinguish it from the other stages. Table 6.4 summarizes these characteristics.

Table 6.3   Distributed Practice: Research Findings and Practical Principles for a Preschool Aquatics Program

Research finding	Practical examples
Distributed practice promotes superior performance.	Keep lessons to 30 min or less. Provide breaks between skills. Use many games, drills, and activities.
Distributed practice promotes superior learning.	Repeat skills every lesson. Use limited practice trials each week.
Younger, inexperienced children learn best under distributed practice.	Use shorter lessons for younger and inexperienced children. Provide more rest between skills for younger children.
Complex and fatiguing skills require distributed practice.	Give more rest for complicated skills. Watch children for fatigue (blue lips, shivering, crying). Break complicated skills into simpler parts. Stress fun and enjoyment.

Table 6.4　A Summary of Learning Stage Characteristics

Characteristics	Learner level		
	Initial	Intermediate	Autonomous
Speed of movement	Slow	Moderate	Fast
Accuracy	Inaccurate	Varied accuracy	Accurate
Movement flow	Awkward	Moderate	Smooth, easy
Movement plan	Narrow	Expanding	Broad, adaptive
Consistency	Consistent	Inconsistent (variable)	Consistent
Adaptability	Inflexible	Moderately flexible	Flexible
Needs augmented feedback	Yes	Yes	No

Initial Stage

In the *initial*, or *cognitive*, stage of learning, the learner makes first attempts to *get the idea of the movement* (Adams, 1971; Gentile, 1972; Robb, 1972). Because the learner's plan (or schema) of movement is limited and rudimentary in the cognitive stage, the learner has only a few, rudimentary movement options. As a result, the beginner's movements are characterized by relative slowness, awkwardness, and inaccuracy (many errors) as she or he attempts to gain control over the muscle actions needed to perform the skill. The novice, contrary to some notions, is comparatively consistent in his or her performance, but that consistency is inflexible and nonadaptive, due to the lack of options in the novice's action plan.

Intermediate Stage

The *intermediate*, or *associative*, stage is a period of acquiring and refining a skill. Whereas the novice establishes a rudimentary movement plan, the intermediate-stage learner must broaden the conditions under which she or he can perform the skill (see chapter 5). She or he also must improve the smoothness and ease with which the skill is performed. During this stage, feedback (see Concept 6.5) about how well the learner is performing must be provided if the learner is to progress. Because the intermediate learner is trying to expand his or her control over the movement plan, the behavior tends to be somewhat erratic and inconsistent.

Autonomous Stage

In the *autonomous*, or *motor*, stage, the learner moves quickly, accurately, and smoothly. The movement seems almost effortless and automatic, due to the learner's extensive experience and practice. Despite being flexible and adaptive to a variety of conditions, the skilled learner is very consistent in performance. During this stage, the learner requires less external feedback from others and detects and corrects his or her own errors. The major tasks for the learner during this stage are minor refinements and performance improvement.

Methods of Instructing at Each Stage of Learning

By becoming aware of the child's learning stage, you can choose the instruction methods most effective for that stage.

Initial Stage

The young swimmer's style of movement can give a clue to her or his stage of learning. If the swimmer shows slow, inaccurate, but fairly consistent movement, you should suspect that the child is still getting the idea of the movement (Gentile, 1972). This indicates this child's need for further demonstration and primary training. The child also may not have a firm grasp of the goal of the movement (see Concept 6.1).

Intermediate Stage

If the child moves quickly but with inconsistent accuracy, he or she is probably at an intermediate stage. Provide extensive practice with a great deal of encouragement, corrective input, and specific feedback about the swimmer's errors. For movements and information on how to provide different types of feedback, see Concept 6.5.

The erratic and inconsistent behavior characteristic of the intermediate stage often displays either *regres-*

sion, an apparent worsening of a skill, or a *plateau*, a lack of improvement, in learning. These two phenomena are frustrating for both the instructor and the child. They often erode the child's motivation, positive practice intentions, and willingness to continue practice. It is helpful if both instructor and child (and parent) understand that these things occur with learning at the intermediate stage. Changing practice sessions by adding more variety or providing more rest or adding motivating games can help to eliminate regressions and plateaus in learning.

Autonomous Stage

The rare child who may have reached the 3rd stage, the *autonomous*, or *motor*, level, still requires your assistance. Learning has not stopped in this final stage. Instead, the kinds of changes the child must make are related to refinement of skills. A child at this learning stage easily can become bored and a behavior problem unless you provide challenging and interesting practice situations.

Within the context of a guided discovery teaching technique, more challenging problems and question stems can easily be given to the young child performing at advanced levels (see chapter 5). You can request the advanced child to come up with more variations on a skill theme or more difficult variations. As a skillful, experienced aquatic readiness instructor, you will be able to use exploration and guided discovery techniques to accommodate young children at all stages of learning within a single class.

FEEDBACK AND REINFORCEMENT
CONCEPT 6.5

At early stages of aquatic readiness learning, positive and precise feedback and reinforcement are crucial to continued progress.

To be successful working with young children, you must understand and use two crucial principles: feedback and reinforcement. The discussions in chapter 5 on positive talk and earlier in this chapter on corrective input are examples of feedback and reinforcement. The following sections explain the concepts and their use more fully.

Feedback

Feedback is information about the process or results of a person's movement. To be effective in the use of feedback, an instructor must understand the two types of feedback—*intrinsic* and *augmented*—and the principle of feedback precision.

Types of Feedback

Feedback is perceived by the young child either naturally (intrinsic) or as a result of enhancement and highlighting (augmented) by the instructor. All learners require feedback information to improve performance. Augmented feedback from the instructor is crucial to learners at the initial and intermediate stages (see Concept 6.4). Learners at the autonomous stage usually learn successfully from both augmented and intrinsic feedback.

Intrinsic Feedback. Intrinsic feedback is naturally perceived information a person obtains either during or after a movement. This feedback can be received from visual, auditory, tactile, kinesthetic, or proprioceptive systems. For instance, when the child feels the water moving across the body (tactile) or feels how the arms come out of the water (kinesthetic) or even sees the lane line to swim in a straight line (visual), the child is using intrinsic feedback. Oftentimes it is important to point out intrinsic feedback, because the young child may not have paid attention to it. For learners at the initial or intermediate stages, intrinsic feedback can be pointed out almost casually. However, more emphasis should be given to intrinsic feedback for autonomous-stage swimmers.

Augmented Feedback. When you provide specific extra information, either verbally, visually, or proprioceptively, you have provided augmented feedback. For instance, some instructors help manipulate children's arms and legs when children are first learning to swim. Others provide more extensive verbal descriptions of how a swimmer is performing. Some instructors use videotape to provide children with accurate pictures of themselves moving in the water (see chapter 4). These are all types of augmented feedback.

There are two main categories of augmented feedback: *knowledge of results* (KR) and *knowledge of performance* (KP) (Gentile, 1972; Schmidt, 1991). When you tell a swimmer something about the *results* of her or his movement (e.g., "You stayed under water 10 seconds" or "You went 10 feet on your glide"), you are providing KR. When the information you give to the swimmer is about the quality or process of the movement (e.g., "You are bending your knees" or "That arm is too straight; it should be bent at the elbow"), you are providing KP. The KR and KP you give the swimmer help to define and strengthen his or her movement plan. KR is often easier to provide (e.g., "You swam 10 feet on your back"). KP is equally important to provide (e.g., "You are pointing your toes on your right leg when you try to swim like a frog"). Figure 6.3 summarizes how feedback can be used for all stages of learning.

Precision of Feedback

The *precision of feedback* is an important factor in the feedback's effectiveness in promoting learning (Adams, 1971). The swimmer needs to hear you say more than simply "Good!" or "That's wrong." On the other hand, you should refrain from being too precise, being too detailed, or providing too much information at one time. Remember that children have a limited vocabulary and that their understanding is much different from adults'. Feedback should be simple and direct: "Kick those legs harder" or "Stretch and make yourself thin." You can also give feedback indirectly or in the form of a question. For instance, if the child is pretending to be a motorboat during a breath control drill, you can ask "Can you be a louder [faster, bigger, etc.] motorboat than that?"

Reinforcement

Feedback that is used for motivation purposes is known as *reinforcement*. Positive feedback is more effective as a reinforcer than is negative feedback. Identify the behavior to be used, not the behavior to be avoided! It is easy to constantly find oneself saying "No," "Don't," and "Not"—identifying the nega-

tive *errors*. It is more difficult, but much more effective, to exclaim, "That's the idea," "That's better," or "You're improving."

Reinforcement is important at all stages of learning. Positive reinforcement is especially important in developing and maintaining positive practice intentions in initial- or intermediate-stage learners. Positive reinforcement can serve the dual roles of increasing motivation (i.e., positive feelings of self-worth and success) and identifying appropriate solutions to movement problems. For example, when a child is told, "Good, Susie, you are moving your arms farther and faster underwater now," the child feels good about accomplishing the task and has learned that longer, faster arm movements are desired and more efficient.

ACHIEVING MOTIVATION
CONCEPT 6.6

Appropriate levels of motivation are important for improving aquatic readiness levels.

Motivation is the conditions or stimuli that arouse or direct behavior (Sage, 1984). Simply put, motivation controls our behavior. The presence of varying motivational factors explains why some children learn to swim quickly and cannot get enough of the water and others never learn to swim and avoid the water at all costs.

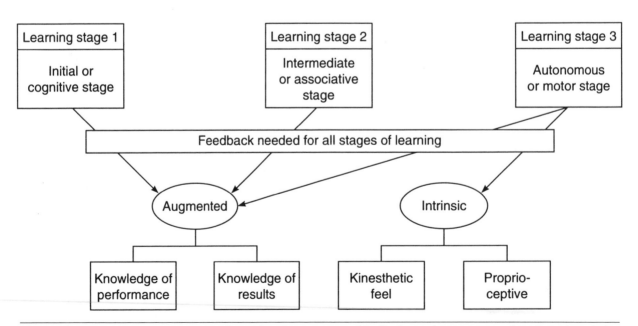

Figure 6.3 Feedback is important to learning, although some types of feedback may be more appropriate than others during a particular stage of learning.

Functions of Motivation

Motivation impels us to accomplish some things and not to do others. Obviously, learning to swim is strongly influenced by motivational factors. There are two basic functions of motivation: arousal and goal achievement.

Arousal

The first function of motivation is to modulate the person's underlying *arousal*, or excitement. When our excitement is too low, we fall asleep. When our excitement is too high, we become agitated and cannot perform correctly.

Optimal arousal and performance occur somewhere between the two extremes. Usually water and swimming activities themselves serve as *motivators* that produce arousal in children. For example, witness the loud and excited voices, the smiling faces, and the plentiful activity inevitably found at a swimming pool or beach. Such behaviors indicate high, but probably fairly optimal, levels of arousal.

In contrast, people who are termed "afraid of the water" actually are excessively aroused by an aquatic environment. Their signs of fear, their passivity, their reluctance to move around water, usually are not signs that these children need to be "psyched up." They need to be relaxed and calmed down instead.

You will have to deal with individual differences in motivation in the aquatic environment. Frequently you will be struggling to calm excited and fearful children while attempting to selectively increase the arousal of listless and unmotivated children. You must discern when a game or activity is having a negative influence on your students, either by causing too much excitement or by being uninteresting. You also must know when and how to increase a class's motivation and when and how to calm a class down.

Goal Achievement

The second function of motivation is the directive, or situation-specific, achievement of a *goal* or satisfaction of a *need* (Sage, 1984). This type of motivation involves specific manipulations of the environment to encourage desired behaviors and discourage inappropriate ones. There are two types of motivators with a *directive* function: incentives and reinforcers.

Incentives. *Incentives* induce or arouse someone to do something. They act as "promises" of later rewards for achieving something. Aquatic readiness

Water is a natural motivator for most children.

instructors have a great many incentives available for their use. Exploration and guided discovery techniques (chapter 5), large play equipment (chapter 7), and games and small equipment (chapter 8) all represent types of incentives that attract children's interest and enthusiasm in the aquatic readiness setting.

Reinforcers. *Reinforcers* (see Concept 6.5) serve to strengthen a response. They act as "rewards" after something has been accomplished. As we mentioned previously, positive reinforcers are more effective in altering behavior, because they reward an action rather than punish one. The aquatic readiness setting is arranged to provide both intrinsic and augmented forms of positive feedback and reinforcement to the child. Activities are geared toward the child's developmental level; gradual, step-by-step progress is encouraged; and evaluation is ongoing, thus providing the children with a positive sense of their accomplishments.

Incentives and reinforcers vary considerably in their effectiveness. Some of the factors that influence their effectiveness include the person administering the motivation, the type of motivation used (e.g., verbal, physical, food), and the socioeconomic status and ethnic background of the learner. Just as with manipulating arousal characteristics of children, you must take great care to structure a positive, success-oriented environment for children. Figure 6.4 illustrates how the concepts related to goal achievement work together to motivate children.

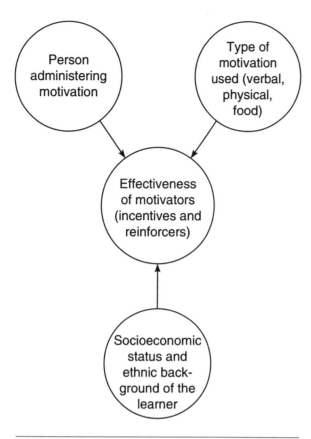

Figure 6.4 Incentives and reinforcers vary in their effectiveness as motivators based on three factors.

Using Motivators in Aquatic Readiness

Instructors and parents can effectively use *motivators* to enhance children's learning. The incentives and reinforcements, however, should be very simple and straightforward. Children respond very effectively to verbal encouragement and praise. They do *not* require physical rewards such as food or medals. In fact, research indicates that physical rewards can reduce the power of praise and cause a reliance on them (Schmidt, 1991). Initially, parents are probably the best administrators of motivators, because they are best known and esteemed by the child. However, after the child gets to know and trust an instructor, the instructor also can become effective in motivating the child. This is accomplished through applying the motivational principles discussed previously.

INDIVIDUAL DIFFERENCES IN LEARNING AND PERCEPTUAL STYLES
CONCEPT 6.7

Learning for aquatic readiness requires attention to individual learning and perceptual styles through a variety of visual, auditory, kinesthetic, and tactile cues.

Important factors influencing aquatic readiness are the individual differences that distinguish one child's behavior from another's. A number of factors makes each child unique from other children. These individual differences complicate the learning process, so that it is often difficult to make accurate generalizations across children. Individual differences discussed in the following sections are variations in learning styles, sensory discrimination abilities, attention to irrelevant stimuli, and intersensory integration.

Learning Styles and Perceptual Preferences

One way children differ is in *learning style*. Differences in learning styles are based on the sense or senses each individual prefers to learn through. For instance, some people prefer learning primarily through seeing, or the *visual* sense. Others learn much more effectively if they *get the feel*, or use the *kinesthetic* sense. Some learn best simply by hearing, or through the *auditory* mode. Finally, some persons learn best using a variety of senses (Buell, Pettigrew, & Langendorfer, 1987).

Swimming instructors of children must be sensitive to these individual differences in learning style and present material and information in a variety of ways. For instance, instead of merely talking about a skill (use the child's auditory sense), also demonstrate the skill (use visual information) and help each child to do the skill (provide kinesthetic feedback). When you use all these sensory modes eclectically, you serve all the different preferences of the children in the class. In addition, each sensory mode can reinforce what has been learned through another mode. Pictures, movies, tapes, games, drills, and gimmicks of all types can help provide multiple learning modes.

Sensory Discrimination Ability

Children have varying degrees of ability to discern sensory and perceptual information, and these developmental differences in perceiving information are important to consider. Gibson (1969) suggested that young children do not *discriminate* information as well as older children. In other words, the younger child may not be able to appreciate a small variation in their behavior that seems obvious to the teacher. Their feet may be coming out of the water on a kick at one time and not at another time, but they may not be able to tell. They also may not be able to discern differences in what the instructor tells them to do. They may think they have their whole head in the water, as instructed, when they have only their mouth and nose submerged.

Attention to Irrelevant Stimuli

Children are often easily distracted by what adults consider to be extraneous information (Gibson, 1969). While you are trying to introduce a new skill, one child may be distracted by several nearby toys, another by the jets bringing water into the pool, and still another may be watching his or her mother up in the pool gallery. This process of being ''captured'' by irrelevant stimuli often is interpreted by adults as a short attention span or poor memory. The aquatic readiness instructor should see this as the child's lack of interest in what an adult thinks is important.

Your challenge, of course, is to make your information more interesting and motivating than all these other distractions! Luckily, as an aquatic readiness instructor you have a variety of tools to use in competing with irrelevant stimuli in the aquatic environment. For instance, the exploratory and guided discovery techniques constructively channel the child's natural curiosity. The use of varied statement and question stems, mixed with repetition, can keep the child involved. Finally, the wealth of games and learning activities presented in the appendix is an excellent source of fun and incentives to use with children.

Intersensory Integration

Finally, Gibson (1969) tells us that young children do not yet integrate information from several sensory sources well. We suggested earlier that you use an eclectic approach of several sensory modes to present information. However, hearing, seeing, and feeling are all considered somewhat separately by the young child, and he or she may have limited ability to link that information together. It is important to help the young child to begin linking information by presenting information in different modes *simultaneously*. For instance, the child who is kicking her or his feet out of the water might not be able to understand that fact from your verbal description alone, but you can grasp the child's feet (giving kinesthetic information) while verbally describing the action (giving auditory information). Similarly, using a videotape can provide visual information in conjunction with either auditory or kinesthetic feedback. Table 6.5 gives examples of possible solutions for dealing with these individual differences.

Table 6.5 Learning Experiences Require Attention to Individual Differences in Learning

Individual difference	Example solution
Learning styles and perceptual preferences	Use a variety of sensory modes in teaching (e.g., tell about the skill *and* show the skill *and* help the children do the skill).
Sensory discrimination ability	Keep comments simple and at child's level of understanding. Use images and cues that children understand (animals, games). Use several modes of presentation simultaneously.
Attention to irrelevant stimuli	Keep distractions to minimum. Remove distractions from child or child from distractions. Keep practice and learning situations as interesting and exciting as possible.
Intersensory integration	Present in different sensory modes. Present same information in different ways at the same time (e.g., show a movie and move the child's limbs as the picture is shown).

SUMMARY

This chapter has highlighted a number of important considerations for structuring the aquatic learning environment for young children and has highlighted crucial information regarding goal setting, practice factors, stages of learning, feedback, motivation, and individual differences in learning and perceptual styles. This information is well supported by theoretical laboratory research but has been organized here to help you apply these principles in concrete and practical situations to optimize the learning environment. Chapters 5, 7, and 8 provide important practical information that reinforces these concepts and will support your efforts to apply this information in your teaching.

Chapter
7
Large Aquatic Equipment

Since the late 1800s we have been creating play structures for children in parks and schoolyards. Only recently has anything but theory (Ellis, 1973; Frost & Klein, 1979) been forwarded to justify the basic features of these structures (Sholtz & Ellis, 1975b). As research has begun to isolate the effects of design features of structures for children's play, publications have appeared to describe the best of those features (Beckwith, 1988; Bowers, 1988; Bruya, 1985c).

This pursuit of more developmentally appropriate play structures will help in the remaking of playground environments to support children's normal growth and development (Bruya, 1988; Bruya & Langendorfer, 1988). Now the concepts used for the design of land-based structures are being applied in the water environment to foster motivation and the improvement of aquatic movement patterns.

In the early 1980s, a pilot project was undertaken that has produced a technique for using large playground-type equipment in the water. The best equipment was found to be "trestle tree" equipment, which is easily movable and can be placed into and removed from the water by one or two people. It was designed in England and made its way to the United States by means of the field of movement education. Although the pieces are separate, they fit together in units that can be reconfigured to meet specific needs.

The pieces tested in the pilot project were

- 2 large trestle tree structures,
- 1 small trestle tree structure,
- 1 arched horizontal ladder,
- 1 ladder,
- 2 bars (usually placed horizontally),
- 1 cargo net,
- 1 slide, and
- two submersible tables (or platforms).

Examples are shown in Figure 7.1.

Following planning, structures should be configured on the deck prior to being placed in the water. The configuration construction is then duplicated in the water. Configurations were chosen dependent on the children and their needs and on the particular educational objective for the day's aquatic readiness experience.

USES FOR LARGE EQUIPMENT
CONCEPT 7.1

Large equipment placed in the aquatic environment for use with aquatic readiness activities can be used for motivational purposes.

Large equipment pieces in the water command the attention of everyone in the aquatic setting. Trestle tree configurations are visually attractive, novel to the children, and also complex (Berlyne, 1958; Hutt, 1976). Such equipment is particularly valuable in the water setting with young children because it provides them with a safe haven or island during instruction, and it is familiar to them by virtue of its similarity to play structures in yards, parks, and school grounds. When the children get into the water on the first day and see the equipment, their obvious intention is to make their way to it. Children who are usually fearful of the water are suddenly focused on the attractive and colorful islands of novel, but seemingly familiar, structures.

This is not to imply that fearful children will suddenly be unafraid when equipment is in the water. Rather, when large equipment and children are present together, children seem to focus primarily on the equipment rather than on the fear of the water that they usually feel while near a pool.

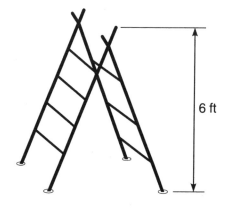 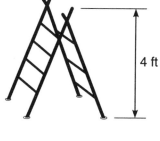

a. Large trestle tree 6 ft

b. Small trestle tree 4 ft

 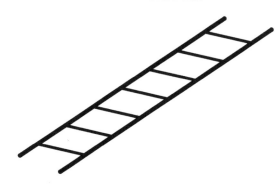

c. Arched horizontal climber

d. Ladder

 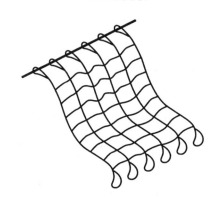

e. 5-ft bar

f. Cargo net

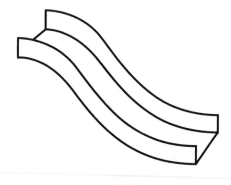 

g. Slide

h. Submersible table

Figure 7.1 Trestle tree structure equipment.

In this way, large equipment can be an important ingredient in a successful aquatic readiness program. The novel but familiar nature of the equipment attracts children (Ellis & Scholtz, 1978), motivating them to move through the water to get to it, and the complexity of the interconnected parts keeps children actively involved (Bruya, 1985c; Weilbacher, 1980) in exploring the environment (see Figure 7.2).

Once in the water and near the equipment, the children seem to feel a need to move on all the parts (Carter, Bruya, & Fowler 1983). Thus, the equipment inspires active child-initiated interactions.

Then, in the normal course of events as they explore and play on and around the equipment, the children are likely to find water splashed in their faces, to be unintentionally partly or fully submersed, and so on. Through these exploratory experiences, the children make gains in aquatic readiness without risk to their rapport with the teacher from prodding

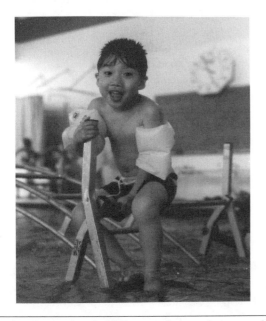

Large equipment is valuable in water because it commands attention from children.

or intentional teacher-initiated submersion. Instead, aquatic readiness activity is stimulated by the children's motivation to use the equipment.

However, because the equipment affects the overall emphasis of the instructional period, it is important to understand the rules for its placement. These rules will be discussed in the next section.

PLACING EQUIPMENT IN THE AQUATIC ENVIRONMENT
CONCEPT 7.2

Configuration rules guide the placement of equipment within the aquatic environment for use in supporting the aquatic readiness curriculum.

The configuration of the equipment in the water follows either of two formats: interconnected or separated. The *interconnected*, or *unified*, format is based on the work of practitioners, researchers, and theorists in the play and movement education literature (Beckwith, 1988; Bowers, 1988; Bruya, 1985d; Gilliom, 1970; Kirchner, Cunningham, & Warrell, 1978). The equipment is closely configured, usually with individual pieces hooked together, or "linked," to form a single large piece of equipment. The equipment is said to be more complex when interconnected (Hutt, 1976; Scholtz & Ellis, 1975a, 1975b).

Interconnected equipment has been shown to be advantageous during play (Bruya, 1985a). It attracts and keeps children actively involved in play for longer periods than equipment that is separated (see Figure 7.3). This is especially evident when the structures are reconfigured at the onset of each day's activities (Weilbacher, 1980). Both visually and motorically, the rearrangement attracts attention, interest, and ultimately the motivation or preference to interact with the equipment (Scholtz & Ellis, 1975a, 1975b). As the newness wears off, the complicated arrangement of the structures provides the motivation

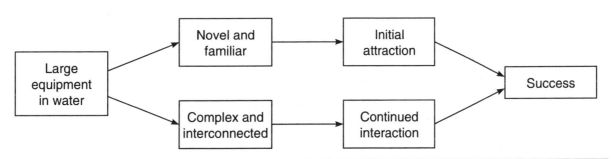

Figure 7.2 The successful use of large equipment in the aquatic readiness program is based on the children's initial attraction to it, and is then sustained by its complexity.

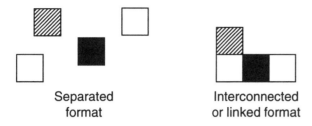

Separated
format

Interconnected
or linked format

Figure 7.3   Children play for significantly longer periods of time when using interconnected equipment (Bruya, 1985a).

to spend additional time exploring the environment (Fiske & Maddi, 1961). Thus, it would seem that increased complexity is the descriptive design concept by which the interconnection of pieces of large equipment works for young children (Munsinger, Kessen, & Kessen, 1964). With interconnected equipment, you can expect your students to spend more time, and get more experience, in the pool. Additional time and experience in the water usually means greater adaptation to its demands, which is a fundamental goal of the aquatic readiness curriculum.

As the children become more adept at working on and off of the island structures, the configuration of pieces can be used to more advantage in a *separated* rather than linked format, particularly when the children are beginning to demonstrate the ability to move from place to place in the water. In this format the individual pieces are separated and progressively placed farther apart.

There are two basic rules governing how far apart equipment should be placed. These rules are discussed in the next sections.

Rule #1: Arrange According to Student Need

The configuration of the equipment in the water is described as its "format," either interconnected or separated (Figure 7.4). Each format is used advantageously during certain instructional phases of the aquatic readiness program and has distinct movement capabilities.

Format changes should be sequenced according to student need—in particular, according to how much physical support a child needs to traverse open water between structures. When children are supported by an adult during traverses between separated pieces of equipment, they perceive the danger and distance to be less than when they move in the water without support. Although all children correctly report that the distance is longer for structures 3 to 6 yards apart than for those that are set closer, they usually will not show reservations about moving to another structure across open water if an adult is there to support them. In fact, most children who move through the water with assistance and support of an adult do not mind traversing a distance between structures of 6 yards and more. It is only when children begin moving without support that they resist traversing open water between structures.

To consistently present open water stimuli to the child, the format can be changed systematically according to the Equipment Format Sequencing Rule Matrix (Table 7.1). This matrix is based on the assumption that a child's willingness to traverse open water depends upon how much physical support the instructor or parent will provide and the distance between structures.

There are nine steps in the matrix. The equipment is linked first as a unit during the instructor-support phase and then reformatted with progressively greater distances between structures. Then as the children are able to move in the water without instructor support, the equipment linking and separation distances are repeated. The key to the sequencing concept is to repeat successful traverses often, as a way to support longer, more difficult traverses.

Equipment should be positioned to provide several options for traversing at each of the levels in Table 7.1. In this way you can move to the next step of the format sequence while providing the next most challenging traverse. Large equipment can be formatted to include distances that meet the needs of all of the students who are using the equipment.

However, formatting the equipment to include the multiple challenges posed by progressively greater

Recommended progressive separation of aquatic structures

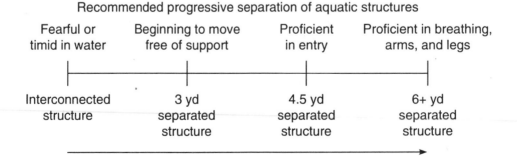

Figure 7.4   As aquatic readiness increases, the configurations of, and the distances between, structures should change.

Table 7.1 Equipment Format Sequencing Rule Matrix

Sequential steps	Instructor support	Instructor nonsupport	Equipment linked	Equipment not linked
Step #1	X		X	
Step #2	X			1.5-yard separation
Step #3	X			3.0-yard separation
Step #4	X			4.5-yard separation
Step #5		X	X	
Step #6		X		1.5-yard separation
Step #7		X		3.0-yard separation
Step #8		X		4.5-yard separation
Step #9		X		+6.0-yard separation

distances of open water does not in itself insure a successful lesson presentation. You must also consider the successful trials or variations performed by the child in the previous task. As outlined in chapter 5 in Figure 5.7, repeated success in the first task increases the confidence of the child as he or she moves to a more difficult second task. Usually, between 5 and 10 successes provide the groundwork for movement to more difficult tasks in the sequence. As is sometimes the case, concomitant benchmark performances also mark readiness to move to more difficult tasks in the equipment format sequence.

Rule #2: Place Equipment According to Student Achievement

Successful repetition of open water traverse challenges as well as concomitantly occurring benchmark performances must be considered to appropriately place a child in the equipment formatting sequence. The intensity of swimmer resistance and willingness to try seem to be based on three factors:

- Past successful traverse of shorter distances
- Successful nonsupported entries
- Successful breathing, arm, and leg patterns

Generally speaking, the more capable the student, the less likely that she or he will balk at traversing increasing distances between structures.

The number of past successful traverses of shorter distances is simply based on record-keeping procedures. You must keep track of, and record, the number of times the child has successfully completed a short traverse, say of 1.5 yards (Step #6), before attempting a larger traverse of 3.0 yards (Step #7). This record-keeping process is especially important in the case of Steps #5 through #9, which include instructor nonsupport (see Table 7.1).

As a benchmark performance, the ability to enter the water with no support is important as an indicator of comfort in the water environment (see chapter 4, Aquatic Readiness Guide, water orientation and adjustment and water entry components). If children are able to demonstrate an entry without support, then they probably are able to recover following submersion. In effect, the act of recovery from submersion is a basic ingredient in the water competence model. Children who can perform submersion recovery are also likely to be able to complete progressively greater traverse distances successfully.

A second benchmark performance that indicates a readiness to traverse progressively greater distances is the ability to successfully manipulate the legs, arms, and breathing patterns at the same time. The ability to complete both of these benchmark performances successfully seems to be the best predictor of ability to traverse open water.

Less ready children, even if they are moving in the water without support, are likely to balk at distances that additively approximate 1.5 yards (see Figure 7.4). This means that less skilled participants who have only recently begun to move independently are likely to view 3 yards as a threatening distance to traverse. Frequently they will lunge on the takeoff, covering most of the distance with momentum from the lunge rather than from propulsion with arms and legs.

As the distance approaches 4.5 yards between structures, aquatic readiness students frequently indicate that they know the distance has been increased, and they will attempt the longer traverse only following several successful traverses of a 3-yard distance. Ability to complete this distance sometimes fluctuates from day to day; this fluctuation is based on commonly occurring factors mentioned earlier in chapter 4.

You can get an indication of a child's willingness to traverse open water at previously successful distances when the child first enters the water. If the entry is made using a flight pattern, such as a jump, then the child is likely to be willing to traverse open water. However, if the child demonstrates an entry pattern regressed from a previous best performance, then the child's willingness to traverse open water is also likely to be reduced.

As large equipment is placed at greater and greater distances from each other using the guidelines provided in Figure 7.4, more ability is required to traverse the distance successfully. By constructing various distances between structures, the development of confidence and the child's ability to successfully cross open water improves progressively.

ALTERNATE USES FOR EQUIPMENT
CONCEPT 7.3

Large equipment in the aquatic environment can be used as a staging or planning area.

Large equipment islands in the water serve as staging platforms where children are removed far enough from the threatening properties of the water to focus and then plan their next aquatic readiness task. Frequently you can gain a perspective on the child's readiness by engaging the child in a short discussion while he or she is on the island. The equipment island provides a place to

- rest,
- observe,
- plan, and
- discuss what will be attempted next.

Besides efficient use of time in the water, one valuable advantage in discussing the next activity with the child is that the child is then active in making the plans about the next task. This provides an element of control for the child, which shortens the time needed by the child to adjust to the activity (Fluegelman, 1976; Orlick, 1978).

Some experts on play assume that valuable adaptations to the environment are made during times of stopping, observing, planning, discussing, and then doing (Beckwith, 1988). The chance for the child to be close by and observe other children in the water is important to the readiness a child feels during play. The child observes skills performed by others and forms ideas for expected outcomes. As the first part of the exploratory process, observation readies the child for participation. The equipment island places them in the middle of activity with no immediate need to perform.

Large equipment's role as a *safe* area within the water cannot be overlooked. Before the use of large equipment, the only areas fearful children perceived as being safe were the sides of the pool and the arms of the instructor when in open water. In the case of a fearful or clinging child, the side of the pool is usually not a satisfactory perch, because lengthy coaxing is usually required to get the child back into the water. If lengthy time is spent in coaxing, valuable experiential time is lost.

With the use of large island structures in the pool, many new perching places are added, which has two additional advantages.

First, the equipment island acts as an intermediate stopping place during a series of open water traverse challenges. When moving from equipment island to equipment island with the support of the instructor, as in Steps #1 to #4 in Table 7.1, the child will

1. physically remove themselves from the instructor,
2. climb onto the structure, and

3. turn on the structure and reenter the water to get back to the instructor.

Because the child often initiates the activity to get on the equipment and then is willing to initiate reentry (maybe in the hope of returning to pool side, in the case of fearful children), the child gets additional practice of needed aquatic skills. The practice of entry skills on the island structure, and the continuation of the lesson while positioned in the middle of the pool, are great instructional advantages, because the inertia represented by the side of the pool does not need to be overcome each time practice is initiated.

The captivated attention of the child on an island in the middle of the pool, as opposed to the reticence of the child clinging to the side of the pool, allows you to concentrate on the child's needs. What frequently occurs as clinging children are placed on the side of the pool is that they roll to their side, stand up, and back away from the water. The equipment island serves as an advantage because valuable time and experience are not lost while the instructor tries to coax a hesitant child back into the water. Thus, the use of large equipment islands in the water can help the instructor and the child focus on the aquatic readiness tasks at hand without interruption.

SUMMARY

The large equipment structures used in the aquatic environment are based on design concepts used in outdoor play structures. These design concepts promote and enhance aquatic development.

Movable equipment (such as trestle tree equipment) is now available for use in the water. These structures can easily be configured to meet children's needs.

Large equipment can serve as a motivator to the children who are in the water. Children are attracted to explore the equipment (and hence the water it's in) by its novelty as a pool item and its complexity.

Configurations most appropriate to readiness activity in children are rule-governed. The rules governing formatting the equipment and placing the children in the formatting sequence are based on aquatic readiness and water competence levels. Large equipment is a safe haven in the water for children and can be used to provide a staging or planning area for aquatic readiness activities. Chapter 8 provides additional concepts, ideas, and examples for promoting aquatic play and games that can go hand-in-hand with the large equipment use discussed in this chapter.

Chapter

8

Learning Experiences and Games for Aquatic Readiness[1]

One of the primary means by which children learn is through play. Their active involvement during play enables them to try new things and become more confident and consistent at the things they already do. No amount of "teaching" by an instructor can accomplish the same thing! Of course, the good instructor uses the play process as part of the teaching process. Chapters 5 and 7 demonstrate ways for instructors to integrate *play* effectively through movement education and large equipment. This chapter introduces valuable means for integrating play principles within aquatic readiness through the use of aquatic learning experiences and games.

IMPORTANCE OF PLAY IN INSTRUCTION
CONCEPT 8.1

Young children learn through active play.

Play is spontaneous behavior performed by anyone, regardless of age. For young children, play in its many forms is particularly important in the learning and developmental processes. Through play the child learns to move effectively, to practice thinking, to live socially with others, and to express feelings. Play can be considered the main avenue by which children develop and learn. Play in the water, therefore, is both a natural means for assisting the child in learning and the most preferred path for helping the child experience the beneficial aspects of water.

GAMES USE IN AQUATIC READINESS
CONCEPT 8.2

Aquatic learning experiences can provide distraction, motivation, practice, feedback, goal setting, and reinforcement for the aquatic learning process.

A *game* has been defined as "an activity in which one or more children engage in competitive or cooperative play with a moving object within the framework of certain rules" (Barrett, 1984b). In this chapter, the terms *learning experiences* and *games* have similar meanings. Both learning experiences and games will have the connotation of a "task designed to reflect a dynamic environment" (Barrett, 1984b). *Games* have a greater degree of structure and organization than *learning experiences*. Regardless of whether they are discussed as *learning experiences* or as *games*, *aquatic games*, as the term is used in this text, are meant to be learning and practice events that may or may not have competitive elements. The main purpose of aquatic games is to improve the child's performance, not to determine a winning person or group. The game must serve the child's need, not vice versa!

Aquatic games serve in several ways to effectively provide aquatic readiness. First, they can be powerful environmental *distractors* for children who may be cautious or fearful in the water. Rather than focus on their fear of the water or on the aquatic setting, the fearful child focuses on the goal of a *game* and, at least momentarily, forgets the fears. Secondly, *games* can become strong *motivators* for enhancing aquatic learning. Motivation occurs when a game is used either as an incentive to encourage a child to try something or as a *reinforcer* to reward the child for accomplishing a task. Finally, games can directly and indirectly augment *learning* by serving as a means for practice, feedback, reinforcement, and setting goals (see Figure 8.1).

AQUATICS AND GAMES HAVE ALWAYS GONE HAND IN HAND
CONCEPT 8.3

Aquatic games traditionally have played a role in learning to swim.

Of course, using games as part of aquatic learning is not something new to aquatic readiness. Gabrielson, Spears, and Gabrielson (1960) suggested several decades ago that games can aid the aquatic learning process. They claimed games can acclimate the swimmer to the water, build the swimmer's confidence in her or his water skills and abilities, improve breath control and breathing skills, improve body position and balance in the water, and enhance coordination and relaxation.

Agencies That Use Games for Aquatic Instruction

Signifying the importance attached recently to water games and activities in promoting aquatic learning, the Canadian Red Cross (1984) published an entire volume of games and water activities. They suggested

that these games can augment the aquatic learning process by providing opportunities for instructors to teach water orientation, physical skills, water safety concepts, and social skills, and that during the process of playing games in the water, children learn about themselves and others while learning to respect ability levels.

The Y Skippers program of the YMCA of the USA (1986) also demonstrates an increased commitment to games and water sports. In fact, the Y states that the focus of instruction has shifted from stroke mechanics to water activities that provide a more balanced approach to aquatic learning. The YMCA cites water games for improving confidence, endurance, skills, and cooperative attitudes.

Commodore Wilbert E. Longfellow, founder of the American Red Cross Water Safety Program, was a strong proponent of conventional water games and activities. One of his favorite mottos was "Keep the fun in fundamentals" (American Red Cross, 1981). Even today the Red Cross claims that games and activities help to overcome the fear of the water that has held back many potential swimmers. They cite games for relieving anxiety and for providing situations that build confidence and enhance skill development. They also suggest that games serve an important role in "tapering off" from the formal instructional phase of a class (American Red Cross, 1981, 1992c).

Limitations on Traditional Use of Games

Traditionally, many swimming instructors have used games as part of a learn-to-swim program. Often, however, the use of games has been limited to serving

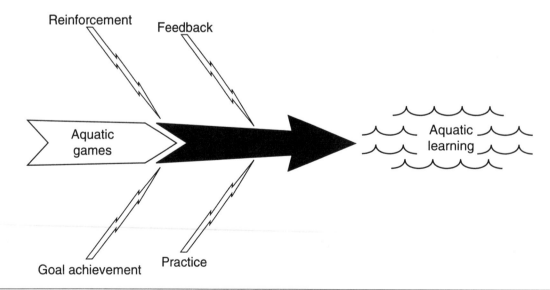

Figure 8.1 Aquatic games promote aquatic learning in a variety of ways.

merely as "time-fillers" or as rewards for good behavior. In fact, traditionally, many instructors reserve the last 5 or 10 minutes of class as "game time." Restricting games to one short period of time misses a golden opportunity to integrate games throughout the aquatic readiness process and make them an integral part of aquatic learning.

Conventional games (Barrett, 1984a) tend to become "institutionalized"—their rules tend to become inflexible and difficult to adapt. As such, games become things to do rather than ways to learn. Unfortunately, conventional games do not accommodate themselves to the changing abilities and individual differences among children. For games to serve a significant role in aquatic readiness, they must be modifiable and adaptive to the needs of the children using them.

BENEFITS OF USING GAMES
CONCEPT 8.4

Aquatic games can play an important role in acquiring aquatic readiness.[2]

Younger children, and infants especially, may benefit from games and water activities at home. Shank (1983) has suggested that fantasy games in the bathtub or a shallow backyard pool provide emotional security for infants and young children as they explore their initial relationship to the water. In fact, Shank (1983) felt that fantasy and make-believe stories are the major way for children to relate to adults in the water, because preschoolers generally do not function well in the traditional teacher-student relationship in which the teacher provides all the directions. Specifically, games can be used to help reduce children's fear of the water and to help them acquire aquatic skills.

Reducing Fear of the Water

Typically, a swimming instructor attempts to help fearful, nonswimming children to progressively get into the water, adapt their movements to the buoyant environment of the water, and gradually submerge different body parts until they can accomplish full-face and head submersion. Traditionally, this progression has been accomplished through direct teaching methods such as verbal explanation, demonstration, exhortation, and even manipulation of the body by the instructor. Particularly if the child is very young or very timid and fearful, such direct teaching by the instructor can be extremely intimidating, and the child might not make any progress at all.

The aquatic game Chin Ball can be used as an alternative technique with nonswimmers to accomplish water adjustment and orientation (YMCA of USA, 1986a, 1986b). This game uses an indirect teaching style. Swimmers try to push a tennis ball as they walk across shallow water. They propel the ball through the water and pass it to a classmate without using the hands, and one or both feet must stay in contact with the bottom. The game also can be used as a relay for older and slightly more skilled children.

To participate in this game, children must enter the water, adapt their body positions, accommodate their senses of balance to the buoyant water, and place part of their faces (their chins) at or near the water surface. In all likelihood, the child will get his or her face splashed in the process of the game. By playing the game, the child accomplishes skills similar to skills taught by the direct instructional approach but has done so indirectly through the game. The teacher has used a secondary goal (pushing the ball through the water) to accomplish the primary goal (the child's acclimating to the water and partially submerging). This is an example of distraction to reduce fear and reluctance.

Aquatic Skill Acquisition

Several recent papers on aquatics for young children show that aquatic games are important aquatic variables to consider in the aquatic skill acquisition process (German, 1987; Langendorfer, 1987d; Langendorfer, Bruya, & Reid, 1987; Langendorfer, German & Kral, 1988). These papers suggest that games and water activities can affect the rate and extent of water learning that young children accomplish. In addition, games are cited to be used with a variety of teaching techniques and styles to enhance learning, practice, and motivation of water safety and aquatic skills. Many games are particularly suited for the developmental level of infants and young children and can enhance the socialization process as well as skill learning (see Figure 8.2).

GAMES FOR ALL LEVELS OF AQUATIC READINESS
CONCEPT 8.5

Games can be used to enhance aquatic readiness at all skill levels.

Use learning experiences and games to facilitate learning no matter what skill level your students are at. Both novice and advanced swimmers enjoy the benefits of aquatic games.

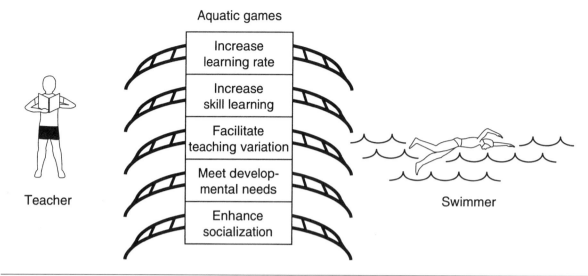

Figure 8.2   Aquatic games build bridges for interactions between the teacher and the swimming student.

A Novice Example

For novice young swimmers, particular swimming skills or water safety techniques can be enhanced by using more advanced games. For instance, the child who feels comfortable in the water and can submerge under water may benefit from a game such as Over and Under (YMCA, 1986a) as an alternative to the traditional bobbing and kickboard drills. Although a direct bobbing drill can have benefits, this game can stress teamwork, following directions, and working competitively.

In Over and Under, students stand in line in the shallow water, all facing in the same direction. The first child in line passes a ball or ring over his or head to the child behind, who passes the object to the next person by submerging and putting the object between her or his legs. This alternating activity continues until the object reaches the last person, who must run or swim the object to the front and begin the activity again. You should stress control of the object and exhalation during submersion, to enhance learning and ensure correct practice of breathing skills.

An Advanced Example

Game play can be a valuable tool even for an advanced swimmer. A range of swimming skills of varied complexity can be used in games for advanced swimmers, because their skill repertoire is relatively full. Usually advanced games require stamina and arm/leg propulsion and involve aspects of submersion, changing position and direction, and familiarity with varied swimming terminology. The game Touch (Canadian Red Cross, 1984) is an example.

In Touch, all swimmers play in either the shallow or the deep end and participate all the time. The instructor or a class member calls out an object, a piece of equipment, or a color in the swimming area for swimmers to try to touch first. Variations include calling specified swimmers' names and/or specifying the type of stroke to be used to reach the target. The game can be either competitive between teams or among individuals or just participant-based so that everyone can play freely.

To use Touch as an introductory game for swimmers who are new to a facility or who are limited in their skill, the shallow end can be used. Also, the names for different swimming pool areas, equipment, and supplies can be practiced. For instance, you might lay out kickboards, pull buoys, PFDs, rescue tubes, ring buoys, goggles, masks, and fins along the pool side to be assured that each swimmer knows the name of each and can readily identify them. In addition, if you make the swimmers go from one end or side of the pool to the other and back again, rapidly over a period of minutes, cardiovascular endurance can be enhanced. At the same time you can determine which swimmers need work on which strokes.

ADAPTATION OF AQUATIC GAMES
CONCEPT 8.6

Aquatic games must be adaptable to the varied skills and needs of the students.

The Over and Under game provides an example of adaptation of a game to fit the skills of the class. It is generally used in shallow water with beginners or novices, but it can be adapted to deep water for use with intermediate and advanced swimmers. The swimmers line up, all facing one direction, in the deep water, but they must tread water during the game. An object (ball, ring, diving brick) is passed back with passes alternating over the head and under the legs. The swimmer at the end must swim the object to the front. In a large class the game could be done as a relay with several groups. If a diving brick or heavy object is used, the rear swimmer can use a lifesaving carry stroke to bring the object to the beginning of the line. You can use Over and Under as an alternative to the traditional lap swimming or timed periods of treading water required by swimming, lifeguarding, and water safety classes.

CHOOSING WATER GAMES: DEVELOPMENTAL AQUATIC GAMES ANALYSIS
CONCEPT 8.7

The process of developmental task analysis is important in choosing and structuring aquatic games for aquatic readiness.

You need to consider several factors before choosing specific water games (see Figure 8.3). First and foremost, you must carefully consider the characteristics and readiness of the children in your class, asking yourself questions that include the following:

- What are the age levels and maturity of the children?
- What handicapping conditions do the children have?
- What specific skill levels does each child have, and how much variability is there among children within the class?
- How many children will participate?

Refer to chapters 3 and 4 for information on evaluating the developmental status of young children in the water. In particular, refer to the Aquatic Readiness Guide (chapter 4) and the Reference Guide to Water Games (later in this chapter and in the appendix) to make sure that the children have the prerequisite skills to successfully and safely participate in the proposed games.

Second, consider the facility in which the games are to be played. The water depth, pool size, water clarity, presence of steps or ramps, and possible facility dangers to children entering and exiting must be considered. If the minimum depth is the standard 3.5 to 4 feet (1.0 to 1.3 meters), many games either cannot be played or must be carefully adapted for young children. Some games require a large space, to be played safely. Others best use a contained area for young children. Obviously, if the class is being

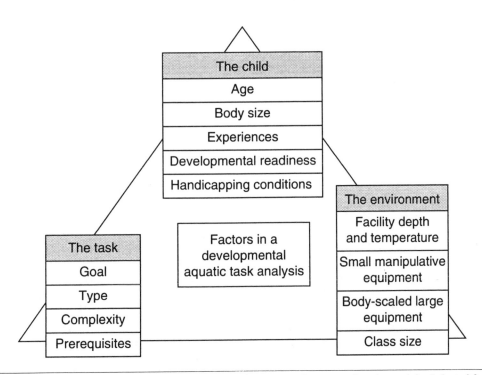

Figure 8.3 Three factors are important to consider when analyzing an aquatic game or learning activity (adapted from Langendorfer, 1987d).

held outside at a beach or lakefront where water clarity is limited, some games may be undesirable. Some games are best played where children can easily enter and exit the pool with ramps or steps, whereas other games require that the children not be able to readily get out of the water. Finally, if the facility has a particular danger zone, such as an area of limited visibility to guards or a sudden drop-off or slippery surface, many games must be limited.

Another related consideration is the availability and appropriateness of equipment. Some games require enough items for each swimmer to have one each. Others can use a single piece of equipment such as a ball or float. Some may not require any equipment. You need to determine this well in advance of the class period. Equipment such as PFDs, flotation devices, balls, fins, goggles, and masks all need to be matched appropriately to the children's sizes. Failure to use correctly sized equipment causes poor performance at best and outright danger to the child at worst.

AQUATIC GAMES ANALYSIS
CONCEPT 8.8

A "games analysis" is an important part of the developmental task analysis in adapting the game to the participants and to the specific purpose.

After considering the child, the facility, and the equipment, carefully consider the game or learning experience, its purpose or purposes, the skills involved, and other special requirements. Initially, consider the specific purpose for using this game at this particular time. Ask yourself the purpose of the game:

- *Practicing* a well-learned or recently learned skill?
- Actually *learning* a new skill?
- Increasing *motivation* for an activity?
- *Distracting* certain swimmers from their fearful reaction?
- *"Time-filling"* so that you can do other things such as evaluation or individual attention—or even so you can avoid teaching?

Once you have examined the purpose and determined it to be appropriate, then consider the individual skills and their combinations within the game. Any game is composed of several skills, some of which are *central* to the purpose of using the game and others of which are *ancillary* (secondary) to its main purpose. Obviously, which skills are central

and which are ancillary will vary as the purpose of the game varies or as you adapt it to different groups of swimmers. Nevertheless, you must ascertain that the swimmers have previously experienced *all* the central *and* ancillary skills, for the game to be effective. For instance, when a game such as Chin Ball (described earlier in this chapter) is used to progress children toward face submersion, the children also must be able to stand up in the water, walk through the water, and not lose their balance due to the new center of buoyancy. If *any* child in the class has not yet mastered walking independently in the water, this particular game will be inappropriate to this class and probably highly unsuccessful.

In cases where the game is used to actually learn a new skill or to distract children from fear, there are *prerequisite* skills that the game requires before the child can participate freely. Again using Chin Ball as an example, if some of the children have not yet learned the prerequisites of entering the pool independently or carrying a small ball under the chin, then they cannot participate successfully in the game, and its use with these children is not appropriate at this time.

Another often misunderstood aspect of games is the competitive environment. Competitive goals in games can affect different participants differently. Research in the area of social facilitation suggests that being in a competitive situation with others negatively affects young and poorly skilled individuals. Therefore, in such a game their performance actually gets worse, and the game is not serving the purpose of learning, practice, or motivation. On the other hand, older and more highly skilled children actually improve their performances when other children are involved and when there is a competitive goal.

The presence of the differential performance effect due to competition can actually serve an interesting evaluative purpose for you. If children playing a competitive game for practice and repetition are observed to *regress* in a skill, that suggests that the skill has not been sufficiently mastered yet. On the other hand, *improved* performances under competitive game situations indicate the ability to use more difficult skills or the same skills in more complex situations.

There is one final aspect of aquatic games and learning experiences you should consider. This factor is related to the complexity of the activity. Complexity is related to a number of factors, such as strategies, competition, rules, number of players, and types of motor skills involved. In general, games for young and inexperienced children need to be simple in all aspects. In other words, they should be straightforward activities, requiring few if any strategies, that children can play without competition and alone—meaning that the child does not have to effectively interact with another child or children in order to play. Simple games may all be played in a group in which all children play simultaneously and in parallel. Only after children are older and more experienced with the water are they ready for complex games.

Games are one important tool for enhancing aquatic skill acquisition. They should not serve as a total substitute for other teaching methods such as demonstration, exploration, or guided discovery. Aquatic games also must be selected with careful consideration of swimmers' ages and skill levels, facility characteristics, equipment, and the specifics of the games. Games also must be used carefully to achieve specific purposes.

The next section illustrates a unique approach to integrating water games and aquatic activities into swimming instruction.

REFERENCE GUIDE TO WATER GAMES
CONCEPT 8.9

Aquatic games can be classified into major functional categories for promoting aquatic readiness.

In the appendix we present a detailed description of 114 water games and aquatic activities for young children. Aside from a Canadian Red Cross text (1984), this is one of the first attempts to present games to aquatic instructors in a cross-referenced format listing *purposes*, *skill level*, *prerequisite developmental skills*, and *descriptions* as pertinent information. Our intention is to provide a unique resource for integrating water games into the teaching of aquatic skills.

We have grouped water games and aquatic activities according to their purposes for skill enhancement and subdivided them according to the age/skill level of the swimmers who will use them (see Table A.2). In addition, for each game the following are specified:

- Game title
- Skill level
- Prerequisite developmental skills required
- Game purpose
- Appropriate water depth
- Class formation
- Game description

- Equipment needed
- Appropriate instructor intervention activities
- Game variations (if appropriate)
- Complexity factors

The games and activities are organized around the following concepts:

- Water orientation and adjustment
- Breath control, breathing, and submersion
- Flotation, buoyancy, and balance
- Body position and change of direction
- Arm/leg propulsion
- Advanced strokes
- Water entry and exit

The subgroupings include skill levels for beginners, novices, advanced swimmers, and mixed levels.

For purposes of this overview, we categorize games in only one conceptual area, in spite of the fact that many games emphasize a number of different skill concepts. In fact, the best games probably reinforce learning and practice for several different skills simultaneously. Nevertheless, we have chosen to categorize each game under the most important, or main, skill concept it involves.

Water Orientation

There are 20 games in the ''Water Orientation'' section. These games are appropriate especially for beginners and younger participants. For the most part, they are organized in shallow water depth, permitting children to stand while participating in the games. Five of the games use rhymes or songs, and three others use an exploration format with minimal instructor commands. The focus is on experiencing and enjoying the water and not on any particular aquatic skills.

Breath Control, Rhythmic Breathing, and Submersion

There are 22 games in the ''Breath Control, Rhythmic Breathing, and Submersion'' section. Some overlap with the ''Water Orientation'' section, because getting used to water around and on the face is properly a water orientation function. Fourteen are oriented primarily toward beginners and are played in shallow water areas (including sinks or bathtubs). Four of the games are songs or rhymes used to entice young learners to submerge part or all of their faces. Due to the difficulty of this conceptual area, gimmicks seem popular with 11 of the 22 activities requiring one or more pieces of equipment to assist the learning process. In several of these games, the instructor takes a more direct role than in water orientation. Several of the games (Magic Candle, Look & Listen), however, make ample use of fantasy in trying to coax the young child to submerge.

Flotation, Buoyancy, and Balance in Water

There are 24 games in the "Flotation, Buoyancy, and Balance in Water" section. These games also overlap with other categories. Because people usually float prone with the face submerged, many of these games emphasize both submersion and flotation. Also, many stress a horizontal body position for floating, thus overlapping with the "Body Position and Change of Direction" category.

Most of these games are intended primarily for beginners, but three emphasize intermediate and advanced flotation skills that would require modification for beginners. The water depth is primarily shallow, with modifications capable for deep water. Two of the skills (Limbo and Push off the Wall) were created especially for teaching back-floating skills.

Body Position and Change of Direction

Only five games are identified as specifically promoting body position and change of direction. Many other games in other categories could be used to practice this concept. Apparently these skills have seldom been considered important for water games.

Arm/Leg Propulsion

There are 19 games, drills, and activities that focus on the ability to propel the body through the water with the limbs. Five of the games specifically deal with kicking activities, particularly the flutter kick. The others include arm and leg movements as part of related activities. Nine rely on some type of equipment, usually kickboards, for organizing the game.

Advanced Strokes

Games for advanced strokes are obviously related to the category of arm/leg propulsion, although at a more advanced level. Of the seven selected for inclusion in the "Advanced Strokes" section, most recommend deep water (although shallow-water ad-

aptations for beginners are usually possible). Only two (Squirt Gun Relay & T-Shirt Relay) require specific equipment. Thus the emphasis is on the swimming strokes themselves. Six include some type of competitive aspect with speed swimming. If your swimmers are not already fairly advanced, you should take care not to reinforce incorrect stroking patterns that might be encouraged by the competitive environment.

Water Entry and Exit

Of the nine water entry games (we found only one strictly for water exit skills), all are organized for beginners and advanced beginners. They focus on climbing, jumping, or sliding into a pool. We found few games that focus on diving and more advanced types of water entry. Two of the games require (minimal) equipment.

USING SMALL EQUIPMENT FOR AQUATIC READINESS
CONCEPT 8.10

Small equipment, like aquatic games, can augment and enhance the aquatic readiness process.

Small equipment, as with games and other teaching techniques, can be used either poorly or effectively in the aquatic environment. To be used effectively, small equipment must fit a specific purpose, be attractive and sized to your children, and be safe in and around the water. To assess whether the equipment fits a given purpose, it is helpful to ask yourself whether using the equipment really is beneficial (i.e., is the child's aquatic readiness promoted by its use?). For a flotation device to be useful, for example, it should be used in water that is too deep for a child to stand, and it should support that child in an inclined or horizontal body position. Use of a flotation device in shallow water where a child can support himself or herself, or where the device supports the child vertically (not in a swimming position) may be detrimental to the child's aquatic readiness.

Small equipment can be homemade or commercially available. Sometimes commercially available equipment actually better suits a purpose different from the one its manufacturer intended. For instance, the inflatable cuffs that fit around children's upper arms are miserable devices for assisting children to float and swim in an inclined position, but they can be very satisfactory when used to explore the concept of buoyancy or breath control.

Regardless of the equipment's origin, each piece must be regularly inspected for safety. Are there any small parts that can dislodge and fit into a young child's mouth? Are there sharp edges, or parts that could break and create sharp edges? Is the equipment deteriorating from exposure to water? If you answer yes to any of these, then the piece of equipment must be either repaired or discarded immediately. For more information about inspecting equipment and the facility, see chapter 9.

Instructors of young swimmers have resorted to using many types of small equipment to help distract, motivate, practice, and reinforce aquatic learning. Most of this equipment has received only sporadic and partial attention by aquatic professionals and aquatic writers.

Langendorfer, Bruya, and Reid (1987) suggested that it might be helpful to classify types of small aquatic equipment into functional categories. Such a taxonomy may aid both the novice and the experienced instructor and the parent in providing appropriate equipment to young children. They classified equipment as (a) flotation devices; (b) distractors and motivators; (c) aids to locomotion; and (d) instructional toys. To that taxonomy might be added the fifth category of breathing apparatus (masks, goggles, snorkels).

Flotation Devices

Flotation devices include a variety of equipment that acts to increase a child's buoyancy. Examples include Coast Guard-approved lifejackets, or PFDs, styrofoam "bubbles" or "eggs," inflatable arm cuffs, ski belts, inflatable rings, inner tubes, foam mats, and even a floating swimming suit with pockets for styrofoam inserts. To be effective, these devices must adequately and safely assist the child's buoyancy *and* should at the same time support at least an inclined body position (see the body position component of chapter 4). As noted earlier, flotation equipment, such as arm cuffs, that primarily holds the child vertically in the water may be detrimental to the child's development of aquatic readiness.

Distractors and Motivators

Distractors and *motivators* are any miscellaneous equipment that children find attractive. They may include balls of various sizes, sponges, submersible flowers, poker chips, rubber animals, boats, miniature figures, or squirt bottles. The purpose of these items is to attract the child's attention and to distract her or him from any dislike or fear for the water. The

Flotation devices include a variety of equipment.

optimal distractor probably varies from child to child, and some may have strong gender identity. For instance, boys might prefer boats and miniature figurines like plastic robots or army figures, and girls might prefer dolls or toys that assist social interaction.

Aids to Locomotion

Aids to locomotion are items that in some manner assist the child's movement through the water. The primary example is flippers, or fins, although hand paddles and gloves may also be useful. Although they are not widely used among young children at present, aids to locomotion may become increasingly

Floating mats are fun for children to use as "boats."

Miscellaneous equipment can be used as distractors and motivators.

popular as more research indicates their usefulness for young children's learning. If you adapt flippers or hand paddles for use with young children, reduce the overall size accordingly, because adult-size equipment is heavy and requires too much strength to use it, and it will cause fatigue, serious regressions in young children's skill, and possibly even injury.

Breathing Apparatuses

Breathing apparatuses are any items that aid the child's breath control. They may include goggles,

masks, snorkels, drinking straws, and water containers. They are used in a variety of ways. Goggles and masks can help the reluctant child submerge and open his or her eyes underwater. The snorkel can encourage rhythmic breathing. The drinking straws can facilitate exhaling and bubble blowing during early breath control acquisition. Containers of water can act as "showers" for the child who is not entering the water. Goggles and masks should be used sparingly with young children, because they usually don't fit a small head properly, and because the child also needs the experience of submerging without an aid.

Instructional Toys

Instructional toys is a category of equipment that overlaps with the previous categories. Any of a number of items can serve the instructional process. A *flotation device* that supports the child who lacks confidence, the *distractor* that helps the fearful child, or the *breathing apparatus* (e.g., a snorkel) that encourages the child to get her or his face near the water and blow bubbles all can promote aquatic readiness. In general, any article that is not damaged by getting wet and that does not pose a danger to a child (of cutting, being swallowed, blocking breathing, etc.) may prove to be an instructional aquatic toy.

Two devices the authors have found to be particularly useful are a large sealed foam mat and a plastic swimming pool. Mats can serve many uses—as a slide or as a large kickboard capable of supporting several children simultaneously, for instance. Children love to slide into the water on them. The plastic swimming pool also has dual use. On the pool deck, filled with warm water, it can serve reluctant children as a wading pool while they acclimate to a water environment. Empty, it can serve as a wonderful boat in the water, carrying one or two small children.

SUMMARY

This chapter has focused on both aquatic learning experiences and games and small equipment for the water environment. The implication for both areas has been that a number of aquatic environmental factors other than traditional teaching may effectively assist the young child in acquiring aquatic readiness and other swimming skills. In combination with the 4-P's curriculum (chapter 3), the Aquatic Readiness Assessment and Readiness Guide (chapter 4), educational aquatic movement education (chapter 5), and setting the aquatic learning environment (chapter 6), this chapter can increase your knowledge and skill as an aquatic readiness instructor.

The final chapter in this text goes beyond the scope of simple instruction and addresses the crucial topic of risk management in aquatic readiness environments and programs. Young children are in the age group with the highest risk of drowning, so it is absolutely imperative that all persons working with young children appreciate the dangers and learn strategies for controlling the risks. We think chapter 9 will assist aquatic instructors, administrators, and parents in doing just that.

NOTES

[1]This chapter was adapted from several papers (Langendorfer, 1987d; Langendorfer, Bruya, & Reid, 1987; Langendorfer, German, & Kral, 1988) and research projects by Elizabeth Willing German and Diana L. Harrod.

[2]This list of games and purposes was compiled by Elizabeth Willing German (1987) and Diana L. Harrod (1990) and used with their permissions.

Chapter
9

Administrative Risk Management

Since the mid-1960s, many aquatic instructors and administrators have sought to establish, operate, and evaluate programs for infants and young children. Parents and other aquatic consumers want to compare and choose among programs appropriate for their infants and young children. Both of these groups will benefit from information presented in this chapter and other chapters of this book (see Figure 9.1). This chapter focuses on a new approach for organizing and operating aquatic programs: *risk management*. This approach is all the more valuable in light of the potential for problems outlined in the example that follows.

Example problem: It is early on a Saturday morning, and the pool area is filled with subdued early morning chatter. The teachers are planning their lessons for the children. The chatter grows as the children begin arriving. It is their 12th lesson, and few are afraid of the water any longer. A great deal of progress has been made by these preschoolers.

As the lesson begins, the children are sitting on the side waiting their turns. Today the children are being taught to enter the water headfirst, or by diving. The teacher has moved the group to the deeper part of the pool. As the teacher begins work with Tommy, Jenny wanders away from the group to an unoccupied part of the pool.

Twice the teacher reminds Jenny to get back with the group. Twice Jenny returns, but again she sneaks away from her group. She knows she can swim—the water is always so warm. Besides, the teacher often has told her mother how well she is doing. The teacher even wrote a letter to Mom and Dad telling them how well she swims. And Daddy had placed the letter on the refrigerator so Grandmother and Grandfather could see it when they came to visit. Besides, she wasn't afraid of the water anyway—she could swim.

She found a place on the wall to practice her dives while the teacher was working with Tommy. The lifeguard on deck didn't see her, either. She dove

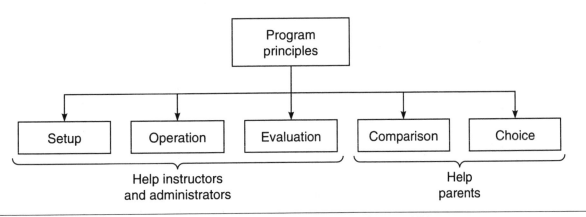

Figure 9.1 Program principles guide decisions about programs for infants and young children.

into the shallow water and struck her head on the bottom, jamming her neck. She had been on the bottom only a short while before her teacher pulled her out. Luckily the supervisor had been smart enough to require the teachers to take coursework in first aid and CPR. In a matter of minutes, Jenny's eyes opened as she sputtered and caught her breath. Her neck was sore for a while, but there appeared to be no permanent damage.

Her parents were frantic but calmed down when they saw that she was conscious. It wasn't until later that they began to understand the problem that now confronted them.

Oh, the problem was small compared to the potential brain damage that could have occurred, but still the damage loomed larger than life to her father; he owned an aquatics equipment supply house, and the water was a big part of their family life. But Jenny didn't want to go back into the water again. This upset her dad because it would limit Jenny's ability to participate in swimming later, but also because it would affect his income. She was going to be his main advertising tool for the business. But now she cried and fought each time her teacher or her parents tried to take her back into the water.

Her mother said, "At least we still have our little girl." Her father said, "I'm glad to have our girl alive and well, but this isn't right! I wonder if I have grounds to sue the supervisor, the teacher, and the pool owners *and win*?" He does have the grounds, and he could win the suit, if a recent court case involving the Seattle Public Schools can be taken as precedent-setting. Equally precedent-setting is the emphasis on documentation of setup, operation, and evaluation of programming for children and youth organized by the Seattle Public Schools to minimize potential injury and lawsuits in the future.

LITIGATION AFFECTING AQUATIC MANAGEMENT
CONCEPT 9.1

A new precedent is developing in litigation, making development and implementation of a total risk management system crucial for the operation of infant and preschool aquatic programs.

In a court case settled for $6.3 million, the courts began to define a new system of rules for establishing negligence. The Seattle Public School District unsuccessfully defended itself against a lawsuit concerning a football neck injury to Chris Thompson (Adams, 1982).

"Failure to Warn"

As could be the case if Jenny's parents decided to sue, the courts ruled in favor of Chris Thompson and his parents on the grounds that the school district and its employees failed to adequately warn him or his parents of the dangers involved. For Chris Thompson the particular danger involved the use of a special tackle (called "spearing"), which, when he executed it improperly, caused his cervical spine (neck) to break.

As with spearing, shallow-water dives should be warned against and can result in neck injuries similar to that suffered by Chris Thompson. Although the situations and settings for the Thompson case and our diving example differ, the failures in the instructional process to provide warning in each of the settings are similar. It should be kept in mind that the ruling in the Thompson vs. Seattle Public School case could very easily be applied to a diving or swimming injury sustained during an aquatics program.

The "failure to warn" category used in the Thompson court case was used as a catchall term for what was really a series of failures (see Figure 9.2): (a) failure to keep injury reports for use in locating potential problem areas (usually aquatics program sponsors do not attend to this need); (b) failure to provide safety clinics for employees to eliminate or deal with potential problems—WSI or Life Saving may be required, although no additional on-site training (such as training in CPR, special preschool aquatic readiness instructional techniques, or preschool aquatic readiness certification) is usually provided; (c) failure to provide a curriculum or safety manual for employees (usually the Red Cross or YMCA manuals that may be available are not specific to preschool aquatic readiness programming); and (d) failure to conduct regular inspections of equipment and facilities (Bruya & Beckwith, 1985) within its jurisdiction (a precaution that is regularly overlooked by aquatics program sponsors).

This ruling and the information that has been developed by the school district following the ruling (Adams, 1982; Seattle Public School District, 1984a, 1984b; Twardus, 1982) made it apparent that much *could* have been accomplished by the Seattle Public Schools prior to the accident, either (a) to prevent potential severe injury through an injury monitoring process or (b) to defend itself against negligence through increased installation and maintenance inspections. Both of these systems, if used in the public schools or in aquatic programs, can contribute to a well-articulated and thorough process for insuring that all phases of an operation are well-documented.

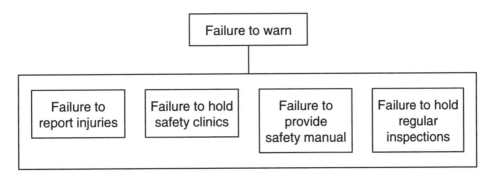

Figure 9.2 The concept of ''failure to warn'' is made up of many components.

Need for Documentation

Based on court rulings and on plain common sense, it is now obvious that documentation systems that were absent in the Thompson case (Seattle Public School District, 1984a, 1984b) are needed for preschool aquatics for both facilities and programs. An aquatic risk management system designed to decrease the risk of large financial loss to the pool and aquatic program sponsors also should attempt, through increased vigilance provided by documentation, to reduce loss due to human injury.

INTRODUCING A RISK MANAGEMENT MODEL
CONCEPT 9.2

Facility and program risk management helps in organizing aquatic programs.

There are several reasons why a risk management system is an effective administration tool. First, such a system is a particularly thorough and effective organization and documentation tool that covers all aspects of an aquatic readiness program. Second, a risk management system focuses on safety and reduces accidents by identifying conditions and situations that may contribute to accidents and injuries in aquatic environments. Finally, a risk management system reduces the risk that staff and agency may incur as the result of an accident or injury, through thorough record keeping and careful attention to reducing risk. In the long run, the system is designed to reduce costs associated with injuries and accidents and to avoid insurance rate increases. Although an agency cannot prevent legal suits, implementation and operation of a thorough risk management system serves to reduce risk and therefore to reduce the likelihood of receiving a negative judgment. Current trends suggest

that the use of a risk management system may even begin to reduce liability insurance costs.

As an organizational and operational procedure, a risk management model is unparalleled. All activities, from hiring personnel and running recruitment campaigns to evaluating progress and issuing certificates, are carefully planned and documented. The system establishes procedures through a comprehensive series of forms and checklists. By following the aquatic readiness risk management system model, the aquatic program for young children can operate both efficiently and safely.

The ideas included in risk management can best be demonstrated when organized in the areas shown in Figure 9.3. Information concerning the planning and preparation of materials that cover each of these systems should be documented. The remainder of this chapter explains the areas comprised by effective risk management.

FACILITY INSPECTION AND REPAIR
CONCEPT 9.3

A planned inspection process is required to ensure maintenance and pool repair.

Considerations for all phases of facility development actually belong in a section that includes risk management procedures for an aquatics program. However, sections related to design and installation processes have been deleted to concentrate instead on the inspection and the maintenance and repair processes common to the needs of most aquatic personnel.

Inspection Process

A regular schedule of inspection should be established and documented to demonstrate concern for

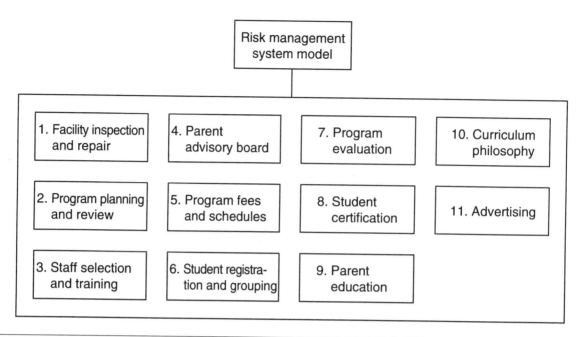

Figure 9.3   Risk management system model.

regular maintenance and repair of problems. Of course, inspection personnel must have training to know what to look for. It also can be helpful to have available inspection forms that list specific areas of concern (see Figure 9.4). This procedure, coupled with a training program, is especially important if more than one inspector will be assigned inspection duties.

Maintenance and Repair Process

Once the pool and support facilities have been constructed and then accepted from the contractor, the responsibility for establishing a procedure to take care of problems that may occur during regular use rests entirely with the sponsor of the facility and its staff. Suggested maintenance schedules for pools and equipment, which are supplied by the manufacturer (see Table 9.1), should be filed and used with an established procedure for insuring maintenance inspections. The court concluded in the Thompson v. Seattle Public Schools lawsuit, mentioned earlier, that the school district was negligent because regular maintenance inspections by an assigned safety officer had not been conducted. This point is particularly important.

Although regular maintenance inspections are a must, it is appropriate that schedules not have specific dates of the month for inspections. A once-a-month or once-a-week general maintenance check inspection

schedule may be the safest for the facility sponsor, with little or no loss in inspection efficiency.

A general inspection schedule provides more latitude while meeting the needs for inspection, because setting specific dates may present problems later during a lawsuit—such as a regular inspection date being missed because of conflict with a holiday, professional meeting, or other legitimate program-related demands. A legal problem can result when a specifically set inspection or maintenance check date is missed for an unavoidable reason, if during that time a child is injured.

If problems are detected during the routinely scheduled maintenance check, it is important to enact and document a procedure for solving the maintenance problem (see Figure 9.5). Any report of a problem should be dealt with immediately. Work orders should be drafted and dated, with copies filed for later use. The filed work order process consists of three separate steps to establish the necessary documentation.

A work order to request a repair (a repair request form) initiates the maintenance problem procedure. This request should include the following information:

- Date
- Location of the needed repair
- Account number to which expenses are to be charged
- An authorizing signature from the designated program safety officer

Margeurite A. Geisa
Pool Facility Maintenance and Repair
Inspection Form

Inspector _____

Inspection schedule: 1/month   1/week   1/day

Last inspection: _____   Current date: _____

Category 1: Water
Temp _____   Alkalinity _____   pH _____   Filter cleaned last _____
Filtering   1   2   3   4   5   6   7   8   9   10
                   works well   doesn't work

Category 2: Air
Temp _____   Humidity _____
Venting   1   2   3   4   5   6   7   8   9   10
                  works well   doesn't work

Category 3: Decks
Clean _____   Dirty _____   Moldy _____   Disinfected last _____
Repair needed _____

Category 4: Locker rooms
Clean smell   Y   N   Clean floors   Y   N   Clean lockers   Y   N
Disinfected last _____
Repair needed _____

Category 5: Showers
Clean smell   Y   N   Clean floors   Y   N   Clean lockers   Y   N
Disinfected last _____
Repair needed _____

Category 6: Toilets
Clean smell   Y   N   Clean floors   Y   N   Clean lockers   Y   N
Disinfected last _____
Repair needed _____

Category 7: Sinks and mirrors
Clean smell   Y   N   Clean floors   Y   N   Clean lockers   Y   N
Disinfected last _____
Repair needed _____

Figure 9.4   An example of a form designed for use in regular maintenance and repair inspections.

Figure 9.6 shows an example of a repair request work order.

The second part of the maintenance problem procedure is the development of a set of instructions to repair the facility or equipment. The labor of repairing the damaged or broken part should be provided promptly by a crew specifically trained to repair the facility.

Thus, the work order repair request and repair instructions, as the focus of the process for accomplishing repairs, should identify the repair task. Also, the repair request form should provide instructions needed for repair, identify the crew assigned to the repair task, identify the time and date upon which the repair should be made, identify the date the repair actually was made, and show the signature of the crew foreman that attests to the fact that the repair was completed.

The last part of the maintenance problem procedure focuses on the follow-up inspection process. The

Table 9.1   Manufacturer's Regular Maintenance Suggested Schedule

Description	Frequency
1. Check water chemistry (chlorine 1.0-1.5 ppm; pH balance 7.4 = 7.6)	4 times a day
2. Check water temperature and heat regulation (80° - 86°)	twice a day
3. Check air temperature regulation (85° - 87°)	twice a day
4. Check chlorinator valve for constant flow regulation (#2)	Daily
5. Check for chlorinator O ring leakage	Daily
6. Check water depth	Daily
7. Check water return system	Daily
8. Check for stone cracks	Daily
9. Diatomaceous earth filters backwash procedure	Heavy use: do twice a day; regular use: do daily
1. Clean deck.	twice a week
2. Vacuum pool bottom and sides.	twice a week
3. Clean rust from chrome ladders and diving board hardware (all metal parts).	twice a week
4. Tighten all diving board, guard chair, and ladder hardware.	twice a week
1. Recharge diatomaceous earth filters.	Heavy use: once a month; regular use: once every 3 months
2. Change chlorine tanks.	Heavy use: once a month; regular use: once every 3 months

form used for this procedure is called the "repair inspection" form and is incorporated as a part of the process following the completion of the repair. Its primary purpose is to insure that the repairs made hold up under the rigors of reinitiated use. Each inspection should be made by the program safety officer and the maintenance and repair supervisor. After each in a series of inspections, the repair inspection form should be signed in the necessary signatory spaces (see Figure 9.7).

In some cases where repairs, or the lack thereof, could decrease swimmers' safety, the maintenance follow-up process becomes extremely important. The follow-up process insures that repairs do not become problems again (see Table 9.2). Increasing the frequency of maintenance inspections following a repair demonstrates responsibility by the sponsoring agent for the state of a repair. This type of repair and follow-up procedure documents that the sponsoring agent has done everything possible to insure safety.

Because of the Thompson v. Seattle Public Schools case, it is more obvious than ever that a fully documented risk management process designed for aquatic facilities is required in programs that service the young child. Documentation provides protection against extreme financial loss that could occur from an injury and subsequent lawsuit. This process is but one step in demonstrating competent response to damaged facilities.

Table 9.2   Maintenance Problem Procedure

Part 1   Repair procedure

1. Identify the repair task.
2. Develop instructions to repair the facility or equipment.
3. See that the assigned repair crew responds to the problem promptly and completes it on schedule.
4. Inspect the repairs and place the repaired part back in operation.

Part 2   Follow-up procedure

1. Increase the frequency of inspections to insure that repairs stay made.
2. Decrease the frequency of follow-up inspections to the level of regularly scheduled inspections.

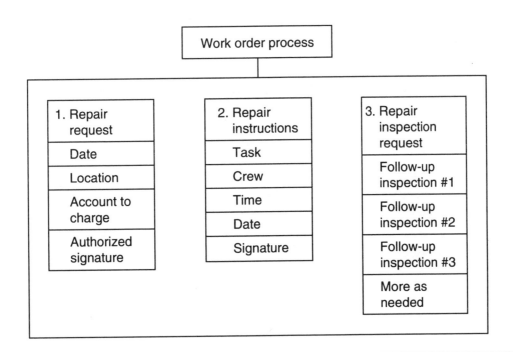

Figure 9.5 A three-part work order process.

W.O. Number _____026_____

Work Order: Repair Request

Donald C. Aquatic Center
Service Dept.
Form No. 1

Date: ___3/1/93___

To: _Main. & Repair Super._   From: _Donald C. Aquatic Safety Officer_

Location: _Shallow water (Aquatic Readiness Pool #1) - North end near entry_
steps - 6" left side of steps - approx. 2' east from the top step

Repair identification and description: _Three pieces of tile are broken in the area._
Please replace the broken deck tiles.

Charge to: ___Aquatic Readiness #7740___ Account

Authorized by: _____William J. Johns_____   *William J. Johns*
                                    Safety Officer

Figure 9.6 A work order repair request.

W.O. Number _____

Work Order: Repair Inspection

J. Robert Aquatic Center
Service Dept.
Form No. 3

Date: _____

Work order repair request number _____ was successfully completed on _____/_____/_____ and has been inspected at the times listed below. These inspections took place to ensure that the repairs that were made were successful (did not reoccur).

Follow-up inspection: Number 1

Date: _____

Safety officer: _____

Maintenance & repair supervisor: _____

Follow-up inspection: Number 2

Date: _____

Safety officer: _____

Maintenance & repair supervisor: _____

Follow-up inspection: Number 3

Date: _____

Safety officer: _____

Maintenance & repair supervisor: _____

Follow-up inspection: Number 4

Date: _____

Safety officer: _____

Maintenance & repair supervisor: _____

Use more follow-up inspections as needed

Figure 9.7 A work order for repair inspection.

PROGRAM PLANNING AND REVIEW
CONCEPT 9.4

Careful planning and review can help prevent future problems.

Anticipating safety problems ahead of time (planning) reduces accidents. The result is injury prevention and management of liability. The risk management system is particularly appropriate for preschool aquatic programming, because these programs are aimed toward an age group that historically has a high accident and drowning rate.

As a program for aquatic readiness of young children is developed and then implemented, documentation of each step can help protect against financial loss through a demonstration of having made every possible attempt to insure that the likelihood of human injury is small. Careful consideration and formation of ideas needed to plan program development materials will help establish a strong public relations program and provide a documented case that planning was competently handled.

Before the planning of an aquatics program for children, two review processes should be established and documented: review by an expert and review by a parents' advisory board (see Figure 9.8). As a part of managing risk, it is advisable to submit the plan for preschool aquatic programming and the plan to manage the risk associated with the preschool aquatic

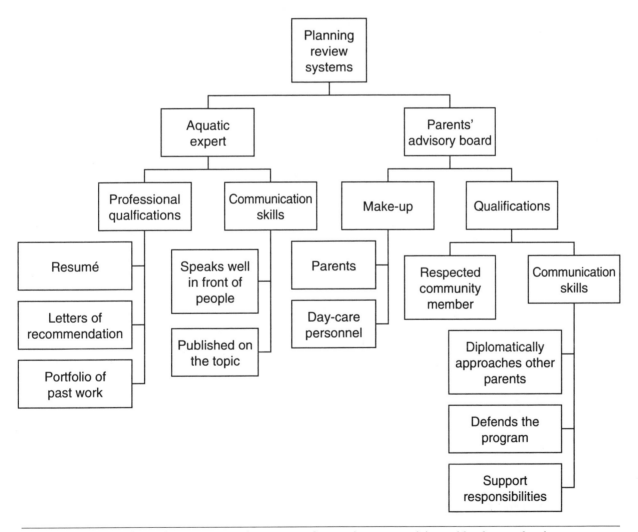

Figure 9.8 The planning review system contains a process for securing expert opinion and local parental assistance.

programming to an outside expert. The purpose of this procedure is to gain valuable review and insight into the system that has been developed and to insure that nothing has been overlooked. Records should be kept concerning expert review, for later review by critics. The process of review by a parents' advisory board will be discussed later in this chapter.

STAFF SELECTION AND TRAINING
CONCEPT 9.5

Program staff must have appropriate credentials and participate in ongoing training and development workshops.

Infant and preschool aquatic programs range from the single person working out of a backyard pool to large metropolitan recreation programs operating dozens of pools and employing hundreds of instructors, lifeguards, and ancillary staff. Each aquatic program has unique circumstances, and the risks involved in operating programs vary widely. A minimum-size staff for *all* aquatic instructional programs is *two* persons: a director and a lifeguard. No program should be operated at any time by a single person.

The Director

An infant/preschool aquatic program requires proper direction and operation. The program director, therefore, must have an established record of expertise in aquatics for young children. This expertise must be carefully documented.

Demonstration of the director's expertise begins with adequate education and proper certification and licensure. For instance, as a minimum, the program director must have a water safety certificate from a nationally recognized and approved program such as Red Cross, YCMA, Scouts, or YWCA. The director must also hold current certification in first aid and cardiopulmonary resuscitation (CPR). Optimally the person should hold at least a bachelor's degree in an appropriate discipline such as physical education, recreation, child development, psychology, or education and be certified as a pool operator (CPO). These and other helpful requirements are shown in Figure 9.9.

It is important that the program director have previous teaching and administrative experience in aquatic programs, especially in ones for young children. Aquatic certification programs often provide important information and skills without adequate training experiences. Newly certified swimming instructors, despite their idealism and enthusiasm, are not sufficiently experienced to direct an aquatic program, particularly not a program for young children. Only experience can teach the program director how to anticipate problems and foresee needed adaptations. An experienced teacher is needed to guide staff development and training while efficiently operating the administrative parts of the program.

It is crucial to document that the program director has maintained current knowledge in aquatics for young children. This may be demonstrated through participation in professional conferences, workshops, or other courses of study; through appropriate professional memberships such as in the Council for National Cooperation in Aquatics, the American Alliance for Health, Physical Education, Recreation and Dance, the National Parks and Recreation Association, or the National Association for the Education of Young Children; and through publications or professional presentations in the area of aquatics for young children.

The documentation of the program director's expertise should be organized as a portfolio. The file should include a job description; a current résumé or vita; current letters of recommendation and commendation; copies of all diplomas, certificates, licenses, and/or professional memberships; and proceedings from conferences and workshops that the director has attended. In addition, previous work experiences should be documented by letters from former employers and co-workers.

Other Staff

Because all programs require at least one other person besides the director/instructor, the qualifications of the additional staff must be documented in a manner analogous to that for the program director. Each file must be individualized depending upon the task for which the individual is employed. First, each staff member's file must contain a copy of the job description. Second, each file must have photocopies of the employee's résumé (including letters of recommendation) and the required certifications, such as swimming instructor or lifeguard training, as indicated in the job description. Finally, any other pertinent materials such as previous job experiences, attendance at in-service training workshops or professional conferences, letters of commendation or thanks from parents, and even social security number and tax withholding papers should be included.

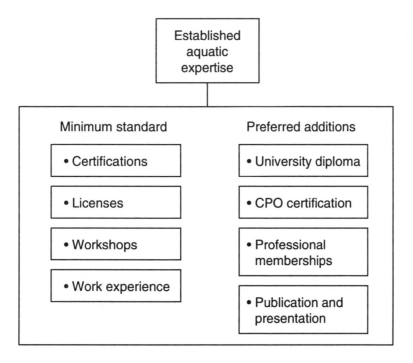

Minimum standard + preferred additions = optimal portfolio qualifications

Figure 9.9   The program director's credentials should be above the minimum standards and closer to the optimal qualifications.

Training

In addition to hiring experienced and properly certified personnel, the staff must be participating regularly in training sessions that keep them abreast of recent information. In addition, they should attend sessions that are designed to improve skills and knowledges for working with infants and young children. A record of attendance, as well as the substance of these sessions, must be documented in each staff member's portfolio.

Staff-Led In-Service Workshops

The organization and content of training sessions can vary widely. In general there are three types of sessions. The first is an in-service workshop organized and run by the program director and staff themselves. These may vary from discussion sessions related to conducting and improving publicity and registration to actual drills related to an emergency action plan. A series of these workshops should be planned to cover all phases of the aquatic program operation.

Expert-Led In-Service Workshops

The second type of training program is an in-service program in which an expert is invited to direct the session. Persons such as a local Red Cross safety services director or YMCA field service agent, local pediatrician, child development expert, nurse, or first aid instructor can profile valuable information related to child health and education, safety, or even certification procedures. Such experts lend additional credibility to the program and can greatly enhance staff knowledges.

Professional Conferences

The third form of training occurs at professional conferences and workshops. A variety of organizations, some of which have been identified earlier, offer local, state, regional, and national conferences and workshops. Because of the variety and quality of persons who conduct and attend such conferences, they are highly recommended for all program staff.

Unfortunately, professional conferences usually involve time, travel, registration, and accommodation expenses that are beyond the means of many aquatic staff members. It is usually helpful to provide incentives to staff members such as release with partial pay or travel costs to attend worthwhile conferences. Agencies or programs should endeavor to budget for both in-service training and conference costs for staff members.

PARENT ADVISORY BOARD
CONCEPT 9.6

An active parent advisory board (PAB) must be organized and participate in all program planning and operations.

Parents of program participants are an important and necessary component of any aquatic program. They can provide advice and input during the planning, scheduling, and operation phases of the program. In addition, parents can serve important public relations and publicity roles that are either too time-consuming or demanding for the professional staff. At the same time, parents can cause turmoil and produce negative publicity about programs due to personality conflicts or lack of information. It is crucial to organize parental input to maximize the positive benefits and minimize negative problems.

An ideal way to organize parental input is through a *parent advisory board (PAB)*. The parent members of the PAB provide credibility to the program and can assist staff members in liaison activities with other parents, administrators, and supporters (see Figure 9.10). The PAB provides important advice on personnel hirings, program offerings, scheduling, fees, program evaluation, and parent education and

orientation programs. For instance, parents can give valuable information about the schedule of classes. Some class times conflict with naps or other popular programs. When parents provide input, the best schedule can be worked out. Criticism of the schedule can then be directed back to the PAB and not toward the program staff.

The critical or complaining parent is a common problem for aquatic professionals. In spite of best intentions, negative parents find fault with many aspects of the program. Left alone, this parent can ''infect'' whole groups of parents, creating a major problem. The PAB can be used to decrease the impact of a critic or complainer. When problems are presented to the aquatics personnel, staff members can remediate most minor difficulties themselves. However, when complaints are serious or ongoing, they should immediately be directed to the chairperson of the PAB. This person, working with the director, can then plan a course of action, contact the chronic complainer, and thus address the problem directly. When the problem is serious and needs immediate attention, the PAB should meet with the professional staff and decide on a plan of action. The PAB acts as the intermediary and lets the complainer know how the problem has been considered and dealt with. In serious cases of complaining, the PAB can direct necessary sanctions against an individual without alienating the professional staff from the parents of the children with whom they work.

Another valuable contribution made by a PAB committee is the review of planned materials to be used in the program. This review process can provide valuable insight into beginning a program or furthering the development of an established program. The

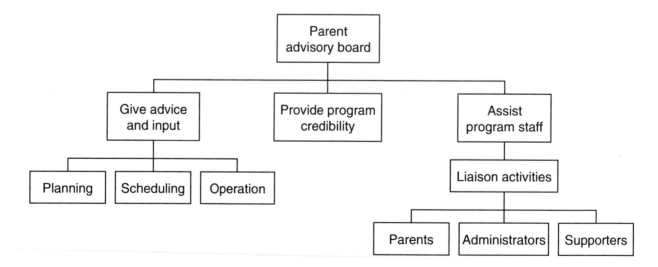

Figure 9.10   The parent advisory board (PAB) is established for the purpose of assisting in the competent presentation of aquatic readiness instruction.

PAB should be composed of interested parents of children who probably will participate in a variety of aquatic programs. It is sometimes helpful to include a preschool director on this review committee, because her or his special expertise may add insight to the planning process (refer back to Figure 9.8).

The advantage of organizing a PAB review process is to provide a sounding board that will consider and review changes in policy. For this reason, it is often better to select (a) outstanding and articulate professionals who can express themselves verbally and/or in the written word and (b) parents who have community stature or who are very vocal themselves and unafraid to approach and talk at length with parents about the positive aspects of the program. Both of these characteristics are particularly necessary in the review process when the PAB becomes involved in educating the rest of the community about the aquatic readiness program.

Documentation of meeting times, places, topics, and specific comments (i.e., minutes) that critique the implementation of the program can greatly enhance the file of material. These should be kept to prove to critics that every avenue was used to insure the quality of the planning process.

PROGRAM FEES AND SCHEDULES
CONCEPT 9.7

A program schedule and fee system must be in place and well documented.

The program time and fee schedule should be developed by the program director in conjunction with the PAB. It must meet the needs of the clientele as well as the availability of the staff and the facility.

Program Schedules

Several factors must be taken into consideration when planning schedules for aquatic readiness instruction. First are the following facility considerations:

- When is the pool available?
- Who else uses the pool and when?
- Are the pool depth, temperature, and equipment appropriate to preschool-age groups in the program?

Second, the size and expertise of the staff must be considered.

- How many instructors are available?

- What levels of expertise and interest do they have?
- When are they available?

Third, factors related to clientele must be examined.

- Who and how many are the program serving?
- What is their socioeconomic status?
- How many children does each adult or parent have?
- How far are they traveling?
- What are the times when they are available?

Finally, program philosophy and goals should be inspected.

- What is the major purpose of the program?
- What kind of limitations are imposed by the certifying agency?
- What are the desired outcomes of the program?

In most programs that provide several instructors, it is practical to schedule several ability groups simultaneously and to offer each level at several different times. Such scheduling also provides flexibility for the family with several young swimmers or for the parent who needs an alternative time for class.

Program Fees

In developing the fee system, the director and the PAB must first consider program costs (including salaries and benefits, pool rental, pool operating costs and overhead, anticipated improvements, profit, and sometimes other hidden costs). In developing and then publicizing the fee schedule, program costs should be documented. The fees then easily can be justified to the critic.

In addition to being financially sound, the fees must be reasonable for the clientele being served. An adjustable fee schedule that takes into account family size or family income is usually a good idea. If a scholarship program (i.e., reduced fees) is included as part of the budget, most parents who can afford the program will not complain if the published fee schedule permits less affluent families to participate through the receipt of scholarships or other aid. A rationale for the use of an adjustable fee schedule must be recorded and retained for later reference. Any change in fee schedule must be documented with a rationale.

Other fee considerations can become problems if not directly addressed. First, parents may assume that their child automatically will gain important skills such as ''swim strokes,'' especially if the fee structure is relatively high. It is important that parents have some realistic understanding of what their fees are buying. The PAB and program administrators should work to educate parents in terms of what can be expected within the particular concepts of aquatic readiness and learning to swim. Second, it is important that parents understand and develop some appreciation for the expense of putting together a program of this type. The process used to accomplish aquatic readiness in children and understanding by parents concerning the nature of the program is a necessary and important part of the documentation process.

STUDENT REGISTRATION AND GROUPING
CONCEPT 9.8

A registration system based on size of instruction group includes documentation of admission priorities and waiting lists.

A consistent and fair registration system, with consideration for appropriate size of instructional groups, helps alleviate public relations problems for the program. The system must work efficiently and accommodate rapid registration according to priorities. These program priorities obviously must evolve from the program philosophy and goals and be developed jointly by the program director and the PAB.

Figure 9.11 illustrates three methods of registering participants. A first-come, first-served policy is often best. In the case where continued or ongoing registration is important, some type of priority for returnees is used. It is often best to provide returnees the opportunity to register earlier or separately from first-time enrollees. This eliminates frustration and feelings of unfairness on the parts of both groups. Waiting lists often must be developed to accommodate interested parents (see Figure 9.12). As with schedules and fees, complaints should be directed to the PAB rather than toward the professional staff. Registration can be completed using phone, forms, or postcards. Records should be kept concerning date of phone contact and/or receipt of registration to demonstrate to critics the competence of the registration system.

Instructional Grouping

Documentation of the implementation process also includes concern for the size of instructional groups. No matter what the policy is regarding which participants sign up first, planners should know how many participants can be handled safely by each instructor. Usually this number is at least partially determined by participant characteristics (age, experience, skill, fear), by instructor characteristics (experience, skill, teaching style), by program characteristics (curriculum, teaching philosophy, goals and objectives), and by facility characteristics (size and equipment).

Usually the best groupings are smaller and are determined by the number needed for activity (i.e., for drills and games that include all skills associated with a physical activity). It should be recognized, however, that increased group size and subsequent increases in the instructor-to-student ratio increase the danger of injury.

Even though, in the case of aquatic programming, the option to use groups as small as two per instructor may seem extreme and even unworkable, it is essential that group assignments be small when teaching infants, toddlers, or preschool-age children who are

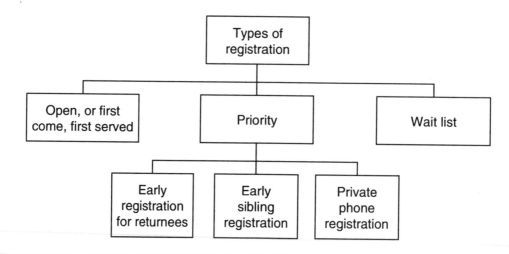

Figure 9.11   The registration system can be used efficiently to fill all sessions and provide fair treatment to all who wish to participate.

Michele Marie Prosser Aquatic Center
Preschool Aquatic Readiness Program
Waiting List

Child's name	Age	Date on list	Brother/ sister in program	Special circumstances	Parents' names	Address	Phone
1							
2							
3							
4							

Figure 9.12   A waiting list form can be used to record children who wish to participate when space becomes available.

not familiar with the specific physical activity and its dangers. Therefore, it is important to document and file the rationale for a group arrangement and group size, because it can prove valuable during later discussions or inquiries, if injury should occur.

STUDENT EVALUATION
CONCEPT 9.9

A thorough assessment, evaluation, and record-keeping system must be maintained by the program staff.

Chapters 2, 3, and 4 suggested that one major problem of aquatic programs for young children has been the failure to assess and evaluate the progress young children make in swimming programs. This failure in accountability presents a major factor for establishing a risk management system. When instructors have not established the skill level of children at the beginning of the program and monitored it throughout instruction, they cannot demonstrate that they have minimized the risk to a young child. The risk increases if the child is asked to perform a task that is too difficult or is permitted to enter a depth of water or use a piece of equipment for which he or she is not yet prepared.

Assessing Student Achievement

An educationally valid program requires pre- and postassessment procedures as well as ongoing formative evaluations. The pretest serves to identify participant needs and insures accurate group placement and accurate placement within instructional progressions. The formative evaluation is used to adequately monitor skill development and teaching throughout the program.

Posttest, or summative, evaluations provide information for certification and a sense of closure to programming and establish expectations for the next scheduled lessons. Following summative evaluation, information is available to provide a letter of progress and a certificate of aquatic readiness level (see Figure 9.13). The certificate is of particular importance because it is used to establish in parents' minds the level of competence at which their child can perform. It qualifies the skill level of the child and indicates levels above which dangers and risks still exist for the child in the water. In essence this can be interpreted as providing adequate warning as called for in the Seattle Public School District (1984b).

Other records, such as attendance, injuries, illness, or unusual occurrences, also must be kept. These are included as part of an adequate risk management system.

An ongoing record-keeping system related to assessment should be established and recorded in the file. The forms that this record system might take include journal entries and note taking. Day-to-day improvements in aquatic skills are recorded in this way. Journal comments about successful techniques to prompt learning are appropriate, as are regressions in performance that may have jeopardized progress.

Recording information about regression can assist the instructor personally and during discussions with parents to focus on progress in skill development rather than to dwell on setbacks. This strategy is important to the child, to the instructor, to the parent, and to program public relations, because regressions

Aquatic Readiness
CERTIFICATE OF MERIT
Awarded by William C. Jr and Patrick John Aquatic Center
Presented to

Gabriel Elizabeth Noran

In recognition of progress toward water safety
and the ability to move without fear of the water.
Our congratulations to you on this accomplishment!

The tested level on 10/23/93 was:

Adjustment: level 3 of 3 levels
Entry: level 5 of 5 levels
Breath control: level 1 of 7 levels
Buoyancy: level 1 of 4 levels
Body position: level 3 of 4 levels
Arm propulsion: level 2 of 4 levels
Arm recovery: level 3 of 5 levels
Legs: level 3 of 5 levels
Combined: level 4 of 5 levels

| Aquatic readiness instructor | Aquatic readiness program director |

Figure 9.13   A certificate of merit to note accomplishments can also be used to advise parents of levels of skill.

in performance occur regularly as a part of the developmental process. Regressions in performance can be stimulated by many small stressors (Roberton & Halverson, 1984); Figure 9.14 lists some of these. (See chapter 6 for explanation of regression and plateaus in performance.)

Assessing Participant Perceptions

Another evaluation system associated with program assessment is used to gain the insight of the participants and caregivers. The program assessment procedure is intended to collect information concerning positive and negative perceptions of program conduct. Through an assessment system, comments collected from parents and children sometimes provide valuable insight into needed changes that can improve the quality of programming.

The instructor's comments also are collected and filed during this part of the evaluation process. This procedure is frequently completed during a debriefing interview. This collection of information from the instructor is particularly important, because her or his view is one of close and intimate relationship to both the specific program and the specific participants.

Assessing Director Concerns

The final evaluation used to improve the program is collected from the director. The information provided through the program director can be invaluable in locating areas of concern and ways to deal with each.

As a compiled set of evaluations, the systems just outlined can provide a rather formidable set of materials. Recording this information, along with a series of targeted program changes, can be very potent in demonstrating competence to critics.

STUDENT CERTIFICATION
CONCEPT 9.10

A comprehensive certification and motivation system must be used in the aquatic readiness program.

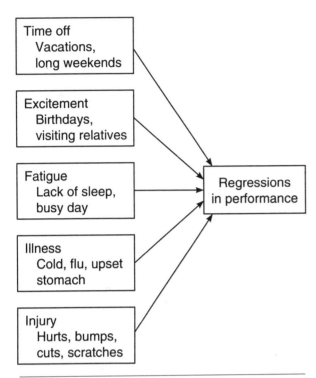

Figure 9.14 Regression in aquatic readiness performance can occur as a result of seemingly small changes in regular routine.

As part of the summative evaluation for concluding any program session, each participant and his or her parents should receive a report of the participant's progress during that session, as exemplified in Figure 9.15. It should include achievements at all appropriate levels of performance for each component and note any special certification received. Accurate use of this reporting system keeps parents informed and aids the staff in group replacement for future sessions.

Chapter 4 has presented the Aquatic Readiness Assessment (ARA) as the recommended instrument for evaluating swimming behavior by young children. This instrument has several advantages for swimmers, parents, and instructors. It contains developmental sequences that make the next levels of achievement for the child readily apparent. The developmental steps organized as a part of the instrument present gradual increments that are developmentally valid and can serve to enhance the child's and parent's motivation. Because the instrument provides sequential information, the instructor is aided in setting up appropriate instructional progressions and group placement (see Readiness Guide in chapter 4).

Use of the ARA also provides more useful information than do traditional certificates. When the child is labeled a ''beginner'' or ''porpoise,'' neither child nor parent really understands what that designation means. With the ARA certificate or report card, each skill component is described, and a child's gain in performance in each of the components can be reported in spite of less progress in a single component.

PARENT EDUCATION
CONCEPT 9.11

All new parents should be required to participate in a parent education program before enrolling their children.

Because parents of infants and young preschoolers are frequently coparticipants in aquatic programs, it is vital that they understand the program philosophy, policies, and procedures. In addition, parents are the primary caregivers for young children and are responsible for the water safety of the child outside of the program. They must receive appropriate information not only about teaching their child to swim but also about how to keep the child safe around *all* aquatic environments at home and in recreation settings.

To insure that all parents are given the opportunity to ask questions about the conduct of the program, it is important to provide information prior to instruction in two ways (see Figure 9.16). Each information providing technique must be monitored and records kept in the files concerning parents to whom information is given.

A great deal of information can be disseminated through a set of materials prepared for and given to parents through a program mailout or through an educational seminar. As a risk management technique, both a parental education session and a packet of material can force the planner to put in writing all policies and descriptions of the program. Then records can be kept that indicate that program sponsors attempted to inform parents of program safety considerations, program policy, and the limitations of the program—all of which parents should understand at the beginning of aquatic readiness instruction.

Of course, copies of the packet of materials also need to be kept on file in case of review by critics. The materials also should be accompanied by a list of signatures indicating which parents have attended the educational seminar session and a list of those to whom packets were mailed. This is a record of those who have *received and read* the packet either during the seminar process or as a result of a mail drop. After parents have had a chance to read the material received through either the seminar or the

Anne Terese Caroline Joanne Dorfer
Aquatic Readiness Progress Report Card
(Based on ARA; Aquatic Readiness Assessment)

Name _____ Date _____

Performance category	Category description	Level number	Date demonstrated
• Water adjustment	1) immense fear of the water; 2) hesitant but minimal fear; 3) entry, no fear	_____	_____
• Entry	1) No voluntary entry; 2) assisted feetfirst entry; 3) unassisted feetfirst entry; 4) assisted headfirst entry; 5) unassisted headfirst entry	_____	_____
• Breath control	1) reflexive breath control; 2) voluntary partial face submersion; 3) spitting/shipping; 4) momentary breath-hold with submersion; 5) repeated breath-hold without stroking; 6) rudimentary breathing with stroking; 7) extended hold/rhythmic breathing with stroke	_____	_____
• Buoyancy	1) no flotation; 2) flotation with assistance; 3) flotation with support; 4) unsupported flotation	_____	_____
• Body position	1) vertical; 2) inclined; 3) level; 4) horizontal	_____	_____
• Arm propulsion	1) no arm action; 2) short downward push; 3) long push-pull; 4) lift propulsion	_____	_____
• Arm recovery	1) no arm action; 2) no overwater; 3) rudimentary overarm; 4) straight overarm; 5) bent elbow overarm	_____	_____
• Legs	1) no leg action; 2) plantar push "bicycling"; 3) rudimentary flutter; 4) bent-knee flutter; 5) straight-leg flutter	_____	_____
• Combined	1) no locomotive behavior; 2) dog paddle; 3) beginner's or human stroke; 4) rudimentary crawl; 5) crawl or other stroke	_____	_____

Instructor _____ Program director _____

Figure 9.15 A report card format used for a summative report to the parents provides them with needed information about their child's skill, and it protects the program and administrators.

mail, a separate signature form included as a part of the packet should be collected from the parents of each child prior to the beginning of the aquatic readiness instruction to insure that packets were read. Thus it can be demonstrated, through two separate recording systems, that responsibility to adequately instruct has been accepted by the personnel running the program.

The parent education phase of a program should be accomplished through both written and oral pre-

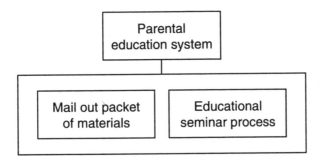

Figure 9.16   The parental education process consists of a mail out packet of materials and a seminar system.

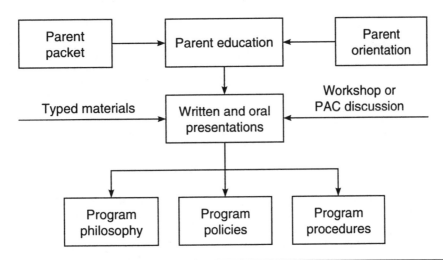

Figure 9.17   A parent education system should be used to present program information to parents in written and oral form.

sentations by the professional staff, the PAB, and health professionals. A parent packet or manual should be prepared and distributed that records all pertinent material (see Figure 9.17).

A parent orientation using different media also should be held each session for new parents. The orientation materials can be distributed at this session and then explained.

Packet materials can be grouped into three main categories. Category 1 includes "things you need to know to attend"; Category 2, "policies that govern the program"; and Category 3, "ancillary materials on child development, parenting, and swimming." See Table 9.3 for specific information that should be included in each category.

The educational seminar, designed to help parents understand the nature of a physical activity program, easily can be prepared using the outline provided in Table 9.3. The seminar period, of about 1 hour in length, lends itself to a systematic discussion of each of the categories (15 minutes each) followed by a 15-minute question-and-answer period.

If a slide show or video can be produced to introduce the components of the program and to demonstrate a typical lesson, this is valuable to help orient parents. The session should also include a trip through

the facility, with a discussion of rules and relevant safety procedures.

At the educational seminar, handouts should be available on each of the topics presented, in case parents have forgotten the packets received through the mail. The invitation to attend the seminar should accompany the registration notification and the packet. Coffee, tea, and other refreshments that can be served at a seminar are nice social amenities. PAB members can provide excellent assistance in serving refreshments.

It is particularly helpful if PAB members are willing to assist in the presentation of seminar topics. Also, through some prearranged process, PAB members should divide up attending parents and make contact with all of them sometime during the course of the meeting. In this way, a more personal feeling of program ownership can be developed. This will also increase understanding and commitment to program goals and objectives while lessening the likelihood of situations leading to lawsuit.

It also is important that the seminar meeting be held somewhere near the physical activity facility. In this way parents have an opportunity to work out parking procedures and determine the time needed to arrive promptly at the start of lessons.

Table 9.3   Parental Packet Materials by Category

Category 1—Necessary information

1. Clothing
2. Dropoff requirements/Pickup locations
3. Parking arrangements
4. Ability groupings

5. Equipment used
6. Safety warnings
7. Medical permission slips
8. Expectations from past experiences

Category 2—Governing policies

1. Philosophy and purpose statement
2. Policy on channels of communication
3. Parents on the pool deck policy
4. Parents advisory board information

5. Filing a complaint
6. Passing along a compliment
7. Substitute teacher policy
8. Meet-the-teacher lesson

Category 3—Child development materials

1. Developmental models
2. Milestones
3. Parenting information

4. Guidelines of professional aquatic organizations
5. Bibliography of related readings
6. Aquatic Readiness Assessment and Readiness Guide

If parents are unable to attend the educational seminar after receiving packets of material in the mail, an alternative means of presenting this information should be arranged. The temptation to only give them written materials, with the suggestion that they read them and ask questions, presents a serious risk management problem. Such an approach fails to inform adequately and, as in the case of recent lawsuits, could significantly increase risk of financial loss.

CURRICULUM PHILOSOPHY
CONCEPT 9.12

The curriculum must be appropriate to a program philosophy oriented toward water orientation and readiness.

The development and implementation of an appropriate curriculum is another step in an aquatic readiness risk management program system. That swimming skills and their instructional principles must be viewed developmentally is the basis for this book. Previous chapters have detailed expectations from developmental and pedagogical perspectives for aquatic programs for young children. A risk management system, as detailed in this chapter, is made more effective when used with an individualized, progressive perspective on learning. It can be used

to collect documentation and to acknowledge a caring and thoughtful approach toward children's learning.

The content of the skills, activities, and games used in the program should reflect the developmental level of the infants and young children. In general, skills should be oriented to water adjustment and readiness and not toward advanced strokes. The general atmosphere should be conducive to learning through play and fun. Approximate adaptations should be made for individual differences due to age, skill, handicapping conditions, or experience. This may be accomplished through age or ability groupings or through individualization strategies such as techniques associated with a station format, the use of task cards, or educational aquatics.

The reader is directed to chapters 4 through 8 for assistance in developing a curriculum oriented toward water orientation and aquatic readiness for the young child. Chapter 4 illustrates the ARA for assessing the beginning and concluding behaviors of children. Chapter 5 provides direction for the use of movement education methods to elicit aquatic readiness using a child-centered approach. Chapter 6 highlights learning factors that the proponents of any teaching approach should consider. Chapters 7 and 8 show how aquatic games and equipment can be used to direct the young child in the water. All of these chapters assist the program staff in developing a curriculum appropriate to the young child.

ADVERTISING
CONCEPT 9.13

Documentation of the advertising process must be undertaken.

Examples of all publicity should be recorded in the file. This information could become useful if questions arise concerning the manner in which advertisement was completed. These examples include mail sent to residences of potential participants, advertisements in local newspapers, signs in local stores, and handouts to previous participants.

• *Mailings.* The content of each of these communications should be recorded in the file. The mail sent to individual homes should probably include a brochure that outlines the program and a letter that invites them to participate. The content of these materials should outline the advantages of participation as well as the dangers inherent in the physical activity setting.

• *Newspaper ads.* A copy of newspaper advertisements also should be placed in the file. The information contained in the advertisement can be extensive or be very short and to the point. Either way, it is advisable to retain a permanent copy of the content.

• *Signs in local stores.* Usually the information included in a poster-type sign is very brief and concise. A brief description of the program should follow the program name, location, and sponsoring agency.

In addition, a phone number should be listed for inquiries for additional information. All information related to this process should be placed in the file.

• *Handouts.* A handout should be provided to all current program participants to indicate the procedure to follow to insure future participation. This information can be used to begin the next registration process, so it is important to place all returned early registration forms (attached to the handouts) in the file.

SUMMARY

Managing the risk of financial loss and loss of life in the aquatic environment is based on legal precedent. "Failure to warn" has assumed new importance. This category includes injury reports, safety clinics, curriculum, and regular inspections. Legal defense is based on a well-articulated documentation system.

Documentation should be focused on inspection of facility, maintenance and repair, and programming. Programming is by far the most complex. It includes documentation systems to manage planning, advertising, implementation, evaluation, and reporting.

Although a system of documentation can burden program personnel, the time spent collecting and filing information pales in light of the potential for human injury or financial loss that could be experienced as a result of a careless oversight. A system to manage the financial and human injury risk can be instrumental in preventing large losses.

Appendix

Water Games for Children

This appendix contains a detailed description of 108 water games and aquatic learning activities for children. Each game specifies the following information in order to assure the developmental appropriateness for the children you use it with:

- Game title
- Primary game purpose
- General skill level of the swimmer
- Specific prerequisite developmental skills needed for successful use of any game
- Appropriate water depth
- Class formation
- Equipment needed (if any)
- Detailed description of each game, including any rhymes or words
- Instructor interventions needed for each game
- Variations (where appropriate) to modify games for individual differences
- Complexity factors that may affect game success
- Reference citation for the source of the game

The games and activities are organized according to their main purposes, which include:

- Water orientation
- Breath control, rhythmic breathing, and submersion
- Flotation, buoyancy, and balance in the water
- Body position and change of direction
- Arm and leg propulsion
- Advanced strokes
- Water entry and exit

Games within each section appear alphabetically by name. In addition, an alphabetic index lists each game along with its main purpose and the skill level for which the game is developmentally appropriate. Note that skill levels for games are classified according to the developmental level that the game generally intends to promote or practice. Developmental prerequisite levels are the levels necessary to achieve *before* attempting a game.

KEY TO SKILL LEVEL NAMES:

Prebeginner = infant, toddler, or preschooler at Stage 1 learning level

Beginner = child at Stage 1 learning level

Intermediate = child at Stage 2 learning level

Advanced = child at Stage 3 learning level

(Refer to chapter 6 for more information about the characteristics of stages or learning levels.)

Table A.1   Alphabetic List of Aquatic Games and Activities

Name	Skill(s) Promoted	Skill Level
Airplane	Flotation, breath control	Beginner
Airplane II	Body position, direction	Beginner
Alligator (Otter)	Water entry (headfirst)	Beginner to intermediate
Alligator Swim	Arm/leg propulsion	Prebeginner to beginner
Bobbing Relay Race	Rhythmic breathing	Beginner to intermediate
Body-Part Tag	Arm/leg propulsion	Intermediate to advanced
Brick Recovery Race	Breath control/holding	Intermediate to advanced
Carousel (a.k.a. Merry-Go-Round)	Buoyancy, balance	Beginner*
Carp and Cranes	Arm/leg propulsion	Beginner to advanced
Charlie Over the Water	Breath control	Intermediate to advanced
Chin Ball	Breath control	Beginner to intermediate
Choo-Choo Train	Water orientation	Prebeginner to beginner*
Circles	Water orientation	Prebeginner*
Combined Stroke on the Back Progression	Arm/leg propulsion	Beginner
Cork Scramble	Arm/leg propulsion	Beginner to advanced
Drop the Puck	Breath control, submersion, propulsion	Beginner to advanced
Easter Egg Coloring Time	Water entry	Prebeginner to intermediate
Echo Tag (a.k.a. Marco Polo)	Flotation, buoyancy	Beginner to advanced
Five Little Ducks	Flotation	Prebeginner to beginner*
Float Tag	Flotation	Beginner to intermediate
Flower Garden	Breath control	Beginner
Flutter Kicking Cues	Leg propulsion	Beginner to intermediate
Front Crawl Stroke—Arm Pull Cues	Arm propulsion	Beginner to intermediate
Gingerbread Cookie	Flotation	Beginner*
Glide and Slide	Flotation, breath control	Beginner
Handicapped Tag	Arm/leg propulsion	Beginner
Hands Up, Hands Down	Water orientation	Prebeginner to beginner*
Head, Shoulders, Knees, and Toes	Body position, change of direction	Beginner
Hokey Pokey	Water orientation	Prebeginner to beginner
Hot and Cold	Leg propulsion	Beginner
Humpty Dumpty	Water entry, breath control	Prebeginner*
If You're Happy and You Know It	Water orientation	Prebeginner to beginner*
Immunity Tag	Body position	Beginner to intermediate
It's Raining, It's Pouring	Water orientation	Prebeginner to beginner*
Jack be Nimble	Water entry, breath control	Prebeginner*
Jack-in-the-Box	Breath control	Prebeginner to beginner*
Jellyfish Center	Water orientation	Prebeginner to beginner
Jumpin'	Buoyancy, balance	Beginner
Jump Into My Circle	Water entry, breath control	Beginner*
Kickboard Killer	Leg propulsion	Beginner to advanced
Kickboard Tug of War	Leg propulsion	Beginner to advanced
Leapfrog	Breath control	Beginner to intermediate
Light Up the Night	Arm/leg propulsion	Intermediate to advanced
Little Green Frog	Breath control	Beginner
Log Tag	Flotation	Intermediate to advanced
London Bridge	Breath control	Prebeginner to beginner
Look and Listen	Rhythmic breath	Prebeginner to intermediate
Magic Candle	Breath control	Prebeginner to beginner*
Motorboat	Breath control, balance	Prebeginner to beginner*
Musical Kickboards	Flotation, body position	Beginner
Name Game	Water orientation	Prebeginner to intermediate
Newspaper Relay	Leg propulsion	Intermediate to advanced
Obstacle Course	Breath control, arm/leg propulsion	Beginner to advanced
One-Arm Swim	Arm/leg propulsion	Intermediate to advanced
Over and Under	Water orientation	Beginner to intermediate

Name	Skill(s) Promoted	Skill Level
Pancakes	Body position	Prebeginner*
Parchute Jump	Water entry, breath control	Beginner to intermediate
The People in the Water (a.k.a. Wheels on the Bus)	Water orientation	Prebeginner to beginner
Ping-Pong Push	Breath control	Beginner
Poison Center	Water orientation	Beginner
Pool Exploration	Water orientation	Prebeginner to beginner
Pop Goes the Weasel	Water orientation	Prebeginner to beginner
Porpoise Tag (a.k.a. Aquatic Red Rover)	Flotation, breath control	Intermediate to advanced
Print	Flotation	Intermediate to advanced
Push Against the Wall	Flotation (back)	Prebeginner*
Ride'Em Cowboys	Buoyancy	Beginner
Ring-Around the Rosy	Breath control	Prebeginner to beginner*
Rocket Booster	Water entry, propulsion	Intermediate
Rocket Ship	Flotation, propulsion	Beginner to intermediate
Salmon Says	Water orientation	Beginner to intermediate
Sharks and Minnows (I)	Flotation, buoyancy	Beginner
Sharks and Minnows (II)	Arm/leg propulsion, rhythmic breathing	Intermediate to advanced
Sinkable/Unsinkable Object Game	Breath control	Nonswimmer to beginner*
Sink Activity	Breath control, water orientation	Beginner*
Sink or Float?	Flotation, buoyancy	Prebeginner
Sink Play	Water orientation	Prebeginner*
Slithering Snake	Water entry	Prebeginner to beginner
Spider Swimming	Arm/leg propulsion	Prebeginner
Splish, Splash	Water orientation, breath control	Beginner
Squirt Gun Relay	Advanced strokes	Beginner to advanced
Sticky Popcorn	Flotation, balance	Beginner to intermediate
Still Pond	Advanced strokes	Intermediate to advanced
Straddleboard Relay	Flotation, buoyancy	Intermediate to advanced
Stroke Switch	Advanced strokes	Intermediate to advanced
Sunken Treasure	Breath control	Beginner to advanced
Superman (I)	Flotation, breath control	Beginner to intermediate
Superman (II)	Body position	Beginner to intermediate
Swimming Spelldown	Advanced strokes	Beginner to advanced
Swizzles	Water orientation	Prebeginner
Teeter-Totter	Breath control, submersion	Prebeginner to beginner
''Timber!''	Flotation, breath control	Beginner to intermediate
Time Machine	Arm/leg propulsion	Intermediate to advanced
Touch	Advanced strokes	Intermediate to advanced
Train	Balance, submersion	Prebeginner to beginner
Trick/Stunt Tag	Water orientation	Beginner to intermediate
T-Shirt Relay	Advanced strokes	Intermediate to advanced
Twenty Ways	Arm/leg propulsion	Beginner to advanced
Up, Up, and Away	Water exit	Beginner
Washcloth Play	Water orientation	Nonswimmer or prebeginner
Water Croquet	Breath control	Intermediate to advanced
Water Limbo	Flotation (back)	Beginner to intermediate
Water Push Ball	Orientation, flotation	Beginner to intermediate
Water Ski Ride	Flotation	Beginner to intermediate
Water Wheelbarrow	Arm/leg propulsion	Intermediate to advanced
The Wave	Breath control	Beginner
Wave to the ''Fishies''	Arm/leg propulsion	Beginner to intermediate
Whale Spitting	Breath control	Prebeginner to beginner
Who Can . . .?	Water orientation	Beginner to intermediate
Zigzag	Advanced strokes	Beginner to advanced

*These beginner activities are most age-appropriate for beginner-level toddlers and preschoolers, due to the simple content and approach.

Table A.2 A List of Aquatic Games by Skill Component and Skill Component Level Promoted

Water Orientation Skills

Choo-Choo Train: Water Adjustment/Orientation Level 3
Circles: Water Adjustment/Orientation Level 3
Hands Up, Hands Down: Water Adjustment/Orientation Level 3
Hokey Pokey: Water Adjustment/Orientation Level 3
If You're Happy and You Know It: Water Adjustment/Orientation Level 2
It's Raining, It's Pouring: Water Adjustment/Orientation Level 2
Jellyfish Center: Water Adjustment/Orientation Level 3
Name Game: Water Adjustment/Orientation Level 3
Over and Under: Water Adjustment/Orientation Level 3
The People in the Water: Water Adjustment/Orientation Level 2
Pool Exploration: Water Adjustment/Orientation Level 2
Pop Goes the Weasel: Water Adjustment/Orientation Level 3
Salmon Says: Water Adjustment/Orientation Level 3
Sink Play: Water Adjustment/Orientation Level 2
Splish Splash: Water Adjustment/Orientation Level 3
Swizzles: Water Adjustment/Orientation Level 3
Trick/Stunt Tag: Water Adjustment/Orientation Level 3
Washcloth Play: Water Adjustment/Orientation Level 2
Water Push Ball: Water Adjustment/Orientation Level 3
Who can . . .?: Water Adjustment/Orientation Level 3

Breath Control, Rhythmic Breathing, and Submersion

Brick Recovery Race (modified): Breath Control Level 4
Bobbing Relay Race: Breath Control Level 5
Charlie Over the Water: Breath Control Level 4
Chin Ball: Breath Control Level 3
Drop the Puck (Water Duck, Duck, Goose): Breath Control Level 4
Flower Garden: Breath Control Level 4
Jack-in-the-Box: Breath Control Level 4
Leapfrog: Breath Control Level 4
Little Green Frog: Breath Control Level 3
London Bridge: Breath Control Level 4
Look and Listen: Breath Control Level 4
Magic Candle: Breath Control Level 2
Motorboat: Breath Control Level 2
Obstacle Course: Breath Control Level 5
Ping-Pong Push: Breath Control Level 3
Ring-Around-the-Rosie: Breath Control Level 3
Sinkable/Unsinkable Object Game: Breath Control Level 3
Sunken Treasure: Breath Control Level 5
Teeter-Totter: Breath Control Level 3
Water Croquet: Breath Control Level 5
The Wave: Breath Control Level 4
Whale Spitting: Breath Control Level 2

Flotation, Buoyancy, and Balance in Water

Airplane: Buoyancy/Flotation Level 3
Carousel (Merry-Go-Round): Buoyancy/Flotation Level 2 to 3
Echo Tag (Marco Polo): Buoyancy/Flotation Level 4
Five Little Ducks: Buoyancy/Flotation Level 2
Float Tag: Buoyancy/Flotation Level 4
Gingerbread Cookie: Buoyancy/Flotation Level 2
Glide and Slide: Buoyancy/Flotation Level 4
Jumpin': Buoyancy/Flotation Level 1
Log Tag: Buoyancy/Flotation Level 4
Musical Kickboards: Buoyancy/Flotation Level 3
Porpoise Tag (Aquatic Red Rover): Buoyancy/Flotation Level 4
Print: Buoyancy/Flotation Level 4

Push Against the Wall: Buoyancy/Flotation Level 2
Ride'Em Cowboys: Buoyancy/Flotation Level 3
Rocket Ship: Buoyancy/Flotation Level 4
Sharks and Minnows (I): Buoyancy/Flotation Level 2
Sink or Float?: Buoyancy/Flotation Level 1
Sticky Popcorn: Buoyancy/Flotation Level 1
Straddleboard (Relay): Buoyancy/Flotation Level 3
Superman (I): Buoyancy/Flotation Level 4
''Timber!'': Buoyancy/Flotation Level 4
Train: Buoyancy/Flotation Level 1
Water Limbo: Buoyancy/Flotation Level 2
Water Ski Ride: Buoyancy/Flotation Level 3

Body Position and Change of Direction

Airplane (II): Body Position Level 2
Head, Shoulders, Knees, and Toes: Body Position Level 3
Immunity Tag: Body Position Level 2
Pancakes: Body Position Level 2
Superman (II): Body Position Level 3

Arm/Leg Propulsion

Alligator Swim: Arm Propulsion Level 1
Body-part Tag: Arm Propulsion Level 3
Carp and Cranes: Arm Propulsion Level 3
Combined Stroke on Back Progression: All Levels
Cork Scramble: Arm Propulsion Level 2
Flutter Kicking Cues: All Arm Propulsion Levels
Front Crawl Stroke Arm Pull Progression: All Arm Propulsion Levels
Hot and Cold: Arm Propulsion Level 2
Kickboard Killer: Arm Propulsion Level 3
Kickboard Tug of War: Arm Propulsion Level 3
Light up the Night: Arm Propulsion Level 4
Newspaper Relay: Arm Propulsion Level 3
One Arm Swim: Arm Propulsion Level 4
Sharks and Minnows (II): Arm Propulsion Level 3
Spider Swimming: Arm Propulsion Level 1
Time Machine: Arm Propulsion Level 3
Twenty Ways: Arm Propulsion Level 3
Water Wheelbarrow: Arm Propulsion Level 4
Wave to the ''Fishies'': Arm Propulsion Level 3

Advanced Strokes

Squirt Gun Relay (Shoot 'Em Down): Combined Stroke Level 3
Still Pond: Combined Stroke Levels 2 to 3
Stroke Switch: Combined Stroke Levels 3 to 5
Swimming Spelldown: Combined Stroke Level 3
Touch: Combined Stroke Level 3
T-Shirt Relay (Change-the-Shirt Relay): Combined Stroke Level 3
Zigzag (Figure-eight): Combined Stroke Level 3

Water Entry and Exit

Alligator (Otter): Water Entry Level 4
Easter Egg Coloring Time: Water Entry Level 3
Humpty Dumpty: Water Entry Level 2
Jack Be Nimble: Water Entry Level 2
Jump Into My Circle: Water Entry Level 3
Parachute Jump: Water Entry Level 3
Rocket Booster: Water Entry Level 5
Slithering Snake: Water Entry Level 2
Up, Up, and Away (Exit game): No prerequisite level

Water Orientation Skills

Choo-Choo Train: Water Entry Level 2; Orientation Level
Circles: Water Entry Level 2
Hands Up, Hands Down: Water Entry Level 2
Hokey Pokey: Entry Level 2
If You're Happy and You Know It: Water Entry Level 2
It's Raining, It's Pouring: Water Entry Level 2
Jellyfish Center: Water Entry Level 2
Name Game: Water Entry Level 2
Over and Under: Water Entry Level 2

The People in the Water: Water Entry Level 2
Pool Exploration: Water Entry Level 1
Pop Goes the Weasel: Water Entry Level 2
Salmon Says: Water Entry Level 2
Sink Play: Water Entry Level 1
Splish Splash: Water Entry Level 2
Swizzles: Water Entry Level 2
Trick/Stunt Tag: Water Entry Level 2
Washcloth Play: Water Entry Level 1
Water Push Ball: Water Entry Level 2
Who can . . . ?: Water Entry Level 2

Choo-Choo Train

Purpose: To improve water adjustment and orientation to the water; to improve mobility and walking movement in the water

Skill level: Prebeginner to beginner (preschool)

Water depth: Shallow (ankle to waist deep)

Class formation: Circle, line, or zigzag

Equipment: None (see variations)

Prerequisite developmental skills:
Water Adjustment/Orientation Level 2
Water Entry Level 2
Breath Control Level 1
Buoyancy/Flotation Level 1
Body Position Level 1
Arm Action Level 1
Leg Action Level 1
Combined Stroke Level 1

Description: Ask children to travel in a circle, lines, or zigzag while moving their arms like the pistons of a steam locomotive. They can also add a whistle, chugging, or other train sounds.

Instructor intervention: Provide instruction and safety.

Variations: Use a hula hoop for the children to hold as they walk in a circle. Suggest a variety of directions and speeds. Let each child be a favorite train car.

Complexity factors: Number of students; depth of water; speed of movement; presence of parents

Source: Runta, N. (1980). *Pre-school swimming instructor's manual.* Findlay, OH: YMCA.

Circles

Purpose: To practice water adjustment and orientation

Skill level: Prebeginner (infants/toddlers)

Water depth: Chest deep or less on parents

Class formation: One-on-one (parent and child)

Prerequisite developmental skills:
Water Adjustment/Orientation Level 2
Water Entry Level 2
Breath Control Level 1
Buoyancy/Flotation Level 1
Body Position Level 1
Arm Action Level 1
Leg Action Level 1
Combined Stroke Level 1

Equipment: None

Description: Placing your right hand under the infant's stomach, with your left hand grasp the arm closest to you. Start turning the infant to your right so she or he skids through the water planing on his or her chest, round and round in one direction. Change directions at intervals suggested by instructor.

Instructor intervention: Provide instructions and safety.

Variations: Same kinds of movements, but have the infant on her or his back or in upright position.

Complexity factors: Water depth; child/parent experience

Source: Prudden, B. (1974). *Teach your baby to swim* (p. 117). New York: Dial Press.

Hands Up, Hands Down

Purpose: To practice water adjustment skills while reinforcing directional terms and knowledge

Skill level: Prebeginner to beginner

Water depth: Waist to chest deep on parents

Class formation: Circle with parents and children facing in

Equipment: None

Prerequisite developmental skills:
Water Adjustment/Orientation Level 2
Water Entry Level 2
Breath Control Level 1
Buoyancy/Flotation Level 1
Body Position Level 1
Arm Action Level 1
Leg Action Level 1
Combined Stroke Level 1

Description: With everyone facing toward center, instructor in center repeats the rhyme:
"Hands up, hands down, splash, splash, splash!
Hands up, hands down, splash, splash, splash!
Hands out, hands in, splash, splash, splash!
Hands out, hands in, splash, splash, splash!
Push down in the water, push down in the water, splash, splash, splash!
Pull, and pull, and pull.
Frog pull, frog pull, frog pull."
Children and parents make actions along with the rhyme. Everyone is encouraged to make as much splash as possible.

Instructor intervention: Provide directions and encouragement and lead rhymes.

Variation: Add different skills (including bubble blowing, face submersion, floating, movement with feet).

Complexity factors: Depth of water, type of skills, presence of parents

Source: Kochen, C., & McCabe, J. (1986). *The baby swim book* (p. 365). Champaign, IL: Human Kinetics.

Hokey Pokey

Purpose: To practice simple water skills and movement in a group setting

Skill level: Prebeginner to beginner

Water depth: Waist to chest deep on children

Class formation: Circle or scattered

Equipment: None

Prerequisite developmental skills:
Water Adjustment/Orientation Level 2
Water Entry Level 2
Breath Control Level 1
Buoyancy/Flotation Level 1
Body Position Level 1
Arm Action Level 1
Leg Action Level 1
Combined Stroke Level 1
(knowledge of right and left)

Description: Children (and parents, if present) form a circle and perform the actions to go with the "Hokey Pokey" song:
"You put your right hand in; you put your right hand out; you put your right hand in; and you shake it all about;
You do the Hokey Pokey and you turn yourself around;
And that's what it's all about!" (and so on)

Instructor intervention: Provide instructions, lead song, and provide model for the actions.

Variation: Change body parts as appropriate to skill level of class.

Complexity factors: Water depth, number and type of body parts used; presence/assistance of parents

Source: YMCA of the USA. (1987). *Y Skippers* (p. 297). Champaign, IL: Human Kinetics.

If You're Happy and You Know It

Purpose: To orient the student to the pool and water environment

Skill level: Prebeginner to beginner

Water depth: Shallow

Class formation: Circle

Equipment: None (record player or tapes if desired)

Prerequisite developmental skills:
Water Adjustment/Orientation Level 2
Water Entry Level 2
Breath Control Level 1
Buoyancy/Flotation Level 1
Body Position Level 1
Arm Action Level 1
Leg Action Level 1
Combined Stroke Level 1

Description: As a group, sing the song
"When You're Happy and You Know It":
"When you're happy and you know it,
[action description]
[demonstrate action];
When you're happy and you know it,
[action description]
[demonstrate action];

When you're happy and you know it and
you really want to show it,
when you're happy and you know it,

[*action description*]

[*demonstrate action*]''

Select from some of the following actions: Clap your hands, splash the water, kick your feet, blow some bubbles, run in place, touch the bottom, float on your tummy, turn all around, etc. (or make up your own). You also may accumulate the actions and do them as a series.

Instructor intervention: Lead song and actions, ensure safety of children, provide encouragement, feedback, and motivation.

Variations: Have each child determine the action and lead the group. Have children perform on the pool side without entering the water.

Complexity factors: Water depth, in water or out; child's enjoyment and experience level of water; types of skills used

Source: Canadian Red Cross. (1984). *Water safety instructor guide and reference* (Vol. 5, p. 42). Toronto: Author.

It's Raining, It's Pouring

Purpose: To help the child become adjusted to having water around or on his or her head

Skill level: Prebeginner to beginner

Water depth: Out of pool (in the shower or at pool side) or waist deep

Class formation: One-on-one or small groups

Prerequisite developmental skills:
Water Adjustment/Orientation Level 1
Water Entry Level 2
Breath Control Level 1
Buoyancy/Flotation Level 1
Body Position Level 1
Arm Action Level 1
Leg Action Level 1
Combined Stroke Level 1

Equipment: Sponges, cups, plastic milk bottle with holes, etc.

Description: While singing the song ''It's Raining, It's Pouring,'' dribble, drop, splash water over the child's head with hands, sponges, cups, etc. Allow the child to make it rain over the instructor's or parent's head as well as her or his own.

Instructor intervention: Provide directions and ensure safety; assist the child in pouring water over herself or himself and others.

Variations: Use empty plastic 2-liter pop bottles with holes punched in the bottom, a watering can, or sponge to simulate a shower. Perform in shower or poolside plastic pool.

Complexity factors: Number of students, level of swimming skill, type of equipment, amount of water, parts of head and face getting wet

Source: Original to S. Langendorfer and D. Harrod.

Jellyfish Center

Purpose: To improve water adjustment skills and water balance

Skill level: Prebeginner to beginner

Water depth: Knee to waist deep

Class formation: Circle

Equipment: Floatable object—balloon or ball

Prerequisite developmental skills:
Water Adjustment/Orientation Level 3
Water Entry Level 2
Breath Control Level 1
Buoyancy/Flotation Level 2
Body Position Level 1
Arm Action Level 1
Leg Action Level 1
Combined Stroke Level 1

Description: Swimmers join hands in a circle. A floatable object (jellyfish) is placed in the center of the circle. The jellyfish cannot be touched by anyone. Through splashing with the feet or pulling on other members in the circle, swimmers attempt to cause others in the circle to touch the jellyfish.

Instructor intervention: Provide instruction and safety; place the jellyfish in the middle of the circle prior to the start of the game.

Variations: Swimmers do not hold hands as they try to move the jellyfish by splashing it with their hands. Play in deep water and have the intermediate/advanced swimmers tread water.

Complexity factors: Water depth, number of students, students' balance skills in the water

Source: Canadian Red Cross. (1984). *Water safety instructor guide and reference* (Vol. 5, p. 42). Toronto: Author.

Name Game

Purpose: To introduce class members to one another; to increase water adjustment and orientation; to practice previously learned skills

Skill level: Prebeginner to intermediate

Water depth: Knee to chest deep, depending upon skill level

Class formation: Line or circle or on pool deck

Equipment: None

Prerequisite developmental skills:
Water Adjustment/Orientation Level 2
Water Entry Level 2
Breath Control Level 1
Buoyancy/Flotation Level 1
Body Position Level 1
Arm Action Level 1
Leg Action Level 1
Combined Stroke Level 1
(Ability to talk and use own name)

Description: With class members (including parents) in formation, the rhyme,
"Names, names, what's in a name?
I've got a name and you've got a name.

What's your name?''

is chanted by the class. The chosen swimmer says her or his name and simultaneously performs a skill. The group then repeats the name three times and attempts to repeat the stunt or skill that the swimmer performed. Each swimmer gets a turn. Instructor and parents can help by giving suggestions for skills and by providing flotation assistance. At the conclusion, a circle is drawn up, and all names are reviewed and skills discussed.

Instructor intervention: Lead the chant; give suggestions for skills; help parents with flotation assistance.

Variation: Children can perform their own skill plus add previous skills performed.

Complexity factors: Water depth, number and type of skills practiced, size of the class, presence of parental assistance

Source: YMCA of the USA. (1987). *Y Skippers* (p. 193). Champaign, IL: Human Kinetics.

Over and Under

Purpose: To practice object-handling skills while standing in water

Skill level: Beginner to intermediate

Water depth: Knee to chest deep

Class formation: One or more lines, all facing same direction

Prerequisite developmental skills:
Water Adjustment/Orientation Level 2-3
Water Entry Level 2
Breath Control Level 1
Buoyancy/Flotation Level 1
Body Position Level 1
Arm Action Level 1
Leg Action Level 1
Combined Stroke Level 1

Equipment: Ball—size can vary.

Description: A ball is given to the first child in line. It is passed over his or her head to the next child, who passes it to the next child by passing it through her or his legs. At end of the line, the last child brings the ball to the front by walking or running, and the process begins again until all have their turn in front.

Instructor intervention: Provide instruction and supervise activities.

Variations: In chest-deep water, the child can submerge as the ball is passed between legs or overhead. Game can become relay race between two or more lines.

Complexity factors: Size of ball, depth of water, presence of competition between/among teams

Source: YMCA of the USA. (1986). *Splash!* (p. 63). Champaign, IL: Human Kinetics.

The People in the Water

Purpose: To help the child learn to move in the water

Skill level: Prebeginner to beginner

Water depth: Out of water (in a shower, at pool side) or knee to waist deep

Class formation: Small group in a circle

Equipment: None

Prerequisite developmental skills:
Water Adjustment/Orientation Level 1
Water Entry Level 1
Breath Control Level 1
Buoyancy/Flotation Level 1
Body Position Level 1
Arm Action Level 1
Leg Action Level 1
Combined Stroke Level 1

Description: While singing the song ''The Fish in the Water'' (to the tune of ''The People on the Bus''), act out the following animals/movements:

Animal	Children's actions	Words
Fish	Jump up and down in the water.	''Up and down''
Waves	Move forward and back in the circle.	''Back and forth''
Flippers	Move left and right.	''Left and right''
Fins	Scoop water in small circles.	''Paddle, paddle''
Porpoise	Tap water with hands.	''Splish, splash''
Otters	Float on back (with assistance if needed).	''Float, float''
Blowfish	Blow bubbles.	(Bubble-blowing sounds)
Whale	Spit water up in air.	(Water-spitting action)

Instructor intervention: Provide instructions and safety; sing and act out song with the children; provide assistance for those who cannot back-float.

Variations: Add additional verses and actions. Do on the pool deck for fearful children.

Complexity factors: Number and skill levels of students, water depth; type of actions

Source: Kelly, K. (1986, March). *Workshop games.* United States Swimming Foundation workshop, Fort Wayne, IN.

Pool Exploration

Purpose: To introduce new children to the pool and water environment for the first time

Skill level: Prebeginner to beginner

Water depth: Out of water to waist deep

Class formation: One-on-one or small group

Prerequisite developmental skills:
Water Adjustment/Orientation Level 1
Water Entry Level 1
Breath Control Level 1
Buoyancy/Flotation Level 1
Body Position Level 1
Arm Action Level 1
Leg Action Level 1
Combined Stroke Level 1

Equipment: All available at pool

Description: Instructor gathers new children (and parents) together and presents the various parts of the swimming area and pool to them. It is important to talk about and touch and play with every part of the pool: gutters, steps, diving boards, safety equipment, deep end, lane lines. The process is intended to remove mystery and fear from the new environment.

Instructor intervention: Lead presentation, encourage questions and exploration.

Variations: Depend upon the environment and children's questions. Can be done in story format.

Complexity factors: Depends upon the pool facility, amount and type of equipment, number and skill levels of students

Source: Original to S. Langendorfer.

Pop Goes the Weasel

Purpose: To improve water adjustment and orientation for the water

Skill level: Prebeginner to beginner

Water depth: Waist to chest deep

Class formation: Circle or scattered

Equipment: None (records or tapes if desired)

Prerequisite developmental skills:
Water Adjustment/Orientation Level 2
Water Entry Level 2
Breath Control Level 1, 2, 3 (depending on variations)
Buoyancy/Flotation Level 2
Body Position Level 1
Arm Action Level 1
Leg Action Level 1
Combined Stroke Level 1

Description: Sing the song "Pop Goes the Weasel":

"Round and round the mulberry bush,
The monkey chased the weasel;
The monkey thought it was all in fun;
Pop goes the weasel!"

On "Pop," all of the children jump up or duck under.

Instructor intervention: Lead activity; provide instruction and safety.

Variations: Perform different swimming actions on "Pop."

Complexity factors: Water depth, number of children, children's skill levels and enjoyment in the water

Source: Runta, N. (1980). *Pre-school swimming instructor's manual.* Findlay, OH: YMCA.

Salmon Says

Purpose: To practice previously learned skills

Skill level: Beginner to intermediate

Water depth: Out of water or waist deep to over the head, depending upon skill level

Class formation: Scattered

Equipment: None

Prerequisite developmental skills:
Water Adjustment/Orientation Level 2
Water Entry Level 1
Breath Control Level 1
Buoyancy/Flotation Level 1
Body Position Level 1
Arm Action Level 1
Leg Action Level 1
Combined Stroke Level 1

Description: This aquatic version of Simon Says is played in much the same way: Leader (called "Salmon") requests other swimmers to copy everything she or he does, as long as the command is preceded by "salmon says . . . ." Depending upon the ages and skill levels of the participants, the speed of commands and the type of skills vary. Violators can be eliminated as in the traditional game, or just pointed out and remain to keep maximum participation.

Instructor intervention: Explain the rules and perhaps be the first "Salmon."

Variations: Issue commands in more rapid order. Play in deep water without touching the bottom.

Complexity factors: Depth of water, types of skills, speed of commands

Source: Canadian Red Cross. (1984). *Water safety instructor guide and reference* (Vol. 5, p. 40). Toronto: Author.

Sink Play

Purpose: To acclimate and adjust fearful child to the water environment; to reduce fear sufficiently to enable child to enter pool

Skill level: Prebeginner (infant, toddler, preschooler)

Water depth: Minimal (sink, tub, plastic pool)

Class formation: One-on-one

Equipment: Small tub or plastic pool, warm water, small colorful tub toys

Prerequisite developmental skills:
Water Adjustment/Orientation Level 1
Water Entry Level 1
Breath Control Level 1
Buoyancy/Flotation Level 1
Body Position Level 1
Arm Action Level 1
Leg Action Level 1
Combined Stroke Level 1

Description: Fill a sink, baby tub, or shallow plastic pool with about 3 inches of warm water. Water area should be sufficient to permit water to be splashed and cover the ears when the child is lying on his or her back.

Instructor intervention: Parent or older sibling who has trust and control of child; patience, positive reinforcement, encouragement, laughter, and guidance.

Variations: As appropriate to get child to play with water (e.g., splashing water, spitting water, pouring cups of water, floating boats or other objects).

Complexity factors: Temperature and depth of water, games and skills requested

Source: Shank, C. (1983). *A child's way to water play* (p. 57). Champaign, IL: Leisure Press.

Splish, Splash

Purpose: To improve water adjustment/orientation and tolerance for water in the face; to practice rudimentary flutter-kick skills

Skill level: Beginner

Water depth: Knee to chest deep

Class formation: Circle

Equipment: Plastic bucket for each circle

Prerequisite developmental skills:
Water Adjustment/Orientation Level 2
Water Entry Levels 2-3
Breath Control Levels 1-3
Buoyancy/Flotation Level 2
Body Position Level 1
Arm Action Level 1
Leg Action Level 1
Combined Stroke Level 1

Description: A plastic bucket is placed floating in the middle of the circle. Class tries to sink the bucket by splashing it full of water as fast as possible.

Instructor intervention: Explain purpose of the game, monitor the bucket, and refloat it when necessary.

Variations: Add more than one circle of splashers. Use larger buckets. Fill the bucket by kicking with feet rather than hands.

Complexity factors: Size of bucket, depth of water

Source: Canadian Red Cross. (1984). *Water safety instructor guide and reference* (Vol. 5, p. 23). Toronto: Author.

Swizzles

Purpose: To practice water adjustment skills

Skill level: Prebeginner (with parents)

Water depth: Waist to chest deep on parents

Class formation: One-on-one (parent and child)

Equipment: None

Prerequisite developmental skills:
Water Adjustment/Orientation Level 2
Water Entry Level 1
Breath Control Level 1
Buoyancy/Flotation Level 1
Body Position Level 1
Arm Action Level 1
Leg Action Level 1
Combined Stroke Level 1

Description: Hold the infant under the arms and lift her or him out of the water so that the legs just come out of the water. Slowly lower the child into the water up to his or her chest, and then back out again. Increase the speed as the child becomes accustomed to this movement.

Instructor intervention: Ensure safety and assist parents to keep children comfortable.

Variation: Make wavelike movements with the child as she or he is going up and down in the water.

Complexity factors: Ratio of children to adults

Source: From: Runta, N. (1980). *Pre-school swimming instructor's manual*. Findlay, OH: YMCA.

Trick/Stunt Tag

Purpose: To practice existing skills and experiment with them in different combinations. In particular, changes in body position and direction can be enhanced.

Skill level: Beginner to intermediate

Water depth: All depths, depending upon swimmer skill levels

Prerequisite developmental skills:
Water Adjustment/Orientation Levels 2-3
Water Entry Level 2
Breath Control Levels 2-3
Buoyancy/Flotation Level 1
Body Position Levels 1-2
Arm Action Level 1
Leg Action Level 1
Combined Stroke Level 1

Class formation: Scattered

Equipment: None necessarily, except buoyed line to restrict play area

Description: Instructor or appointed class member is "it." "It" calls out body parts to hold out of the water or stunts to perform. Any participant not performing stunt can be tagged and becomes next "it."

Instructor intervention: Explain rules, ensure safety of participants, and referee questionable decisions.

Variations: May be used as a warm-up at beginning of class period. Swimmers can be eliminated, become "it," or become part of team "it."

Complexity factors: Depth of water, type and difficulty of skills, number of skill combinations

Source: Sheffield, L. (1927). *Swimming simplified* (p. 240). New York: Barnes.

Washcloth Play

Purpose: To accustom the child to having water on his or her face

Skill level: Nonswimmer or prebeginner

Water depth: None to very shallow

Class formation: One-on-one

Equipment: One to two washcloths, small water container or tub, towels for drying

Prerequisite developmental skills:
Water Adjustment/Orientation Level 1
Water Entry Level 1
Breath Control Level 1
Buoyancy/Flotation Level 1
Body Position Level 1
Arm Action Level 1
Leg Action Level 1
Combined Stroke Level 1

Description: The child is brought near the water. A wet washcloth is provided, and the child is encouraged to play with it (pick it up, suck on it, splash it). Parent demonstrates washing body parts; child is encouraged to imitate. Child's body parts also can be washed.

Instructor intervention: Provides modeling behaviors for parents and ensures safety. Provides patience, positive reinforcement, encouragement, laughter, and guidance.

Variations: Play peek-a-boo with cloth; make a tent; wear a wet hat. Works well in combination with Sink Play and Sinkable/Unsinkable Object games.

Complexity factors: Water temperature, amount of water on cloth

Source: Shank, C. (1983). *A child's way to water play* (p. 60). Champaign, IL: Leisure Press.

Water Push Ball

Purpose: To improve the swimmer's ability to move in the water; to become adjusted to water being splashed on body and in face

Skill level: Beginner to intermediate

Water depth: Knee to chest deep

Class formation: Circle

Equipment: Ball

Prerequisite developmental skills:
Water Adjustment/Orientation Level 2
Water Entry Level 2
Breath Control Level 1
Buoyancy/Flotation Levels 1-2
Body Position Level 1
Arm Action Level 1
Leg Action Level 1
Combined Stroke Level 1

Description: In a circle around a ball, the children try to move the ball by splashing and pushing water with their hands. The children try not to touch the ball with any part of their bodies.

Instructor intervention: Provide directions and safety; make sure that certain children who may be apprehensive about having water splashed in their faces have a chance to participate.

Variations: Have many balls in the group. Divide the class into groups. Intermediate swimmers use a plastic cage ball in deeper water, and the swimmers can use their hands to move it from one side of the pool to the other. Intermediate swimmers can also divide into two teams and try to push the ball to the other team's goal—the cage ball is not allowed to be lifted out of the water.

Complexity factors: Number of students, levels of the students' skills, depth of water, size of ball, level of competition

Source: Brown, C. (1986, March). *Workshop games*. United States Swimming Foundation workshop, Fort Wayne, IN.

Who Can . . . ?

Purpose: To *practice* new or existing skills using an exploration format. May include skills for water orientation, entry/exit, propulsion, change of direction and position, breath control, submersion, water balance (see chapter 5).

Skill level: Beginner to intermediate

Water depth: Waist deep or deeper

Class formation: Scattered

Prerequisite developmental skills:
Water Adjustment/Orientation Level 2
Water Entry Level 2
Breath Control Level 2
Buoyancy/Flotation Level 2
Body Position Level 2
Arm Action Level 1
Leg Action Level 1
Combined Stroke Level 1

Equipment: None necessary; buoyed line(s) can keep swimmers in restricted area; other equipment can be used as appropriate to skills

Description: Instructor (or selected class member) calls out a "Who can . . . ?" question (e.g., "put face in water," "float like a turtle," "surface-dive headfirst," "flutter-kick 20 feet on front with face in," "jump the farthest from the side," "swim from one side to the other without stopping"). Continue questions until the desired numbers of skills are practiced and all swimmers have been successful.

Instructor intervention: Guide discovery for swimmers. Pose appropriate types and level of skills as questions.

Variations: Pose combinations of skills for advanced skills.

Complexity factors: Depth of water, type and difficulty of skills, number of skill combinations

Source: Council for National Cooperation in Aquatics. (1965). *Water fun for everyone* (pp. 38-39). New York: Association Press.

Breath Control, Rhythmic Breathing, and Submersion

Brick Recovery Race (modified): Breath Control
Level 5
Bobbing Relay Race: Breath Control Level 5
Charlie Over the Water: Breath Control Level 5
Chin Ball: Breath Control Level 2
Drop the Puck (Water Duck, Duck, Goose): Breath
Control Level 3
Flower Garden: Breath Control Level 4
Jack-in-the-Box: Breath Control Level 2
Leapfrog: Breath Control Level 4
Little Green Frog: Breath Control Level 2
London Bridge: Breath Control Level 3
Look and Listen: Breath Control Level 4

Magic Candle: Breath Control Level 2
Motorboat: Breath Control Level 2
Obstacle Course: Breath Control Level 5
Ping-Pong Push: Breath Control Level 2
Ring-Around-the-Rosy: Breath Control Level 3
Sinkable/Unsinkable Object Game: Breath Control
Level 3
Sunken Treasure: Breath Control Level 4
Teeter-Totter: Breath Control Level 4
Water Croquet: Breath Control Level 5
The Wave: Breath Control Level 3
Whale Spitting: Breath Control Level 2

Brick Recovery Race (modified)

Purpose: To recover a moderately heavy object underwater; to practice underwater skills

Skill level: Intermediate to advanced

Water depth: Chest deep to over head, depending upon skill level of class

Class formation: Lines (e.g., relay teams)

Equipment: Diving bricks

Prerequisite developmental skills:
Water Entry Level 3-5
Combined Movements Level 4
Water Adjustment/Orientation Level 3
Water Entry Level 5
Breath Control Levels 4-5
Buoyancy/Flotation Levels 3-4
Body Position Levels 2-4
Arm Action Levels 2-3
Leg Action Levels 2-3
Combined Stroke Level 4
Surface Dive
Underwater Swimming

Description: Swimmers line up at side of pool, either individually or as teams. Diving bricks are submerged a distance from the side and at a depth corresponding to the skill level of the class. Individuals or teams try to swim out, surface dive, recover brick, and swim the brick back.

Instructor intervention: Provide instruction, review necessary skills, and place bricks appropriately. During game, watchful supervision is critical to ensure safety. Swimmer must *not* use hyperventilation to increase breath-holding time!

Variations: Brick rescuers can work in pairs, one to recover brick and the other to swim to shore. For beginners, waist to chest depths can be used with a feetfirst recovery. Also, smaller objects, such as hockey pucks, can be recovered.

Complexity factors: Depth of water, weight and size of object, distance of swim, use of partners

Source: YMCA of the USA. (1986). *Progressive swimming instructors guide* (p. 58). Champaign, IL: Human Kinetics.

Bobbing Relay Race

Purpose: To practice repeated submersions and rhythmic breathing along with pushoff from bottom and recovery of balance

Skill level: Beginner to intermediate

Water depth: Waist to chest deep or over head (depending upon skill level)

Class formation: Lines or waves

Equipment: None

Prerequisite developmental skills:
Water Adjustment/Orientation Level 3
Water Entry Level 3
Breath Control Level 4
Buoyancy/Flotation Levels 3-4
Body Position Levels 2-4
Arm Action Levels 2-3
Leg Action Levels 2-3
Combined Stroke Level 4

Description: Swimmers enter the water individually or in groups (depending upon formation). They progress across the pool by repeatedly submerging and then pushing off the bottom and jumping to the surface with help of the arms. It is important to emphasize getting a breath upon surfacing each time and exhaling underwater. The depth of submersion depends upon the depth of the water and the swimmer's skill.

Instructor intervention: Provide instructions and feedback about exhaling, inhaling, and maintaining balance, as well as safety.

Variations: Can be done as a relay. Can add a surface dive to begin each submersion, for more advanced swimmers.

Complexity factors: Depth of water, distance to cover, goal of activity, number of swimmers

Source: Beach and Pool. (1947). *Aquatic games, pageants, and stunts* (pp. 10-11). New York: Hoffman & Harris.

Charlie Over the Water

Purpose: To practice a number of intermediate and advanced skills in a tag game

Skill level: Intermediate to advanced

Water depth: Chest deep to over head

Class formation: Circle initially, then scattered

Equipment: Sinkable objects (ring, puck, poker chip), one for each swimmer

Prerequisite developmental skills:
Water Adjustment/Orientation Level 3
Water Entry Level 3
Breath Control Levels 3-4
Buoyancy/Flotation Levels 3-4
Body Position Levels 2-4
Arm Action Level 2+
Leg Action Level 2+
Combined Stroke Level 4
(Surface diving skill)

Description: One class member, called "Charlie," is "it." Class members form a circle around Charlie, standing or treading water, depending on depth. Together they chant:

"Charlie over the water;
Charlie over the sea;
Charlie catch a tuna;
but he can't catch me!"

During the first line, all swimmers drop a ring or puck in front of them. At the word *me*, all dive to get their pucks (including Charlie) and try to swim back to a side with the puck. Charlie retrieves his or her own puck and then tries to tag someone before they reach a side. First person tagged becomes next "Charlie."

Instructor intervention: Provide instruction, help with rhyme, ensure safety, and give feedback where needed.

Variations: Swimmers line up on one side of the pool and have to surface-dive to get object and swim to the other side before Charlie catches them. Swimmers are safe once they retrieve object and are doing a selected stroke. Increase the number of "Charlies" used as "it." Alter the distance and number of safe sides that swimmers can go to.

Complexity factors: Depth of water, number of children, type of object to be retrieved, number of "Charlies," distance and number of "safe" sides

Source: YMCA of the USA. (1986). *Progressive swimming program instructors guide* (p. 57). Champaign, IL: Human Kinetics.

Chin Ball

Purpose: To practice movements with the face in and around the surface of the water

Skill level: Beginner to intermediate

Water depth: Thigh to chest deep

Class formation: Lines for relays

Equipment: Small ball (tennis, table tennis, racquetball)

Prerequisite developmental skills:
Water Adjustment/Orientation Level 2
Water Entry Level 2
Breath Control Levels 2-3
Buoyancy/Flotation Level 2
Body Position Level 2+
Arm Action Level 1
Leg Action Level 1
Combined Stroke Level 1

Description: Each swimmer pushes a tennis or table-tennis ball with chin, mouth, or face across the pool to another team member while walking on the bottom and holding hands behind the back. The relay continues until all have participated at least once.

Instructor intervention: Provide instructions, start relay, and control play. Provide feedback where appropriate.

Variations: Can carry and pass ball by tucking it between chin and chest. Intermediates can play in deep end by swimming. Can play as exploration without teams.

Complexity factors: Depth of water, number of players, competition

Source: YMCA of the USA. (1986). *Progressive swimming program instructors guide* (p. 15). Champaign, IL: Human Kinetics.

Drop the Puck (Water Duck, Duck, Goose)

Purpose: To practice breath control, submersion, arm and leg propulsion movements, and change of directions

Skill level: Beginner to advanced

Water depth: Knee to head deep, depending on skill

Class formation: Circle

Equipment: Hockey puck or sinkable ring

Prerequisite developmental skills:
   Water Adjustment/Orientation Level 3
   Water Entry Level 3
   Breath Control Level 3
   Buoyancy/Flotation Level 2
   Body Position Level 3
   Arm Action Levels 1-2
   Leg Action Levels 1-2
   Combined Stroke Levels 1-2

Description: Students stand in circle. "It" has hockey puck or sinking ring on outside of circle. "It" drops puck behind one of the participants, who must submerge and recover it. After picking the puck up, she or he must chase "it" by swimming (or running) around the circle back to their original place.

Instructor intervention: Provide instructions, encouragement, and feedback, and ensure safety. Keep swimmers in a circle.

Variations: Use more than one "it." Two "its" must swim in tandem and be chased by two participants in tandem.

Complexity factors: Depth of water, number of "its," size and type of sinkable object

Source: American National Red Cross. (1981). *Swimming and aquatic safety* (p. 165). Washington, DC: Author.

Flower Garden

Purpose: To practice and improve breath control and submersion

Skill level: Beginner

Water depth: Thigh to chest deep

Class formation: Scattered

Equipment: Weighted plastic flowers or similar objects

Prerequisite developmental skills:
   Water Adjustment/Orientation Level 2
   Water Entry Level 3
   Breath Control Level 3
   Buoyancy/Flotation Levels 2-3
   Body Position Level 1
   Arm Action Level 1
   Leg Action Level 1
   Combined Stroke Level 1

Description: "Plant" flowers (weighted) on the bottom of the pool. Ask the "gardeners" (children) to pick up as many flowers as they can.

Instructor intervention: Provide instructions, safety, and encouragement; "plant" the flowers on the bottom of the pool.

Variations: Use other sinkable objects. Have the children try to pick up objects in novel ways.

Complexity factors: Depth of water, number of students, body parts used

Source: Brown, C. (1986, March). *Workshop games*. United States Swimming Foundation workshop, Fort Wayne, IN.

Jack-in-the-Box

Purpose: To practice breath control and submersion

Skill level: Prebeginner to beginner

Water depth: Waist to chest deep

Class formation: One-on-one or in pairs

Equipment: None

Prerequisite developmental skills:
Water Adjustment/Orientation Level 2
Water Entry Levels 3-4
Breath Control Level 3
Buoyancy/Flotation Levels 2-3
Body Position Level 1
Arm Action Level 1
Leg Action Level 1
Combined Stroke Level 1

Description: Have one child place his or her hand on your head, and you go under the water. Then pop back up as a jack-in-the-box would. Next place your hand on her or his head and have the child go under. Don't force the child under, but apply a little pressure and he or she will usually go under.

Instructor intervention: Provide instruction and safety; assist the ''jack-in-the-boxes.''

Variations: Have the students hold a body part (foot, hand, ears, etc.) as they go under and pop up still holding that part of the body.

Complexity factors: Water depth, number of submersions, body parts held, length of submersion

Source: Runta, N. (1980). *Pre-school swimming instructor's manual*. Findlay, OH: YMCA.

Leapfrog

Purpose: To practice breath control and submersion skills

Skill level: Beginner to intermediate

Water depth: Knee to waist deep

Class formation: Line

Equipment: None

Prerequisite developmental skills:
Water Adjustment/Orientation Level 3
Water Entry Level 3
Breath Control Level 3
Buoyancy/Flotation Level 2
Body Position Level 2
Arm Action Level 1
Leg Action Level 1
Combined Stroke Level 1

Description: One swimmer stands on the bottom of the pool with hands on knees in a crouch position. The second swimmer, the "frog," places his or her hands on the shoulders of the other swimmer and leaps over her or his back, landing in front. The two swimmers take turns being the "frog."

Instructor intervention: Provide instructions and safety; be aware that some swimmers may feel trapped or held underwater, which may make this game inappropriate for swimmers who are not comfortable going underwater (Level 3 or 4 in Breath Control).

Variations: Have several swimmers in a line, and they all take turns leaping over the group one by one. Play in deep water with advanced swimmers. Make this game part of a relay race.

Complexity factors: Number of students, skill level of students, depth of the water

Source: Canadian Red Cross. (1984). *Water safety instructor guide and reference* (Vol. 5, p. 44). Toronto: Author.

Little Green Frog

Purpose: To practice breath holding and submersion with assistance

Skill level: Beginner

Water depth: Knee to chest deep (depending on presence of parents)

Class formation: Circle (with parents)

Equipment: None

Prerequisite developmental skills:
Water Adjustment/Orientation Level 2
Water Entry Level 2
Breath Control Level 2
Buoyancy/Flotation Level 2
Body Position Level 1
Arm Action Level 1
Leg Action Level 1
Combined Stroke Level 1

Description: Children (with parents) form a circle facing the center. The instructor leads the rhyme:
"Baa Roomp went the little green frog one day!
Baa Roomp went the little green frog.
Baa Roomp went the little green frog one day!
His eyes went blink, blink, blink!"
Each time "Baa Roomp" is said, the children submerge their faces. At "blink, blink, blink," they blink eyelids rapidly to get rid of the water.

Instructor intervention: Provide instructions and encouragement and lead rhyme.

Variations: Children can rhythmically breathe on each "Baa Roomp" as well as submerge. Add whole-body bobbing and recovery for more advanced swimmers.

Complexity factors: Depth of water, number and extent of submersions

Source: YMCA of the USA. (1987). *Y Skippers* (p. 191). Champaign, IL: Human Kinetics.

London Bridge

Purpose: To practice breath control and submersion

Skill level: Prebeginner to beginner

Water depth: Waist to chest deep

Class formation: Groups of three children

Equipment: None (records or tapes may be used)

Prerequisite developmental skills:
Water Adjustment/Orientation Level 2
Water Entry Level 3
Breath Control Level 3
Buoyancy/Flotation Levels 1-2
Body Position Level 1
Arm Action Level 1
Leg Action Level 1
Combined Stroke Level 1

Description: Have two children facing hold hands. This forms the bridge. The third child walks back and forth under the bridge as the song "London Bridge Is Falling Down" is sung. When the last line of the song is said, all three children submerge under the water.

Instructor intervention: Provide instructions and feedback and ensure safety.

Variations: Have the children swim through the London Bridge. Create a line of London Bridges with pairs of children in a row. Children make the London Bridge out of their legs and their partners swim through it.

Complexity factors: Number of children, depth of the water

Source: Miner, M.F. (1980). *Water fun* (pp. 116-117). Englewood Cliffs, NJ: Prentice Hall.

Look and Listen (Fish Talk)

Purpose: To practice rhythmic breathing while doing kicking drills

Skill level: Prebeginner to intermediate

Water depth: Waist to chest deep or over head

Class formation: Waves

Equipment: Kickboards

Prerequisite developmental skills:
Water Adjustment/Orientation Level 3
Water Entry Level 3
Breath Control Levels 3-4
Buoyancy/Flotation Levels 3-4
Body Position Levels 2-4
Arm Action Levels 1-2
Leg Action Level 3
Combined Stroke Level 2+

Description: Swimmers move across designated areas, kicking on kickboards. They pretend to be talking and listening to fish as they kick. To talk to fish, each child puts face in water and exhales vigorously, making bubbles; to listen to fish, they turn their face to the side (as they get a new breath). Instructor can maintain fantasy by asking the children what they saw or heard the fish say.

Instructor intervention: Provide instructions and lead fantasy play.

Variations: Vary the ear with which the child listens to the fish. Vary the kicks to other styles besides flutter (whip, dolphin, scissors). Do at pool side or in plastic pool on the deck for young or fearful beginners.

Complexity factors: Depth of water, distance to kick and breathe, presence of kickboard or standing

Source: YMCA of the USA. (1987). *Y Skippers* (p. 192). Champaign, IL: Human Kinetics.

Magic Candle

Purpose: To practice breath control and exhalation

Skill level: Prebeginner to beginner

Water depth: Any depth

Class formation: One-on-one (can use parent as partner)

Equipment: None (instructor's fingers)

Prerequisite developmental skills:
Water Adjustment/Orientation Level 2
Water Entry Level 2
Breath Control Level 1
Buoyancy/Flotation Level 1
Body Position Level 1
Arm Action Level 1
Leg Action Level 1
Combined Stroke Level 1

Description: Instructor holds up finger and engages the child in a fantasy: "See this birthday candle? Can you blow it out?" If the child doesn't respond, instructor can demonstrate that the finger "disappears" (tucked inside fist quickly) when blown on. Progressively lower candle until it becomes a *magic candle* that burns underwater. To blow it out underwater, the child must forcefully exhale into water, making bubbles. The quick movement of the hand and wrist upon "blowing out" the candle gives the young child the illusion of the finger disappearing, especially underwater.

Instructor intervention: Lead fantasy, encourage child's participation, and progress depth of "candle" at child's pace.

Variation: Use number of fingers to match the child's age.

Complexity factors: Depth of submersion of "candle," number of fingers used

Source: Original to M. Dougan and S. Langendorfer.

Motorboat

Purpose: To learn and practice breath control while having water around the face; to practice balance in water

Skill level: Prebeginner to beginner

Water depth: Thigh to waist deep

Class formation: Circle or scattered

Prerequisite developmental skills:
Water Adjustment/Orientation Level 2
Water Entry Level 2
Breath Control Level 1
Buoyancy/Flotation Level 2
Body Position Level 1
Arm Action Level 1
Leg Action Level 1
Combined Stroke Level 1

Equipment: None (kickboards for intermediates)

Description: Children facing around the circle. Instructor leads the chant:

"Motor boat, motor boat, go so slow;
Motor boat, motor boat, go so fast;
Motor boat, motor boat, step on the gas!"

During the chant, the children put their chins and mouths at the water surface and blow bubbles. At "go so slow," the bubble blowing by the children should be soft, and the children should walk slowly around circle. At "go so fast," the bubble blowing gets harder, and they walk faster. At "step on the gas," they should do forceful exhalation and try to run rapidly around the circle.

Instructor intervention: Explain procedures, lead chants, and encourage children.

Variations: Can include full-face submersion for intermediates. The game can be played in lines (waves). Can play while kicking on kickboards.

Complexity factors: Depth of water, skills included

Source: Kochen, C., & McCabe, J. (1986). *The baby swim book*. Champaign, IL: Human Kinetics.

Obstacle Course

Purpose: To practice underwater swimming skills

Skill level: Beginner to advanced

Water depth: Waist deep to over head (depending on skill level)

Class formation: One-on-one

Prerequisite developmental skills:
Water Adjustment/Orientation Level 3
Water Entry Level 3
Breath Control Level 4
Buoyancy/Flotation Levels 3-4
Body Position Level 2
Arm Action Level 2
Leg Action Level 2
Combined Stroke Level 2

Equipment: Diving bricks, kickboards, buoyed lines, rope, hula hoops, mats, tot docks, poker chips, buckets, balls, other pool equipment as desired

Description: Instructor creates obstacle course with kickboards, buoyed lines, hula hoops, diving bricks, and floating mats. Instructor can specify certain skills for certain parts of the course in order to provide skill-specific practice. Swimmers first try to swim through course without stopping, then swim through for time.

Instructor intervention: Create obstacle course to match skills of class; provide instructions, hints, and feedback during running of course and careful supervision throughout.

Variations: Shallow-water course emphasizing above-water skills can be developed for beginners. Teams can relay through course against the clock or against other teams.

Complexity factors: Depth of water, length of course, type of equipment, and stunts required

Source: YMCA of the USA. (1986). *Progressive swimming program instructors guide* (p. 48). Champaign, IL: Human Kinetics.

Ping-Pong Push

Purpose: To practice exhalation in water by manipulating light balls or floating objects

Skill level: Beginner

Water depth: Waist

Class formation: One-on-one, lines, or waves

Equipment: Table-tennis (Ping-Pong) balls

Prerequisite developmental skills:
Water Adjustment/Orientation Level 2
Water Entry Level 2
Breath Control Level 2
Buoyancy/Flotation Level 2
Body Position Level 1
Arm Action Level 1
Leg Action Level 1
Combined Stroke Level 1

Description: Swimmers individually or in groups blow a table-tennis (Ping-Pong) ball across the water surface. When done in relay fashion, each swimmer tries to get her or his ball to a teammate as quickly as possible.

Instructor intervention: Provide instruction and organization and ensure safety.

Variations: Perform as a relay. Perform in pairs, facing one another, trying to blow the ball past opponent. Blow the ball with bubbles or a spout of water instead of a stream of air.

Complexity factors: Depth of water, goal of game, number of partners

Source: Original to S. Langendorfer.

Ring-Around-the-Rosy

Purpose: To practice basic movement and submersion in water in a group setting with music

Skill level: Prebeginner to beginner

Water depth: Waist to chest deep

Class formation: Circle

Equipment: None (can use records or tapes)

Prerequisite developmental skills:
Water Adjustment/Orientation Level 2
Water Entry Level 2
Breath Control Levels 2-3
Buoyancy/Flotation Level 1
Body Position Level 1
Arm Action Level 1
Leg Action Level 1
Combined Stroke Level 1

Description: In circle, which may include parents for very young children, sing ''Ring-Around-the-Rosy'' tune:

''Ring-around-the-rosy,
Pocket full of posies
Ashes, ashes [water, water],
We all fall down [or substitute other skill name].''

At the line, ''We all fall down,'' submerge together.

Instructor intervention: Lead song, give directions, and lead submersion and other skills; provide encouragement and feedback.

Variations: Include other skills besides submersion (bubble blowing, front and back float).

Complexity factors: Water depth, number and age of swimmers; presence of parents or assistants

Source: YMCA of the USA. (1987). *Y Skippers* (p. 195). Champaign, IL: Human Kinetics.

Sinkable/Unsinkable Object

Purpose: To experiment with buoyancy concept, improve water orientation, and introduce breath control/brief submersion

Skill level: Nonswimmer to beginner

Water depth: Minimal (tub, steps, tot dock, shallow end)

Class formation: Scattered or paired with parent

Prerequisite developmental skills:
Water Adjustment/Orientation Level 2
Water Entry Level 2
Breath Control Levels 1-2
Buoyancy/Flotation Level 2
Body Position Level 1
Arm Action Level 1
Leg Action Level 1
Combined Stroke Level 1

Equipment: Table-tennis balls, corks, spoons, pennies, bottle caps, thread spools, pencils, soap bars, match sticks, leaves, toy boats

Description: Collect a variety of sinkable and floating objects. Ask young child to guess which objects will float and which will sink. Let child explore with the objects in the water. Ask the child to propel floating objects across water by blowing and exhaling. Ask the child to submerge to pick up sinking objects.

Instructor intervention: Provide equipment and direct questions; encourage breath control and submersion; provide directions to parents.

Variations: Use exhalation and submersion skills. Use dilute solution of detergent for blowing soap bubbles.

Complexity factors: Water depth, type of objects, number and depth of submersions

Source: Shank, C. (1983). *A child's way to water play* (pp. 60-61). Champaign, IL: Leisure Press.

Sunken Treasure

Purpose: To practice submersion and underwater swimming and movement skills

Skill level: Beginner to advanced

Water depth: Ankle deep to very deep, depending upon skill level

Class formation: Scattered (initially at pool side)

Prerequisite developmental skills:
Water Adjustment/Orientation Level 2
Water Entry Level 3
Breath Control Level 4
Buoyancy/Flotation Level 2
Body Position Level 1
Arm Action Level 1
Leg Action Level 1
Combined Stroke Level 1

Equipment: Pennies, coins, or poker chips

Description: Pennies or other coins or facsimiles (poker chips) are scattered all over the bottom of the pool. Swimmers, on command, can enter the pool and search for them. In mixed skill groups, swimmers are restricted to deep end, beginners to shallow. When recovering the coin or chip from the bottom, swimmer goes to side and places coin in her or his own container or space. At the end, coins can be added up to see who recovered the most "sunken treasure."

Instructor intervention: Hide coins, provide directions, ensure safety, and give feedback and encouragement.

Variations: Swimmers work in pairs, one diving and the other swimming the coins to the side. Require swimmers to recover two or three coins in each dive before surfacing.

Complexity factors: Depth of water, size of area holding coins, water clarity, size of coins/chips

Source: Ryan, J. (1960). *Learning to swim is fun* (p. 72). New York: Ronald Press.

Teeter-Totter

Purpose: To practice breath control and submersion; to discourage the children to hold their noses while submerging; to teach bobbing under the water

Skill level: Prebeginner to beginner

Water depth: Shallow

Class formation: In partners

Equipment: None

Prerequisite developmental skills:
Water Adjustment/Orientation Level 2
Water Entry Level 3
Breath Control Level 2
Buoyancy/Flotation Level 2
Body Position Level 1
Arm Action Level 1
Leg Action Level 1
Combined Stroke Level 1

Description: In partners, the children hold hands. The partners take turns going under the water. When one child is under, the other child is above the water, similar to the action on a teeter-totter.

Instructor intervention: Provide instruction and safety; encourage the children to go farther under the water until their entire heads are submerged.

Variations: Instead of partners, have the class in one large group, and select children to go under as a small group. Have the children prone-float instead of submerging under the water.

Complexity factors: Number of children

Source: Original to D. Harrod.

Water Croquet

Purpose: To improve breath holding, surface diving, and underwater swimming skills

Skill level: Intermediate to advanced

Water depth: Waist deep to over head

Class formation: Line or scattered

Equipment: Hula hoops that are tied down by a weight; hula hoops can be at different heights

Prerequisite developmental skills:
Water Adjustment/Orientation Level 3
Water Entry Level 3
Breath Control Level 5
Buoyancy/Flotation Level 4
Body Position Levels 3-4
Arm Action Level 3
Leg Action Level 3
Combined Stroke Level 3
(Underwater swimming)

Description: Weighted hula hoops are arranged around the pool. One at a time, class members swim through as many hula hoops as possible with one breath. Students take turns and must stand still wherever they stop. First student to complete the ''croquet course'' by swimming through all of the hoops is the winner.

Instructor intervention: Provide instruction, ensure safety, and give feedback where necessary. Must *not* permit children to hyperventilate when swimming underwater.

Variations: Swimmers retrieve objects underwater while swimming through the hula hoops. Advanced swimmers use masks, fins, and snorkels while surface-diving through hula hoops.

Complexity factors: Depth of water, number of children, number of hula hoops, number of objects to retrieve

Source: Original to D. Harrod.

The Wave

Purpose: To improve breath control and submersion skills

Skill level: Beginner

Water depth: Waist to chest deep

Class formation: Small groups, in a circle

Equipment: None

Prerequisite developmental skills:
Water Adjustment/Orientation Level 2
Water Entry Level 3
Breath Control Level 3
Buoyancy/Flotation Level 2
Body Position Level 1
Arm Action Level 1
Leg Action Level 1
Combined Stroke Level 1

Description: In groups of three or four, children form a circle by holding hands. A designated leader squeezes the hand on his or her left side, at which point that swimmer takes a breath and ducks under the water. The submerged swimmer then squeezes the hand on her or his left, and the process is repeated until all are underwater. The leader is the last swimmer under the water. When he or she goes under, the leader then squeezes the hand on her or his left again, and ''the wave'' continues.

Instructor intervention: Provide instruction, ensure safety, and give feedback where necessary.

Variations: Have several students go underwater at the same time. Vary the speed of ''the wave.'' Have children go in two directions at once.

Complexity factors: Water depth; number and ability of children

Source: Original to S. Langendorfer and D. Harrod.

Whale Spitting

Purpose: To become accustomed to water in the mouth and acquire spitting and shipping skills

Skill level: Prebeginner to beginner

Water depth: None to waist deep

Class formation: One-on-one or small group

Equipment: None

Prerequisite developmental skills:
Water Adjustment/Orientation Level 2
Water Entry Level 3
Breath Control Level 1
Buoyancy/Flotation Level 1
Body Position Level 1
Arm Action Level 1
Leg Action Level 1
Combined Stroke Level 1

Description: Instructor puts water in his or her mouth and spits it out high and far, which is similar to a whale shooting water out of its spout. The students are now asked to imitate a whale.

Instructor intervention: Demonstrate ''whale spitting.''

Variations: The students can be challenged by the instructor asking them to spit as high or as far as possible. The child can pick up a diving ring and then be asked to spit through it.

Complexity factors: Child's ability to spit water, distance, presence of a target

Source: Original to S. Langendorfer.

Flotation, Buoyancy, and Balance in Water

Airplane: Buoyancy/Flotation Level 3
Carousel (Merry-Go-Round): Buoyancy/Flotation Levels 2 to 3
Echo Tag (Marco Polo): Buoyancy/Flotation Level 4
Five Little Ducks: Buoyancy/Flotation Level 2
Float Tag: Buoyancy/Flotation Level 4
Gingerbread Cookie: Buoyancy/Flotation Level 2
Glide and Slide: Buoyancy/Flotation Level 4
Jumpin': Buoyancy/Flotation Level 1
Log Tag: Buoyancy/Flotation Level 4
Musical Kickboards: Buoyancy/Flotation Level 3
Porpoise Tag (Aquatic Red Rover): Buoyancy/Flotation Level 4

Print: Buoyancy/Flotation Level 4
Push Against the Wall: Buoyancy/Flotation Level 2
Ride 'Em Cowboys: Buoyancy/Flotation Level 3
Rocket Ship: Buoyancy/Flotation Level 4
Sharks and Minnows (I): Buoyancy/Flotation Level 2
Sink or Float?: Buoyancy/Flotation Level 1
Sticky Popcorn: Buoyancy/Flotation Level 1
Straddleboard (Relay): Buoyancy/Flotation Level 3
Superman (I): Buoyancy/Flotation Level 4
''Timber!'': Buoyancy/Flotation Level 4
Train: Buoyancy/Flotation Level 1
Water Limbo: Buoyancy/Flotation Level 2
Water Ski Ride: Buoyancy/Flotation Level 3

Airplane

Purpose: To improve swimmers' ability to move in the water in an inclined prone position

Skill level: Beginner

Water depth: Waist to chest deep

Class formation: Scattered, lines, or wave

Equipment: Kickboards, two per child

Prerequisite developmental skills:
Water Adjustment/Orientation Level 3
Water Entry Level 3
Breath Control Levels 2-3
Buoyancy/Flotation Level 1
Body Position Level 2
Arm Action Level 1
Leg Action Levels 1-3
Combined Stroke Level 1

Description: Each child has two kickboards, one under each arm, resembling airplane wings. Instruct the child to prone-float while holding onto the kickboards. The child can kick her or his feet to propel around the pool.

Instructor intervention: Provide directions, encouragement, and physical assistance where needed.

Variations: The children can blow bubbles in the water to imitate the noise of an airplane motor or jet. If there are not enough kickboards for each child to have two, have the children work as partners; one child can be the airplane, holding onto the kickboards and kicking, and the other the pilot, who walks around the pool steering the airplane by holding onto the kickboards.

Complexity factors: Depth of water, number of students per kickboards

Source: Original to D. Harrod.

Carousel (Merry-Go-Round)

Purpose: To practice various movements through water; to improve balance in the water

Skill level: Beginner

Water depth: Knee to waist deep

Class formation: Circle (double circle if large class)

Prerequisite developmental skills:
Water Adjustment/Orientation Level 3
Water Entry Level 3
Breath Control Level 3
Buoyancy/Flotation Levels 2-3
Body Position Level 1
Arm Action Level 1
Leg Action Level 1
Combined Stroke Level 1

Equipment: None

Description: In a circle, the students pretend they are on horses such as those found on a merry-go-round. The students can bob up and down (submerging under) in the water as they ride on the merry-go-round. The instructor can ask the students to perform different locomotor skills (running, leaping, galloping, jumping, hopping) and to change directions (forward, backward, sideward).

Instructor intervention: Provide instruction and safety; call out different skills or directions.

Variation: Various swimming skills such as floating (front or back), kicking (with or without kickboards), etc., can be performed on the merry-go-round.

Complexity factors: Water depth, number of students, skill level of the students

Source: Brown, C. (1986). *Workshop games*. United States Swimming Foundation workshop, Fort Wayne, IN.

Echo Tag (Marco Polo)

Purpose: To practice balance and buoyancy in water in tag-game format

Skill level: Beginner to advanced

Water depth: Shallow to deep, depending upon skill level

Class formation: Scattered

Equipment: None

Prerequisite developmental skills:
Water Adjustment/Orientation Level 3
Water Entry Level 3
Breath Control Level 1
Buoyancy/Flotation Level 2
Body Position Level 1
Arm Action Level 1
Leg Action Level 1
Combined Stroke Level 1

Description: "It" is blindfolded or has eyes closed and calls out words, phrases, or other sounds, which have to be repeated ("echoed") by others. "It" attempts to locate others by sound and tag them. Swimmers can swim underwater to avoid detection but must echo all sounds made by "it."

Instructor intervention: Explain rules of game, help to referee, ensure safety, but mainly stay out of the way.

Variations: Phrases can be water safety slogans (e.g., "Always swim with a buddy"; "Never swim alone"; "In a boat, wear a lifejacket"; etc.). Have more than one "it." Play in deep water over everyone's head (for advanced only).

Complexity factors: Depth of water, number of "its"

Source: Canadian Red Cross. (1984). *Water safety instructor guide and reference* (Vol. 5, p. 33). Toronto: Author.

Five Little Ducks

Purpose: To practice water entry, breath control, submersion, and prone float

Skill level: Prebeginner to beginner

Water depth: Knee to chest deep

Class formation: Circle

Prerequisite developmental skills:
Water Adjustment/Orientation Level 2
Water Entry Level 3
Breath Control Level 3
Buoyancy/Flotation Levels 2-3
Body Position Level 1
Arm Action Level 1
Leg Action Level 1
Combined Stroke Level 1

Equipment: None

Description: Perform actions to the nursery rhyme:
"Five little ducks swimming in the lake,
The first one said: 'Watch the waves I make.'
The second duck said: 'Swimming is such fun.'
The third duck said: 'I'd rather sit in the sun.'
The fourth duck said: 'Let's swim away.'
The fifth duck said: 'Oh, let's stay.'
Then along came a motorboat, with a POP, POP, POP!
And five little ducks swam away from the spot."

Instructor intervention: Provide instruction and safety, say and act out nursery rhyme with children.

Variations: Add activities that the "ducks" could act out.

Complexity factors: Water depth, number of students, presence of parents, types of activities

Source: Brown, C. (1986). *Workshop games.* United States Swimming Foundation workshop, Fort Wayne, IN.

Float Tag

Purpose: To practice flotation in a game situation

Skill level: Beginner to intermediate

Water depth: Waist to neck deep

Class formation: Scattered

Equipment: None

Prerequisite developmental skills:
Water Adjustment/Orientation Level 3
Water Entry Level 3
Breath Control Level 4
Buoyancy/Flotation Levels 3-4
Body Position Level 3
Arm Action Level 1
Leg Action Level 1
Combined Stroke Level 1

Description: Three or more children participate, with one being "it." "It" tries to tag any person to replace him- or herself. Swimmers are safe when they are performing any type of float: jellyfish, turtle, prone, back, survival.

Instructor intervention: Provide directions, supervise play, and ensure safety.

Variations: Play in pairs, with both persons linking hands during float. Specify one type of float at any time for specific skill practice. Increase number of people who are "it." Use flotation devices (PFDs or others) to assist flotation.

Complexity factors: Depth of water, number of "its"

Source: Ryan, J. (1960). *Learning to swim for fun* (pp. 72-77). New York: Ronald Press.

Gingerbread Cookie (Sailing, Sailing)

Purpose: To practice floating as motionlessly as possible using fantasy play

Skill level: Beginner

Water depth: Knee to neck deep

Class formation: Scattered or one-on-one

Equipment: None

Prerequisite developmental skills:
Water Adjustment/Orientation Level 3
Water Entry Level 3
Breath Control Level 3
Buoyancy/Flotation Levels 3-4
Body Position Levels 2-3
Arm Action Level 1
Leg Action Level 1
Combined Stroke Level 1

Description: Children are asked to pretend to be gingerbread persons who cannot move while floating for fear of breaking off a gingerbread arm or leg. With instructor assistance, each class member attempts to float prone or supine as motionlessly as possible. Class all claps for each person's attempt.

Instructor intervention: Provide instructions, assist each swimmer, and help maintain fantasy.

Variations: Add, for tag game, a "fox" who will eat up any gingerbread person who is not floating (see Float Tag). Use flotation device or partner to assist flotation.

Complexity factors: Depth of water, length of time for float, type of float requested, use of flotation device

Source: YMCA of the USA. (1987). *Y Skippers* (p. 196). Champaign, IL: Human Kinetics.

Glide and Slide

Purpose: To improve prone float and glide and length of breath control

Skill level: Beginner

Water depth: Knee to chest deep

Class formation: Single line or wave

Equipment: None

Prerequisite developmental skills:
Water Adjustment/Orientation Level 3
Water Entry Level 3
Breath Control Levels 4-5
Buoyancy/Flotation Level 4
Body Position Levels 2-3
Arm Action Level 1
Leg Action Level 1
Combined Stroke Level 1

Description: Swimmers push off from the side or shallow bottom and glide as far as possible in torpedo position. Upon slowing the glide, the swimmer pulls the knees up and stands. Compare the distances among class members or between trials.

Instructor intervention: Explain activity and ensure safety; discuss means for gliding further; point out who has glided farthest; provide other appropriate feedback.

Variations: Add leg kick and arm motions to glide. Push off only from bottom rather than from side. Perform glide or kick-glide skills in supine position.

Complexity factors: Depth of water, presence and type of side from which to push off

Source: YMCA of the USA. (1986). *Splash!* (p. 62). Champaign, IL: Human Kinetics.

Jumpin'

Purpose: To practice balance in the water while jumping; to recover from sudden submersion

Skill level: Beginner

Water depth: Knee to chest deep

Class formation: Scattered

Equipment: Any soft object (balloons, lifejackets); structure and rope for suspending objects

Prerequisite developmental skills:
Water Adjustment/Orientation Level 2
Water Entry Level 3
Breath Control Levels 2-3
Buoyancy/Flotation Level 2
Body Position Level 1
Arm Action Level 1
Leg Action Level 1
Combined Stroke Level 1

Description: Balloons and other soft objects are suspended above the surface of the water out of reach of swimmers when standing. The swimmers attempt to jump and hit the objects with a hand. Objects can be suspended in several ways: from a rope across the pool, from the ceiling, etc.

Instructor intervention: Provide instruction and safety; suspend objects.

Variations: Challenge the swimmers to hit the objects with different parts of their bodies. In deep water, have students tread water and thrust themselves up out of the water to hit the objects.

Complexity factors: Water depth, height of objects, size of objects

Source: Canadian Red Cross. (1984). *Water safety instructor guide and reference* (Vol. 5, p. 46). Toronto: Author.

Log Tag

Purpose: To practice back floating and changing position (horizontal to vertical or prone to supine) and improve front swimming (combined movement)

Skill level: Intermediate to advanced

Water depth: Chest deep to over head

Class formation: Opposing lines

Equipment: None

Prerequisite developmental skills:
Water Adjustment/Orientation Level 3
Water Entry Level 3
Breath Control Level 4
Buoyancy/Flotation Levels 3-4
Body Position Levels 2-3
Arm Action Level 1
Leg Action Level 1
Combined Stroke Level 2

Description: Class participants are divided into two groups at opposite ends/sides of the pool. One swimmer is the "log" and floats in the center while the others move from their "safe" areas. "Log" suddenly rolls over or stands up and gives chase. She or he tries to tag others before they reach their safety area.

Instructor intervention: Provide instructions, enforce rules, and ensure safety. Can be first "log."

Variations: Participants can be eliminated, replace the log, or join the log as a team. "Safe" can be back or front float instead of area.

Complexity factors: Depth of water, length of the facility, number of participants, number of "logs"

Source: Swimming Pool Data and Reference Annual. (1960). *Aquatic games, pageants, and stunts* (p. 20). New York: Hoffman & Harris.

Musical Kickboards

Purpose: To practice assisted flotation

Skill level: Beginner

Water depth: Knee to chest deep

Class formation: Circle

Equipment: Kickboards for each swimmer, cassette or record player, tape or record

Prerequisite developmental skills:
Water Adjustment/Orientation Levels 2-3
Water Entry Level 3
Breath Control Level 3
Buoyancy/Flotation Level 3
Body Position Level 1
Arm Action Level 1
Leg Action Level 1
Combined Stroke Level 1

Description: With instructor clapping, singing, or playing music, the swimmers walk around the circle with kickboards in the center. When the music stops, each child must grab a kickboard and float holding onto it (front or back). Flotation time can vary from 5 to 60 seconds.

Instructor intervention: Provide instruction, start and stop music, and control action.

Variations: Remove one kickboard each time, which will eliminate one swimmer, who will have to float *without* a board. Each round, one more class member will have to do it without a board, until the last round when all have to float without it. Extend floating time each round until 60 seconds is reached.

Complexity factors: Depth of water, length of float time, number of kickboards

Source: Canadian Red Cross. (1984). *Water safety instructor guide and reference* (Vol. 5, p. 43). Toronto: Author.

Porpoise Tag (Aquatic Red Rover)

Purpose: To improve treading water, underwater swimming, surface diving, and breath-holding skills

Skill level: Intermediate to advanced

Water depth: Waist deep or greater

Class formation: Scattered

Equipment: None

Prerequisite developmental skills:
Water Adjustment/Orientation Level 3
Water Entry Level 2
Breath Control Levels 4-5
Buoyancy/Flotation Levels 3-4
Body Position Level 2
Arm Action Level 3
Leg Action Level 3
Combined Stroke Level 3

Description: Designate one or two as "it." They tread water in the middle of the pool. Participants hold onto the side and try to swim to the other wall to be safe. When approached by "it," they must swim underwater to avoid being tagged.

Instructor intervention: Explain rules, appoint first "it," enforce rules, referee, and ensure safety.

Variations: Elimination of tagged participants, tagged participants become "it," or replace "it." Other skills can be substituted for surface diving, such as back-floating or particular strokes.

Complexity factors: Depth and width of pool, type of skills, number of "its"

Source: Sheffield, L. (1927). *Swimming simplified* (p. 240). New York: Barnes.

Print

Purpose: To improve swimmers' ability to move in the water

Skill level: Intermediate to advanced

Water depth: Knee to waist deep

Class formation: Scattered

Equipment: None

Prerequisite developmental skills:
Water Adjustment/Orientation Level 3
Water Entry Level 3
Breath Control Level 5
Buoyancy/Flotation Level 3
Body Position Levels 3-4
Arm Action Level 3
Leg Action Level 3
Combined Stroke Level 3

Description: Have the children form individual letters of the alphabet (such as I, T, O, X) or numbers while floating or standing in the water.

Instructor intervention: Provide directions and ensure safety; challenge the students to form various letters.

Variations: Have the students form letters (partners—S, A, B; groups—R, M) or words in small groups. Have one group form a letter or word while others guess it. Use equipment (reaching pole, ring buoy, paddle, kickboard) to assist in forming letters.

Complexity factors: Depth of water, number of students, level of students

Source: Canadian Red Cross. (1984). *Water safety instructor guide and reference* (Vol. 5, p. 41). Toronto: Author.

Push Against the Wall

Purpose: To practice back-float position and kicking with assistance

Skill level: Prebeginner with parent

Water depth: Waist to chest deep

Class formation: one-on-one with parent

Equipment: None (parent for each child)

Prerequisite developmental skills:
Water Adjustment/Orientation Level 2
Water Entry Level 2
Body Position Level 3
Breath Control Level 1
Buoyancy/Flotation Levels 2-4 (supine)
Body Position Level 2
Arm Action Level 1
Leg Action Levels 2-3
Combined Stroke Level 1

Description: Children are coaxed onto back position with head resting on parent's shoulder and feet touching the wall. Parent provides extra support under shoulders and hips, as needed. Child should push vigorously off wall and begin kicking while the parent guides them to other side of pool or swim area. Just before reaching wall, they can be encouraged to roll over, push off from parent's thigh, and grasp wall. Encouragement by parent and instructor can emphasize high hips (or belly button) and looking at the ceiling for some imaginary object (spider, fly, picture, little man, etc.).

Instructor intervention: Provide direction, assistance to parents, and encouragement to children; ensure safety.

Variations: Use kickboard or other flotation device between child's head and parent's shoulder as child gets more comfortable. Lead up to kicking on back with board and no parent.

Complexity factors: Parent support, distance to be covered

Source: Kochen, C., & McCabe, J. (1986). *The baby swim book*. Champaign, IL: Human Kinetics.

Ride 'Em Cowboys

Purpose: To practice balancing in the water; to improve water adjustment skills

Skill level: Beginner

Water depth: Knee to chest deep

Class formation: One-on-one, scattered

Prerequisite developmental skills:
Water Adjustment/Orientation Level 2
Water Entry Level 3
Breath Control Level 1
Buoyancy/Flotation Levels 2-3
Body Position Level 2
Arm Action Level 1
Leg Action Levels 2-3
Combined Stroke Level 1

Equipment: Styrofoam barbell

Description: Child sits on one end of a styrofoam barbell holding on to the "neck" of the horse. The parent/instructor will have to assist the swimmer in maintaining his or her balance. The parent/instructor can place a hand under the bottom of the barbell and make the "horse" move in the water. The "horse" can also "jump" when the barbell is tilted backward.

Instructor intervention: Provide instructions and safety; assist the child in controlling the "horse."

Variation: Use a kickboard as the "horse."

Complexity factors: Water depth, ratio of students to parents/instructors

Source: Wertz, H. (1986). *Workshop games.* United States Swimming Foundation workshop, Fort Wayne, IN.

Rocket Ship

Purpose: To practice a progression of prone-float skills leading into prone locomotion

Skill level: Beginner to intermediate

Water depth: Waist to chest deep

Class formation: Single line or wave

Equipment: None

Prerequisite developmental skills:
Water Adjustment/Orientation Level 3
Water Entry Level 3
Breath Control Level 3
Buoyancy/Flotation Levels 2-4
Body Position Level 3
Arm Action Levels 1-3
Leg Action Levels 1-3
Combined Stroke Levels 1-3

Description: Students line up and pretend to be rocket ships. Instructor describes Stage 1 Rocket (prone glide); Stage 2 Rocket (prone kick glide); and Stage 3 Rocket (prone combined beginner and human stroke). Instructor and class in unison "count down" to "blast off." At "blast off," each child pushes off from pool edge or bottom. Each stage adds one skill (glide, then kick, then arms). Compare distance covered from trial to trial.

Instructor intervention: Describe rules; lead "count down."

Variations: Use mask and snorkel. Use same or similar progression on the back.

Complexity factors: Depth of water, presence of side from which to push off

Source: Original to S. Langendorfer.

Sharks and Minnows (I)

Purpose: To practice rudimentary skills, balance, and movement in shallow water

Skill level: Beginner

Water depth: Knee to chest deep

Class formation: Scattered

Equipment: Buoyed line to contain the tag area

Prerequisite developmental skills:
Water Adjustment/Orientation Level 3
Water Entry Level 3
Breath Control Level 3
Buoyancy/Flotation Level 3
Body Position Level 3
Arm Action Levels 1-3
Leg Action Levels 1-3
Combined Stroke Levels 1-3

Description: Swimmers (minnows) spread out in shallow end and try to avoid being caught by the Shark. Safe areas may include a buoyed line or side of pool. In unison, the minnows call out, "What time is it, Shark?" Shark calls out random times (4 o'clock, 7 o'clock, etc.), and the minnows move (swim or step) the time toward Shark. When the shark calls out "Dinner time," she or he tries to catch the minnows before they reach safety. Minnows can walk, run, or swim to safe areas. Minnows tagged can become sharks, sit out, or simply return to game.

Instructor intervention: Provide instructions; can serve as first Shark; ensure safety for all participants.

Variations: Add extra sharks. Choose one or more skills (e.g., back flotation) as the way to be "safe."

Complexity factors: Depth of water, size of area, size of safe area, number of sharks, total number of players

Source: Canadian Red Cross. (1984). *Water safety instructor guide and reference* (Vol. 5, p. 31). Toronto: Author.

Sink or Float?

Purpose: To increase the children's understanding of floating and sinkable objects

Skill level: Prebeginner

Water depth: None to waist deep

Class formation: Circle

Prerequisite developmental skills:
Water Adjustment/Orientation Level 1
Water Entry Level 1
Breath Control Level 1
Buoyancy/Flotation Level 1
Body Position Level 1
Arm Action Level 1
Leg Action Level 1
Combined Stroke Level 1

Equipment: Dishpan, baby bathtub, or plastic swimming pool, variety of objects (coins, poker chips, corks, balls), hand towels, plastic tablecloth

Description: Fill a large dishpan or baby bathtub with water, and place it at poolside. Standing around the table, explain in elementary terms the concept of flotation and density (i.e., that some objects float because they are less dense than water, and that objects that are denser than water sink). Have a variety of objects that sink and float (rock, small balls, sponge, crayon, plastic straw, etc.). Have the children determine if the object sinks or floats by "testing" it in the water. Then have children test themselves in different positions in shallow water.

Instructor intervention: Provide directions and feedback and pose exploratory questions.

Variations: Have the children try to guess whether an object will sink or float before "testing" it. Have the children find items to "test."

Complexity factors: Number of students, level of the students' understanding

Source: Original to D. Harrod.

Sticky Popcorn

Purpose: To practice balance in water when jumping in air, especially together with class members

Skill level: Beginner to intermediate

Water depth: Knee to waist deep

Class formation: Scattered

Equipment: None

Prerequisite developmental skills:
Water Adjustment/Orientation Level 3
Water Entry Level 3
Breath Control Level 1
Buoyancy/Flotation Level 2
Body Position Level 1
Arm Action Level 1
Leg Action Level 1
Combined Stroke Level 1

Description: Swimmers scatter across shallow water and begin bouncing up and down "like popcorn." Classmates who touch must join hands and keep "popping." When more than two classmates join up, they become a big sticky popcorn ball.

Instructor intervention: Provide directions, encourage bouncing, and ensure safety.

Variations: Add other skills to bouncing, such as submersion or floating during the jumping.

Complexity factors: Water depth, skills required, number of players

Source: Canadian Red Cross. (1984). *Water safety instructor guide and reference* (Vol. 5, p. 27). Toronto: Author.

Straddleboard Relay

Purpose: To practice balance and buoyancy in the water under game conditions

Skill level: Intermediate to advanced

Water depth: Chest deep to over head

Class formation: Lines

Equipment: Kickboards

Prerequisite developmental skills:
Water Adjustment/Orientation Levels 3-4
Water Entry Levels 3-5
Breath Control Level 4
Buoyancy/Flotation Levels 3-4
Body Position Levels 1-2
Arm Action Level 2
Leg Action Level 2
Combined Stroke Level 2

Description: Swimmers try to cover a selected distance while straddle-seated on a kickboard. Arms and feet are used to propel them through the water. A swimmer who falls off his or her "horse" must remount and continue.

Instructor intervention: Provide instructions, begin play, provide supervision, and ensure safety.

Variations: Played as a team relay; swimmers go across pool and give board to next person. Done as backstroke relay, holding board between legs and paddling with arms only. Done with beginners or novices wearing flotation devices.

Complexity factors: Depth of water, distance covered, skills

Source: Council for National Cooperation in Aquatics. (1965). *Water fun for everyone* (p. 68). New York: Association Press.

Superman (Superwoman or Superkid) (I)

Purpose: To increase skill in prone float and length of breath holding

Skill level: Beginner to intermediate

Water depth: Waist to chest deep

Class formation: Single line or wave

Equipment: None

Prerequisite developmental skills:
Water Adjustment/Orientation Level 3
Water Entry Level 3
Breath Control Level 5
Buoyancy/Flotation Levels 3-4
Body Position Level 3
Arm Action Level 1
Leg Action Level 1
Combined Stroke Level 1

Description: Children pretend to be Superman (-woman, -kid) by assuming prone extended position in the water. They push off and try to glide as far as possible (as if they were flying).

Instructor intervention: Provide encouragement and feedback about front-float position.

Variations: Gliding on the back (upside-down Superman). Class goes as group, in waves, individually, or two-by-two.

Complexity factors: Depth of water, side to push from

Source: YMCA of the USA. (1987). *Y Skippers* (p. 197). Champaign, IL: Human Kinetics.

"Timber!"

Purpose: To practice submersion and flotation skills

Skill level: Beginner to intermediate

Water depth: Waist deep

Class formation: Scattered

Equipment: None

Prerequisite developmental skills:
Water Adjustment/Orientation Level 3
Water Entry Level 3
Breath Control Level 3
Buoyancy/Flotation Level 3
Body Position Level 3
Arm Action Level 1
Leg Action Level 1
Combined Stroke Level 1

Description: Swimmers stand at least arm's length apart from one another. Upon the shout "Timber!" each tries to fall like a tree into the water. Each time the instructor can request hands at sides or over head and to "timber" into prone or supine float. After floating for varying periods of time, swimmers recover and start over.

Instructor intervention: Provide instructions, call out "Timber!" and assist hesitant swimmers with encouragement and feedback.

Variations: Fall to front or back, hands over heads, or to side; fall from side of pool into deeper water, for intermediates.

Complexity factors: Depth of water, hands position, length of float

Source: YMCA of the USA. (1987). *Y Skippers* (p. 198). Champaign, IL: Human Kinetics.

Train

Purpose: To practice balance in the water working as a group

Skill level: Prebeginner and beginner

Water depth: Knee to waist deep

Class formation: Single file line

Equipment: Kickboard, floating mat, floating toys, hula hoops

Prerequisite developmental skills:
Water Adjustment/Orientation Level 3
Water Entry Level 3
Breath Control Level 1
Buoyancy/Flotation Level 3
Body Position Level 1
Arm Action Level 1
Leg Action Level 1
Combined Stroke Level 1

Description: Swimmers stand behind one another facing in same direction. Each swimmer holds the waist of the swimmer in front. The line becomes a train, with the first in line being the engine, the last the caboose; those in between can choose their type of railroad car. Making train sounds, the whole line winds around through the shallow end, sometimes going slow, sometimes going fast. Train can go uphill (everyone on tip toes), downhill (bend knees), through a tunnel (instructor places arms, kickboard, or mat over heads). Take turns, giving different children opportunities to be engine and caboose.

Instructor intervention: Provide instructions, encourage fantasy play, help all have turn, and ensure safety.

Variations: Add obstacles such as hula hoops to submerge through. Perform in deeper water wearing flotation devices.

Complexity factors: Depth of water, level of skills stressed, use of flotation devices

Source: Canadian Red Cross. (1984). *Water safety instructor guide and reference* (Vol. 5, p. 21). Toronto: Author.

Water Limbo

Purpose: To learn and practice proper position for back float and glide

Skill level: Beginner to intermediate

Water depth: Progressively from dry land to pool side to knee deep to chest deep

Class formation: One-on-one or partners

Equipment: Pole or kickboard

Prerequisite developmental skills:
Water Adjustment/Orientation Level 3
Water Entry Level 3
Breath Control Level 3
Buoyancy/Flotation Level 2 (supine)
Body Position Level 2
Arm Action Level 1
Leg Action Level 1
Combined Stroke Level 1

Description: Instructor explains and demonstrates "limbo" dance (attempt to arch back and duck under horizontal pole) on dry land. Supporting the back of child's head and shoulders, position the child in "limbo" position with high hips and back, and assist her or his walk under the pole held by class members. Repeat with all class members on dry land. Then repeat using pool side and finally in about waist-deep water. The instructor can substitute kickboard for pole. Emphasize same high-hips position in water as on land. Give lots of support first to the head and shoulders until each child is comfortable.

Instructor intervention: Describe, demonstrate, and provide manual support to each child in and out of water.

Variations: Provide more or less support depending upon child's skill and confidence. Have limbo contest to see who can bend over farthest—on land and in water.

Complexity factors: Height of pole, degree of instructor support, depth of water, swimmer experience and comfort

Source: Original to S. Langendorfer.

Water Ski Ride

Purpose: To practice prone floating with assistance

Skill level: Beginner to intermediate

Water depth: Waist deep to overhead

Class formation: Line

Equipment: Water ski rope

Prerequisite developmental skills:
Water Adjustment/Orientation Levels 3-5
Water Entry Level 3
Breath Control Levels 4-5
Buoyancy/Flotation Levels 3-4
Body Position Level 2
Arm Action Level 1
Leg Action Level 1
Combined Stroke Level 1

Description: The swimmer holds on tightly to a ski rope handle. The instructor on deck holds the other end of the ski rope. On the signal "Hold tight, here we go!" the instructor pulls the child in the water. The speed of the ride depends upon the ability of the student and depth of the water.

Instructor intervention: Provide instructions and safety, pull the water ski rope, and provide encouragement.

Variations: Pull the swimmers on their backs. Have the children kick their feet while holding onto the rope. Use a flotation device for beginners.

Complexity factors: Depth of water, number of students, length of rope, speed of pull

Source: Wertz, H. (1986). *Workshop games*. United States Swimming Foundation workshop, Fort Wayne, IN.

Body Position and Change of Direction

Airplane II—Buoyancy/Flotation Level 2
Head, Shoulders, Knees, and Toes—Buoyancy/Flotation Level 2

Immunity Tag—Buoyancy/Flotation Level 2
Pancakes—Buoyancy/Flotation Level 1
Superman (II)—Buoyancy/Flotation Level 3

Airplane II

Purpose: To improve swimmers' ability to maintain an inclined prone position

Skill level: Beginner

Water depth: Knee to chest deep

Class formation: Scattered

Equipment: Kickboard

Prerequisite developmental skills:
Water Adjustment/Orientation Level 3
Water Entry Level 3
Breath Control Level 1
Buoyancy/Flotation Level 2
Body Position Level 2
Arm Action Level 1
Leg Action Level 1
Combined Stroke Level 1

Description: Each child has two kickboards. The child holds a kickboard under each arm, to resemble airplane wings. Instruct the child to prone-float while holding onto the kickboards. The child can kick to propel around the pool.

Instructor intervention: Provide directions and safety.

Variations: The children can blow bubbles in the water to imitate the noise of an airplane motor. If there are not enough kickboards for each child to have two, have the children pair up. One child can be the airplane and the other the pilot, who walks around the pool steering the airplane by holding onto the kickboards.

Complexity factors: Number of students per kickboards

Source: Original to S.J. Langendorfer.

Head, Shoulders, Knees, and Toes

Purpose: To encourage changes in body position and balance while standing and moving in waist- to chest-deep water

Skill level: Beginner

Water depth: Waist to chest deep

Class formation: Lines or semicircle

Equipment: None

Prerequisite developmental skills:
Water Adjustment/Orientation Level 2
Water Entry Level 2
Breath Control Level 3
Buoyancy/Flotation Levels 1-2
Body Position Level 1
Arm Action Level 1
Leg Action Level 1
Combined Stroke Level 1

Description: Children stand facing instructor or other "leader" in shallow water. The leader gives rapid-fire directions for which body parts to touch. Children try to touch body parts with both hands as rapidly as the parts are called out. Touching knees and toes may require brief submersion.

Instructor intervention: Provide directions and lead the game initially. Encourage the timid ones to try to get wet.

Variations: Touch body parts to surface of water or to kickboard floating in front of child.

Complexity factors: Depth of water, speed of commands, use of kickboard

Source: YMCA of the USA. (1986). *Progressive swimming program instructors guide* (p. 15). Champaign, IL: Human Kinetics.

Immunity Tag

Purpose: To practice and explore different body positions in the water while holding a body part out of the water

Skill level: Beginner to intermediate

Water depth: Shallow to moderate (depending upon skill level)

Class formation: Scattered

Equipment: None

Prerequisite developmental skills:
Water Adjustment/Orientation Level 3
Water Entry Level 3
Breath Control Levels 2-3
Buoyancy/Flotation Level 2
Body Position Level 2
Arm Action Level 2
Leg Action Level 2
Combined Stroke Level 2

Description: One child is "it." Instructor calls out a body part, which has to remain out of the water in order for the swimmer to be safe from tag by "it." Tagged swimmer becomes new "it."

Instructor intervention: Provide instructions, call out body parts, encourage innovative solutions, provide feedback, and ensure safety.

Variations: Play in deeper water with intermediates or advanced swimmers, where they cannot stand and must swim to support the body part out of water. Play with more than one "it."

Complexity factors: Depth of water, number of "its," difficulty of skills used

Source: Cureton, T. (1949). *Fun in the water* (p. 85). New York: Association Press.

Pancakes

Purpose: To experience and practice rolling over from front to back and vice versa

Skill level: Prebeginner (infants and young children with parental assistance)

Water depth: Waist to chest deep (depends on parent assist)

Class formation: Circle, with parents holding children

Equipment: None (record player with tune—optional)

Prerequisite developmental skills:
Water Adjustment/Orientation Level 2
Water Entry Level 2
Breath Control Level 1
Buoyancy/Flotation Levels 1-2
Body Position Level 1
Arm Action Level 1
Leg Action Level 1
Combined Stroke Level 1

Description: Parents hold children in circle with feet toward center. Together all sing (to the tune of "I'm a little teapot"):

"I'm a little pancake on my back.
I'm a little pancake nice and flat.
I'm a little pancake on my back.
Flip me over just like that!"

Child starts out on back, and at last sentence, parent gently rolls her or him over onto stomach. As the children gain skill, they can roll themselves, and parents can release momentarily so they can swim forward to parent on stomach.

Instructor intervention: Provide basic directions, lead tunes, and provide feedback to parents.

Variations: Make up other lyrics (tugboat, fish, etc.), and practice rolling from front to back, from vertical to horizontal, etc.

Complexity factors: Parental assistance, skills involved beyond rolling

Source: Kochen, C., & McCabe, J. (1986). *The baby swim book* (pp. 370-371). Champaign, IL: Human Kinetics.

Superman (II)

Purpose: To practice and improve horizontal body position during front and back float

Skill level: Beginner to intermediate

Water depth: Waist to chest deep, depending upon skill level

Class formation: Scattered, circle, one-on-one

Equipment: None

Prerequisite developmental skills:
Water Adjustment/Orientation Level 3
Water Entry Level 2
Breath Control Level 3
Buoyancy/Flotation Level 3
Body Position Levels 2-3
Arm Action Level 2
Leg Action Level 2
Combined Stroke Level 2

Description: Children pretend to be Superman (-woman) flying and assume the extended flying position with arms extended and legs straight. Can be adapted to the back float also, although position needs to be modified.

Instructor intervention: Provide instructions, assist swimmers, and provide feedback about positions.

Variations: Float on back for time. Float with partners holding hands (for security).

Complexity factors: Depth of water, length of float, type of float

Source: YMCA of the USA. (1987). *Y Skippers* (p. 197). Champaign, IL: Human Kinetics.

Arm and Leg Propulsion

Alligator Swim—Level 1
Body-Part Tag—Level 3
Carp and Cranes—Level 3
Combined Stroke on Back Progression—All Levels

Cork Scramble—Level 2
Flutter Kicking Cues—All Levels
Front Crawl Stroke—Arm Pull Cues—All Levels
Hot and Cold—Level 2

Kickboard Killer—Level 3
Kickboard Tug of War—Level 3
Light up the Night—Level 4
Newspaper Relay—Levels 3-4
One-Arm Swim—Level 4
Sharks and Minnows (II)—Level 3

Spider Swimming—Level 1
Time Machine—Level 3
Twenty Ways—Level 3
Water Wheelbarrow—Level 4
Wave to the ''Fishies''—Level 3

Alligator Swim

Purpose: To help the child experience having his or her feet off the bottom of the pool

Skill level: Prebeginner or beginner

Water depth: Child must be able to place hands on bottom of steps or bottom of pool with face out of the water

Class formation: One-to-one or small group

Equipment: None

Prerequisite developmental skills:
   Water Adjustment/Orientation Level 3
   Water Entry Level 2
   Breath Control Level 3
   Buoyancy/Flotation Level 2
   Body Position Level 2
   Arm Action Level 1
   Leg Action Level 1
   Combined Stroke Level 1

Description: Students place their hands on the bottom of the steps or bottom of the pool, with their faces out of the water. The students can walk along the bottom of the pool by moving their hands and kicking their feet.

Instructor intervention: Provide assistance and ensure safety.

Variations: Students can be asked to place their faces in the water and blow bubbles, spit water, look for fish, rings, etc. Students can be asked to support themselves with one hand as they wave to the instructor or parents.

Complexity factors: Number of students, depth of pool

Source: Original to S. Langendorfer and D. Harrod.

Body-Part Tag

Purpose: To practice different forms of swimming and moving in water with limited use of limbs

Skill level: Intermediate to advanced

Water depth: Knee deep to over head, depending on skill level

Class formation: Scattered

Prerequisite developmental skills:
   Water Adjustment/Orientation Level 3
   Water Entry Levels 3-5
   Breath Control Level 4
   Buoyancy/Flotation Levels 3-5
   Body Position Levels 3-4
   Arm Action Level 2
   Leg Action Level 3
   Combined Stroke Level 3

Equipment: None

Description: One swimmer is "it" and tries to tag other members of class. As each member is tagged, he or she becomes "handicapped" by losing the use of whatever limb or body part is touched during the tag. The "handicaps" accumulate until the person can no longer move or swim and becomes "it."

Instructor intervention: Provide instructions and demonstration, control game action, and ensure safety.

Variations: Use more than one "it." Work two teams against one another (see Carp and Cranes).

Complexity factors: Depth of water, number of "its"

Source: Swimming Pool Data and Reference Annual. (1960). *Aquatic games, pageants, and stunts* (p. 18). New York: Hoffman & Harris.

Carp and Cranes

Purpose: To practice rapid movement or swimming in game setting

Skill level: Beginner through advanced

Water depth: Waist deep to over head, depending upon skill level

Class formation: Two lines facing, about 10 to 15 feet apart

Prerequisite developmental skills:
Water Adjustment/Orientation Level 3
Water Entry Levels 3-5
Breath Control Level 4
Buoyancy/Flotation Level 3
Body Position Level 2
Arm Action Level 3
Leg Action Level 3
Combined Stroke Level 3

Equipment: None

Description: One group are the Carp, other are the Cranes. Instructor calls out either "Carp" or "Crane," who become "it" and try to capture the other team before they reach their home side. Caught persons join the other side.

Instructor intervention: Provide instructions, control pace of game, referee, and ensure safety.

Variations: Played in deep end with swimmers or with beginners wearing PFDs. Require a specific stroke to be used by all players during chase.

Complexity factors: Depth of water, distance apart, distance to safety, strokes permitted

Source: Council for National Cooperation in Aquatics. (1965). *Water fun for everyone.* New York: Association Press.

Combined Stroke on Back Progression

Purpose: To improve propulsion on the back in the water

Skill level: Beginner

Water depth: Shallow

Class formation: Line, group

Equipment: Kickboard

Prerequisite developmental skills:
Water Adjustment/Orientation Level 3
Water Entry Level 3
Breath Control Level 3
Buoyancy/Flotation Level 2
Body Position Level 2
Arm Action Levels 1-2
Leg Action Levels 1-2
Combined Stroke Levels 1-2

Description:
A) Arm pull
   1. Sculling/finning—move hands back and forth by legs
   2. Elementary backstroke arm pull (demonstrate and practice on land first)
      a. Phase 1—Up
         a) Zipper up sides
         b) Sneak up and tickle armpits
      b. Phase 2—Out
         a) Stretch arms out
         b) Flap wing out to side—be a bird
         c) Make a "T," not a "Y"
      c. Phase 3—Together
         a) Push arms to body
         b) Flap wings down to side—torpedo
B) Kick
   1. Flutter kick (see flutter-kick cues)
   2. Elementary backstroke kick (demonstrate and practice sitting on a bench or on side of pool first)
   Phase 1—drop heels toward the bottom of the pool
   Phase 2—move feet out to the side
   Phase 3—straighten legs and have feet touch out in front

Instructor intervention: Provide instructions, safety, and cues for the children.

Variations: Have the children vary the speed, direction, and distance.

Complexity factors: Water depth, number of students, kickboard

Source: Original to S. Langendorfer and D. Harrod.

Cork Scramble

Purpose: To practice water entry and propulsion skills in nonteaching setting

Skill level: Beginner to advanced

Water depth: Knee deep to over head, depending upon skill level

Class formation: Lines on side of pool

Prerequisite developmental skills:
Water Adjustment/Orientation Level 3
Water Entry Level 3
Breath Control Level 3
Buoyancy/Flotation Levels 2-3
Body Position Levels 2-4
Arm Action Level 2
Leg Action Level 2
Combined Stroke Level 2

Equipment: Corks or other small floating objects (table-tennis balls, tennis balls, floating rings, etc.)

Description: Corks or other small, floating objects are scattered in center of pool. On signal, swimmers enter water and try to quickly gather up corks. Swimmer who gets the most (or the first) is winner and gets to toss in corks on second round.

Instructor intervention: Provide instruction, spread corks, start game, and control action.

Variations: Relays can retrieve corks. Partners must retrieve corks without letting go of hands. Require specific stroke for recovering corks.

Complexity factors: Depth of water, size and number of corks, distance swum, number of players

Source: Cureton, T. (1949). *Fun in the water* (p. 86). New York: Association Press.

Flutter Kicking Cues

Purpose: To develop an effective flutter kick

Skill level: Beginner to intermediate

Water depth: Shallow

Class formation: Line, group

Equipment: Kickboard

Prerequisite developmental skills:
Water Adjustment/Orientation Level 3
Water Entry Level 3
Breath Control Level 3
Buoyancy/Flotation Level 3
Body Position Level 2
Arm Action Level 1
Leg Action Level 2
Combined Stroke Level 1

Description: Flutter Kick Cues
1. Robot Kick—straight legs with slight bend in knees
2. Baby Kicks—shallow kick
3. Ballerina Legs—straight legs with slight bend in knees, with pointed toes
4. Kick from the hips, not the knees
5. Practice kicking with a kickboard, mat, styrofoam barbell, etc. (with and without a partner)
6. Small baby splashes, not gigantic ones
7. Have the student place his or her hands around your neck. Extend your arms out so that your hands grasp the child's legs above the knees. Move the child's legs in the kick motion, and say "kick, kick, kick."

Instructor intervention: Provide instructions, safety, and feedback.

Variations: Have the children vary the speed, direction, and distance.

Complexity factors: Number of students

Source: Original to D.L. Harrod.

Front Crawl Stroke—Arm Pull Cues

Purpose: To improve the front crawl stroke arm pull

Skill level: Beginner to intermediate

Water depth: Shallow

Class formation: Line, group

Equipment: Floatable object

Prerequisite developmental skills:
Water Adjustment/Orientation Level 3
Water Entry Levels 3-5
Breath Control Level 4
Buoyancy/Flotation Levels 3-4
Body Position Levels 2-4
Arm Action Levels 3-4
Leg Action Level 2
Combined Stroke Level 3

Description: Front Crawl Stroke Arm Pull
1. Reach hand out in front to touch an object.
2. Extend hand back to touch thigh or swim suit.
3. Pull phase: hand, wrist, elbow.
4. Recovery phase: elbow, wrist, hand.
5. ''Wave'' to recover arm out of the water.
6. Catch water in front and push it to your feet.
7. Arms take turns ''pulling'' the water.
8. Arms in water at 10 and 2 o'clock.
9. Drag thumb through armpit during recovery phase.

Instructor intervention: Provide instruction, safety, and feedback.

Variations: Have the children vary the speed, direction, and distance.

Complexity factors: Number of students

Source: Original to D. Harrod.

Hot and Cold

Purpose: To practice flutter kick fast and slow, shallow and deep, from the side of the pool

Skill level: Beginner

Water depth: Shallow

Class formation: Seated line on the side

Equipment: Small sinkable object (ring, poker chip, etc.)

Prerequisite developmental skills:
Water Adjustment/Orientation Level 3
Water Entry Level 2
Breath Control Levels 3-5
Buoyancy/Flotation Level 4
Body Position Levels 3-4
Arm Action Level 2
Leg Action Level 2
Combined Stroke Level 2

Description: Class sits on the side of the pool. While one member is turned away from the pool with eyes closed, a ring or poker chip is submerged somewhere. When the person enters the pool, the class kicks hard and deep when the person gets near the submerged object and shallow and softly when they move away from it.

Instructor intervention: Give directions, hide object first time, provide assistance, and ensure safety.

Variations: "It" could be blindfolded while in the water. Class could be all the way in water up to necks and hang on side to kick. Different kicks beside flutter (scissors, whip, dolphin) could be used.

Complexity factors: Size of object, depth of pool, size of class

Source: Council for National Cooperation in Aquatics. (1965). *Water fun for everyone* (pp. 32-33). New York: Association Press.

Kickboard Killer

Purpose: To practice kicking skills under an endurance condition

Skill level: Beginner to advanced

Water depth: Any depth (vary with skill level)

Class formation: Pairs

Equipment: Kickboard or sealed foam mat

Prerequisite developmental skills:
Water Adjustment/Orientation Level 3
Water Entry Level 3
Breath Control Level 5
Buoyancy/Flotation Level 4
Body Position Levels 3-4
Arm Action Level 3
Leg Action Level 3
Combined Stroke Level 3

Description: As with Kickboard Tug of War, swimmers pair up across kickboard. On command they kick *toward* one another while holding onto the kickboard, trying to push their partner backward. Begin with 5-second kick and progress to longer times.

Instructor intervention: Provide instruction and start/stop command as well as provide stipulations for other kicks.

Variations: Vary the kicks from flutter to whip to dolphin to scissors. Use large foam mat, and include more than two children.

Complexity factors: Type of kick, number of kickers, length of time for kick

Source: Council for National Cooperation in Aquatics. (1965). *Water fun for everyone*. New York: Association Press.

Kickboard Tug of War

Purpose: To practice kicking skills under an endurance condition

Skill level: Beginner to advanced

Water depth: Any depth (vary with skill level)

Class formation: Pairs or teams in lines

Equipment: Kickboard or buoyed line

Prerequisite developmental skills:
Water Adjustment/Orientation Level 3
Water Entry Level 3
Breath Control Levels 4-5
Buoyancy/Flotation Levels 3-4
Body Position Levels 3-4
Arm Action Level 3
Leg Action Level 3
Combined Stroke Level 3

Description: Swimmers pair off on opposite sides of kickboard. On command, they grasp their end of the kickboard and begin kicking vigorously, trying to pull their partner over an imaginary line.

Instructor intervention: Provide instructions, stop and start commands, and provide feedback to participants.

Variations: Use buoyed line and use teams for Tug of War. Combine kicking and pulling or walking in game. Try different types of kicks.

Complexity factors: Depth of water, team versus pairs

Source: YMCA of the USA. (1986). *Progressive swimming program instructors guide* (p. 15). Champaign, IL: Human Kinetics.

Light Up the Night

Purpose: To practice swimming while holding a lit candle without extinguishing it

Skill level: Intermediate to advanced elementary-aged children

Water depth: Deep

Class formation: Relay lines

Prerequisite developmental skills:
Water Adjustment/Orientation Level 3
Water Entry Level 4-5
Breath Control Level 5
Buoyancy/Flotation Level 4
Body Position Levels 3-4
Arm Action Levels 5-6
Leg Action Levels 4-5
Combined Stroke Level 5

Equipment: Candles and matches

Description: Swimmers try to swim with legs and single-arm propulsion across set distance of water. Swimmers start in water and swim with little or no splash. If candle goes out, swimmer must go back to start and try again.

Instructor intervention: Provide instructions, demonstration, and strategy where appropriate. Ensure safety and control action.

Variations: Run as relays in competition with each other. Pass candle from one swimmer to the next in relay without extinguishing it. Specify adapted stroke to be used by all swimmers.

Complexity factors: Depth of water, size of candle, type of stroke used

Source: Jeffries, R. (1984). Unpublished materials from Ashland Family YMCA 1st Annual Silly Relay Meet, Ashland, OH.

Newspaper Relay

Purpose: To practice back floating and kicking in game setting.

Skill level: Intermediate to advanced

Water depth: Waist deep to over head

Class formation: Relay lines or waves

Equipment: Newspapers for all swimmers or teams

Prerequisite developmental skills:
Water Adjustment/Orientation Level 3
Water Entry Levels 3-5
Breath Control Level 5
Buoyancy/Flotation Level 4
Body Position Level 3
Arm Action Level 3
Leg Action Level 3
Combined Stroke Level 4

Description: Swimmers try to cover set distance on their backs while reading a newspaper aloud and without getting it soaking wet

Instructor intervention: Provide instructions, begin games, and provide feedback throughout.

Variations: Do as a relay with newspaper passed from swimmer to swimmer. Attempt while swimming adapted sidestroke. Hold endurance contest to see who can swim farthest without newspaper being soaked.

Complexity factors: Length of swim, number of players, goal of game

Source: Council for National Cooperation in Aquatics. (1965). *Water fun for everyone* (pp. 62-63). New York: Association Press.

One-Arm Swim

Purpose: To practice various movements in the water

Skill level: Intermediate to advanced

Water depth: Knee deep to over head

Class formation: Line

Equipment: None

Prerequisite developmental skills:
Water Adjustment/Orientation Level 3
Water Entry Levels 4-5
Breath Control Level 4
Buoyancy/Flotation Level 4
Body Position Level 4
Arm Action Levels 4-5
Leg Action Level 4
Combined Stroke Level 4

Description: Have the students swim with only one arm or kick with one leg.

Instructor intervention: Provide instructions and safety.

Variations: Have the students hold an object in one hand while swimming. Use a pull buoy to prevent the swimmers from using their legs while swimming.

Complexity factors: Number of swimmers

Source: Runta, N. (1980). *Preschool swimming instructor's manual*. Findlay, OH: YMCA.

Sharks and Minnows (II)

Purpose: To practice rapid swimming skills in a game setting

Skill level: Intermediate to advanced

Water depth: Waist deep to over head

Class formation: Line

Equipment: None

Prerequisite developmental skills:
Water Adjustment/Orientation Level 3
Water Entry Levels 3-5
Breath Control Level 5
Buoyancy/Flotation Level 4
Body Position Level 3
Arm Action Level 4+
Leg Action Level 3+
Combined Stroke Levels 3-4

Description: Minnows are on one side or end of pool and have to swim to the other side or end without being tagged by the shark. The minnow is safe swimming underwater unless caught by a shark and brought to the surface. Tagged minnows become sharks.

Instructor intervention: Provide instructions, suggest strategy, and ensure safety by controlling action and carefully supervising.

Variations: Use more than one shark initially. Select different strokes as ''safe'' ways to move through shark-infested waters.

Complexity factors: Depth and distance to be swum, number of sharks, number of minnows

Source: Swimming Pool Data and Reference Annual. (1947). *Aquatic games, pageants, and stunts* (p. 10). New York: Beach and Pool.

Spider Swimming

Purpose: To explore the pool by moving along the wall in the water; to teach children how to move to safety (ladder, steps) in case of an accidental fall in

Skill level: Prebeginner

Water depth: Any depth (uses pool side/gutter)

Class formation: One-to-one or small group, in a line against the wall

Equipment: None

Prerequisite developmental skills:
Water Adjustment/Orientation Level 2
Water Entry Level 2
Breath Control Level 1
Buoyancy/Flotation Level 2
Body Position Level 1
Arm Action Level 1
Leg Action Level 1
Combined Stroke Level 1

Description: Students hold on to the wall with feet against the wall. The students move along the wall by sliding their hands and feet.

Instructor intervention: Provide assistance and safety.

Variations: Students can be asked to move in different directions, through hula hoops, and under a bridge (mat, instructor's arm). Students can sing "Eensy, Weensy Spider" as they move along the wall.

Complexity factors: Number of students

Source: Original to S. Langendorfer and D. Harrod.

Time Machine

Purpose: To progressively learn and practice lead-ups to front crawl

Skill level: Intermediate to advanced

Water depth: Shallow to deep

Class formation: Circle, lines in lanes

Equipment: None

Prerequisite developmental skills:
Water Adjustment/Orientation Level 3
Water Entry Levels 3-5
Breath Control Level 3+
Buoyancy/Flotation Level 3
Body Position Level 2+
Arm Action Level 3
Leg Action Level 3
Combined Stroke Levels 2-3

Description: This game is a progression from dog paddle to beginner (human) stroke to crawl in a fantasy setting. Using "story" format, instructor tells swimmers they will enter a "time machine" for this drill. "How do you suppose the cave man swam? He probably copied a wolf or sabre-tooth tiger!" Try swimming like a wolf [i.e., dog paddle]!" etc.

Instructor intervention: Provide instructions, leadership, feedback, story.

Variations: Have the children act out different stories.

Complexity factors: Age and skill level of the children

Source: Original to S. Langendorfer (adapted from a drill by Rosemary Dawson).

Twenty Ways

Purpose: To explore different ways of moving through water

Skill level: Beginner through advanced

Water depth: Shallow to deep, depending on skill level

Class formation: Scattered or one-on-one

Equipment: None

Prerequisite developmental skills:
Water Adjustment/Orientation Level 3
Water Entry Level 3
Breath Control Level 3
Buoyancy/Flotation Levels 3-4
Body Position Level 3
Arm Action Level 3
Leg Action Level 3
Combined Stroke Level 3

Description: Swimmers are challenged to show as many ways of moving through the water as possible. Beginners can use skills supported by the bottom while intermediate and advanced must show swimming skills. Instructor is allowed to demonstrate movements for entering, leaving, going through or under the water.

Instructor intervention: Provide instructions and act as official judge on number of skills demonstrated.

Variations: Work as a group or in two competing teams to come up with skills. Limit swimming skills to one type (entering, propulsion on front or on back).

Complexity factors: Water depth, complexity of skills

Source: Canadian Red Cross. (1984). *Water safety instructor guide and reference* (Vol. 5, p. 56). Toronto: Author.

Water Wheelbarrow

Purpose: To practice arm and leg movements of swimming strokes

Skill level: Intermediate to advanced

Water depth: Waist deep to over head

Class formation: In partners

Equipment: None

Prerequisite developmental skills:
Water Adjustment/Orientation Level 3
Water Entry Level 3+
Breath Control Level 5
Buoyancy/Flotation Level 4
Body Position Levels 3-4
Arm Action Level 4
Leg Action Level 4
Combined Stroke Level 4

Description: This game is similar to wheelbarrow races, in that within each set of partners, one swimmer acts as the "arms" and the other person as the "legs" for the swimming stroke. The person being the "legs" must hold on to the ankles of the "arms."

Instructor intervention: Provide instructions and assistance and ensure safety.

Variations: Use a variety of swimming strokes. Combine two strokes together, such as breaststroke arm pull with a flutter kick.

Complexity factors: Number of students, swimming level of the students, students' knowledge of the swimming strokes

Source: Original to D.L. Harrod.

Wave to the "Fishies"

Purpose: To improve the finning motion of the hands during back float/glide

Skill level: Beginner to intermediate

Water depth: Shallow

Class formation: Line

Equipment: None

Prerequisite developmental skills:
Water Adjustment/Orientation Level 3
Water Entry Level 3+
Breath Control Level 4
Buoyancy/Flotation Level 4
Body Position Level 3
Arm Action Level 3
Leg Action Level 3
Combined Stroke Level 3

Description: Have the children standing in the pool. Tell them, "We are going to lie on our backs and kick to the other end. We are going to pretend there are "fishies" at the bottom of the pool." Tell the students to move their hands in a sculling movement as they wave to the "fishies."

Instructor intervention: Provide instructions and safety.

Variations: Have the children vary the speed, distance, and direction (feetfirst and headfirst).

Complexity factors: Number of students

Source: German, L.W. (1978). *North Canton preschool handbook*. North Canton, OH: YMCA.

Advanced Strokes

Squirt Gun Relay (Shoot 'Em Down)—Combined
    stroke level 3
Still Pond—Combined stroke level 2-3
Stroke Switch—Combined stroke level 3-6
Swimming Spelldown—Combined stroke level 3

Touch—Combined stroke level 3
T-Shirt Relay (Change-the-Shirt Relay)—Combined
    stroke level 3
Zigzag—Combined stroke level 3

Squirt Gun Relay

Purpose: To practice advanced strokes in a game
relay format

Skill level: Beginner to advanced

Water depth: Shallow to deep, depending upon
skill level

Class formation: Relay lines or waves

Prerequisite developmental skills:
    Water Adjustment/Orientation Level 3
    Water Entry Level 3
    Breath Control Level 5
    Buoyancy/Flotation Level 4
    Body Position Level 3
    Arm Action Level 3
    Leg Action Level 3
    Combined Stroke Level 3

Equipment: Squirt guns, plastic targets that will knock over

Description: Swimmers cross pool with stroke selected by instructor. At the other wall, they pick up a
squirt gun and try to knock down a light plastic target with water. They then return with same selected
stroke, and the next team member goes.

Instructor intervention: Provide instruction and demonstration, direct stroke selection, and supervise
action.

Variations: Perform strokes and squirt gun shooting as individuals and not teams. Do as a medley of
strokes. Beginners can walk or perform other types of movement.

Complexity factors: Distance, depth, strokes required

Source: Jeffries, R. (1984). Unpublished materials from First Annual Ashland Family YMCA Silly Relay
Meet, Ashland, OH.

Still Pond

Purpose: To swim effectively and efficiently in a game setting

Skill level: Intermediate to advanced

Water depth: Variable

Class formation: Scattered

Equipment: None

Prerequisite developmental skills:
Water Adjustment/Orientation Level 3
Water Entry Levels 3-5
Breath Control Level 5
Buoyancy/Flotation Level 4
Body Position Level 3
Arm Action Level 3
Leg Action Level 3
Combined Stroke Level 3

Description: One student is ''it'' with eyes closed and back turned to others while the others stand at end. ''It'' begins to count. Students begin swimming forward with a selected stroke. At some point in the count, ''it'' calls ''Still pond . . . no more moving!'' and turns around and opens her or his eyes. Anyone seen moving and not floating motionless is ''caught.'' Game continues until someone manages to swim the entire length of the pool and becomes the next ''it.''

Instructor intervention: Provide instruction, demonstration, and feedback. If not ''it,'' must supervise action of game and ensure safety.

Variations: All students must use same stroke. Students who get caught are penalized a short distance instead of eliminated or sent all the way back.

Complexity factors: Depth of water, length of pool

Source: Beach and Pool. (1947). *Aquatic games, pageants, and stunts* (p. 9). New York: Hoffman & Harris.

Stroke Switch

Purpose: To practice swimming a variety of strokes as designated by the instructor

Skill level: Intermediate to advanced

Water depth: Moderate to deep

Class formation: Lines or waves

Equipment: None

Prerequisite developmental skills:
Water Adjustment/Orientation Level 3
Water Entry Level 3
Breath Control Level 5
Buoyancy/Flotation Level 4
Body Position Level 3
Arm Action Level 3
Leg Action Level 3
Combined Stroke Level 3

Description: Swimmers dive in and swim across pool on start command. Strokes are switched at end of each lap as designated by instructor. Number of consecutive laps can be varied.

Instructor intervention: Provide instructions, start action, and designate stroke switch, either before or during each turn.

Variations: Increase number of laps. Individualize stroke switch for each swimmer depending upon need. Run as switching medley relay, with each swimmer doing a different stroke in each round.

Complexity factors: Length of lap, number of laps, type of strokes

Source: YMCA of the USA. (1986). *Progressive swimming program instructors guide* (p. 58). Chicago, IL: Human Kinetics.

Swimming Spelldown

Purpose: To practice skills and stunts commensurate with skill level

Skill level: Beginning to advanced

Water depth: Waist deep to over head, depending upon skill level

Class formation: Scattered

Equipment: None

Prerequisite developmental skills:
Water Adjustment/Orientation Level 3
Water Entry Level 3
Breath Control Level 5
Buoyancy/Flotation Levels 3-4
Body Position Levels 3-4
Arm Action Level 3
Leg Action Level 3
Combined Stroke Level 3

Description: Students are spread around either shallow or deep end, depending upon skill level. Leader (may be instructor the first time) calls out stunt or demonstrates it. Students all attempt stunt or skill. Students who are unsuccessful with stunt either drop out or count up number of stunts achieved.

Instructor intervention: Provide direction, demonstration, and leadership. Feedback to students is important.

Variations: Students can count the number of skills achieved instead of dropping out. Students can be offered a group of skills within a concept area, and they can choose one or more to try.

Complexity factors: Depth of water, type of stunts requested

Source: American Red Cross. (1968). *Swimming and water safety* (pp. 132-134). Washington, DC: Author.

Touch

Purpose: To practice selected strokes for speed in a game setting

Skill level: Intermediate to advanced

Water depth: Variable

Class formation: Two lines on sides of pool

Prerequisite developmental skills:
Water Adjustment/Orientation Level 3
Water Entry Level 3
Breath Control Level 5
Buoyancy/Flotation Level 4
Body Position Level 3
Arm Action Level 3
Leg Action Level 3
Combined Stroke Level 3

Equipment: Varied equipment around pool left at edges or floating

Description: Swimmers are divided into two groups at opposite sides of pool. A leader calls out the name of one swimmer from each team and an object in pool to touch. At "Go," they swim as quickly as possible to the object and then return to their spot. The teams can accumulate points for fastest swimmers.

Instructor intervention: Provide instructions, call names and objects, keep score, and control action.

Variations: Let all swimmers on the team swim to touch object called. First swimmer to reach object carries it back to her or his side. Prescribe stroke(s) to be used by all swimmers.

Complexity factors: Depth of water, distances, strokes used

Source: Council for National Cooperation in Aquatics. (1965). *Water fun for everyone* (p. 51). New York: Association Press.

T-Shirt Relay

Purpose: To practice swimming strokes while wearing an impediment (T-shirt)

Skill level: Intermediate to advanced

Water depth: Moderate to deep

Class formation: Lines (relays)

Equipment: None (unless doing kickboard relay with T-shirt)

Prerequisite developmental skills:
Water Adjustment/Orientation Level 3
Water Entry Level 3
Breath Control Level 5
Buoyancy/Flotation Levels 3-4
Body Position Level 3
Arm Action Level 3
Leg Action Level 3
Combined Stroke Level 3+

Description: Swimmers are divided into relay teams. The first member of the team wears a T-shirt and swims a prescribed stroke an established distance. At end of the lap, he or she must pull the T-shirt off and pass it to the next swimmer, who repeats the lap. The team that finishes first wins. Repeat with swimmers performing other strokes.

Instructor intervention: Provide instructions and control action of the swim.

Variations: Two swimmers wear one T-shirt and swim together. Different strokes are required, or swimmers do medley (each does a different stroke).

Complexity factors: Length of swim, strokes requested, size of T-shirt

Source: YMCA of the USA. (1986). *Progressive swimming program instructors guide* (p. 29). Chicago, IL: Human Kinetics.

Zigzag

Purpose: To practice prone strokes

Skill level: Beginning to advanced

Water depth: Variable

Class formation: Lines spaced 2 or 3 yards apart

Equipment: None

Prerequisite developmental skills:
Water Adjustment/Orientation Level 3
Water Entry Level 3
Breath Control Level 5
Buoyancy/Flotation Level 4
Body Position Level 3
Arm Action Level 3
Leg Action Level 3
Combined Stroke Level 3

Description: Class members stand facing in same direction. First member in line swims in a figure eight, weaving through classmates using a selected stroke. After his or her turn, the swimmer returns to the end of the line, and the next swimmer repeats the figure-eight swim.

Instructor intervention: Provide instructions, arrange the formations, and control the action.

Variations: Try relay races between lines or timed trials of swimmers through figure-eight course.

Complexity factors: Distance of swim, type of stroke

Source: YMCA of the USA. (1986). *Splash!* (p. 65). Champaign, IL: Human Kinetics.

Water Entry and Exit

Alligator (Otter)—Water Entry Level 4
Easter Egg Coloring Time—Water Entry Level 3
Humpty Dumpty—Water Entry Level 2
Jack Be Nimble—Water Entry Level 2
Jump Into My Circle—Water Entry Level 3

Parachute Jump—Water Entry Level 3
Rocket Booster—Water Entry Level 5
Slithering Snake—Water Entry Level 2
Up, Up, and Away—(Exit game)

Alligator (Otter)

Purpose: To learn and practice headfirst entries
into water

Skill level: Beginner to intermediate

Water depth: Shallow to moderate

Class formation: One-on-one or several lines

Equipment: Foam mat if available, rubber ring

Prerequisite developmental skills:
Water Adjustment/Orientation Levels 2-3
Water Entry Level 3
Breath Control Level 3+
Buoyancy/Flotation Levels 2-4
Body Position Level 2
Arm Action Level 1
Leg Action Level 1
Combined Stroke Level 1

Description: Instructor demonstrates how hungry alligator slides on belly into water to get a fish breakfast (or other meal). Encourages child to imitate: Can provide assistance by pulling from wrists. Child initially does not need to submerge face. Provide an imaginary fish to eat upon entry. Foam mat helps to smooth entry and avoid bumping knees.

Instructor intervention: Demonstrate, encourage fantasy, and provide feedback to child.

Variations: Can use "otter" if "alligator" image frightens child. Can ask more skilled child to go to bottom to retrieve ring (fish). Slide feetfirst, backward, on back, etc.

Complexity factors: Use of mat, face submersion, ring retrieval

Source: Original to S. Langendorfer.

Easter Egg Coloring Time

Purpose: To practice rudimentary entries into water

Skill level: Prebeginner to intermediate

Water depth: Shallow, preferably with steps or ramp

Class formation: Line along side of pool

Equipment: None (flotation device)

Prerequisite developmental skills:
Water Adjustment/Orientation Level 2
Water Entry Level 2
Breath Control Level 3
Buoyancy/Flotation Level 3
Body Position Level 2
Arm Action Level 1
Leg Action Level 1
Combined Stroke Level 2

Description: Children pretend to be Easter eggs with the pool as the coloring dye. Children choose their favorite color or color of the swim suit. When instructor or parent calls out color, child jumps or slides into water. Upon entering water, child must right, turn, and paddle back to the side and get out.

Instructor intervention: Provide instructions, call out colors, and provide assistance and feedback to parents and children.

Variations: All children can jump at each color. Parents can provide the minimal assistance needed.

Complexity factors: Depth of water, other skills after jump

Source: YMCA of the USA. (1987). *Y Skippers* (p. 289). Champaign, IL: Human Kinetics.

Humpty Dumpty

Purpose: To practice entering water with a sitting jump

Skill level: Prebeginner with parents

Water depth: Waist to chest deep

Class formation: Line along side with parents in water

Equipment: None

Prerequisite developmental skills:
Water Adjustment/Orientation Level 2
Water Entry Level 2
Breath Control Level 3
Buoyancy/Flotation Level 2
Body Position Level 2
Arm Action Level 1
Leg Action Level 1
Combined Stroke Level 1

Description: Instructor and parents chant rhyme:

"Humpty Dumpty sat on a wall;
Humpty Dumpty had a great fall;
Humpty Dumpty swam back to the wall."

Parents rock child throughout rhyme. At "great fall," parent pulls child into the water and assists her or him back to wall during last line. As child improves in skill, parent can reduce the assistance provided and increase depth and length of submersion.

Instructor intervention: Provide instruction to parents and lead the rhyme. Provide feedback to parents and children.

Variations: Parent can jump with child. Parent can reduce amount of assistance as child progresses.

Complexity factors: Number of entries tried, depth of submersions, amount of assistance provided

Source: YMCA of the USA. (1987). *Y Skippers* (p. 189). Champaign, IL: Human Kinetics.

Jack Be Nimble

Purpose: To practice jumping into water

Skill level: Prebeginner with parents

Water depth: Waist to chest deep

Class formation: Lined up on side with parents in water

Equipment: None

Prerequisite developmental skills:
Water Adjustment/Orientation Level 2
Water Entry Level 2
Breath Control Level 3
Buoyancy/Flotation Level 2
Body Position Level 1
Arm Action Level 1
Leg Action Level 1
Combined Stroke Level 1

Description: Instructor and parents chant rhyme:

"Jack [Jill] be nimble;
Jack [Jill] be quick;
Jack [Jill] *jump* over the candlestick."

At the last line, children are encouraged to jump into the pool to parents. Upon entry and submersion, they should turn and paddle back to the side, with assistance if necessary.

Instructor intervention: Provide instructions, lead rhyme, and provide feedback to parents and children.

Variations: Parents can jump in with child. Parents can catch child if submersion is frightening. Add other skills such as back float or turtle float after jump.

Complexity factors: Assistance by parents, depth of water, presence of other skills

Source: Kochen, C., & McCabe, J. (1986). *The baby swim book* (pp. 368-369). Champaign, IL: Human Kinetics.

Jump Into My Circle

Purpose: To practice jump entries from pool side

Skill level: Beginner with parents

Water depth: Waist to chest deep

Class formation: Line on pool side with parents in water

Equipment: Hula hoops, one for each adult

Prerequisite developmental skills:
Water Adjustment/Orientation Level 2
Water Entry Level 2
Breath Control Level 3
Buoyancy/Flotation Level 2
Body Position Level 1
Arm Action Level 1
Leg Action Level 1
Combined Stroke Level 1

Description: Children stand or sit on pool side. Adult has hula hoop on water surface and counts "1, 2, 3." Child is encouraged to jump into hoop with brief submersion encouraged. If child grabs side of hoop, adult can assist him or her back to side.

Instructor intervention: Provide instruction and feedback and ensure safety.

Variations: Parents can hold hand of child throughout jump. Child can jump from varying heights, including from sitting and standing on a diving block.

Complexity factors: Depth of water, amount of assistance from parent

Source: YMCA of the USA. (1987). *Y Skippers* (p. 190). Champaign, IL: Human Kinetics.

Parachute Jump

Purpose: To practice jumping into the pool, submerging to the bottom, and returning to the side and climbing out

Skill level: Beginner to intermediate

Water depth: Shallow to moderate

Class formation: Single line or wave

Equipment: None

Prerequisite developmental skills:
Water Adjustment/Orientation Level 2
Water Entry Level 2
Breath Control Level 3
Buoyancy/Flotation Level 2
Body Position Level 1
Arm Action Level 1
Leg Action Level 1
Combined Stroke Level 2

Description: Swimmers line up along shallow edge of pool. Instructor describes that they are in plane and are parachute jumpers. Upon instructor calling out names, or going in order, swimmers yell their own name, jump into the water, submerge to the bottom, push off, and return to the side and climb out.

Instructor intervention: Provide instructions. Can control order and speed of entries. For fearful beginners, can provide support and assistance during jump.

Variations: Give support individually to beginners. Pretend to be "frogmen" jumping from speedboat.

Complexity factors: Height of jump, turns, backward jumps, length of time spent underwater after jump

Source: YMCA of the USA. (1987). *Y Skippers* (p. 194). Champaign, IL: Human Kinetics.

Rocket Booster

Purpose: To practice and improve diving skills in combination with deep-water swimming skills such as underwater swimming and advanced strokes

Skill level: Intermediate

Water depth: Over head (diving depth)

Class formation: Single line or waves from wall

Equipment: None required

Prerequisite developmental skills:
Water Adjustment/Orientation Level 3
Water Entry Levels 3-4
Breath Control Level 5
Buoyancy/Flotation Levels 3-4
Body Position Level 2
Arm Action Level 2
Leg Action Level 2
Combined Stroke Level 3

Description: Swimmers sit (kneel, squat, stand) along side of pool in deep end. Upon signal or command (count down), swimmers blast off into water by diving. Goal is to see who can glide the farthest underwater without surfacing or kicking/pulling. When returning to original side, swimmer can use any designated stroke.

Instructor intervention: Explain rules, emphasize goal and safety considerations, and provide feedback to swimmers on form of dive, glide, and return swimming stroke.

Variations: Progress the type of dive used (sit to kneel to squat to stand) and change the type of advanced stroke used.

Complexity factors: Starting position, presence of line/object to dive over

Source: YMCA of the USA. (1986). *Y Skippers* (p. 195). Champaign, IL: Human Kinetics.

Slithering Snake

Purpose: To improve water entry ability

Skill level: Prebeginner to beginner

Water depth: Waist to chest deep

Class formation: One-on-one, line

Equipment: Gutter/wall of the pool

Prerequisite developmental skills:
Water Adjustment/Orientation Level 2
Water Entry Level 2
Breath Control Levels 2-3
Buoyancy/Flotation Level 2
Body Position Level 1
Arm Action Level 1
Leg Action Level 1
Combined Stroke Level 1

Description: Child sits on the side of the pool and puts one hand on the wall/gutter by his or her side. The other hand reaches across body and is placed next to the first hand. The child turns to face the wall and slowly lowers into the water.

Instructor intervention: Provide instructions and safety.

Variations: Depending on the pool facility, the children can "slither" into the pool down the steps or a handicap ramp.

Complexity factors: Climbing ability of students

Source: Original to D. Harrod.

Up, Up, and Away

Purpose: To improve water exit ability

Skill level: Beginner

Water depth: Waist to chest deep

Class formation: One-on-one, line

Equipment: Gutter/wall of the pool

Prerequisite developmental skills:
Water Adjustment/Orientation Level 2
Water Entry Level 2
Breath Control Level 1
Buoyancy/Flotation Level 1
Body Position Level 1
Arm Action Level 1
Leg Action Level 1
Combined Stroke Level 1

Description: The child uses the side of the pool to climb up over the gutter of the pool. The child puts both hands on the wall and extends both arms upward. Next, the child puts one foot in the gutter and lifts body out of the pool. Parent should assist very young child.

Instructor intervention: Provide instructions and safety.

Variations: The teacher can assist the children by having them use his or her knee as a step.

Complexity factors: Students' climbing ability, type of gutter, height of deck

Source: Original to D. Harrod.

References

Adams, J.A. (1971). A closed loop theory of motor learning. *Journal of Motor Behavior*, **3**, 111-150.

Adams, S.H. (1982). Court hits hard again with new liability twists. *Athletic Purchasing and Facilities*, **6**(5), 12-166.

American Academy of Pediatrics. (1985). Policy statement: Infant swimming programs. *AAP News*, **1**, 15.

American Red Cross. (1977). *Adapted aquatics*. New York: Doubleday.

American Red Cross. (1981). *Swimming and aquatic safety*. Washington, DC: Author.

American Red Cross. (1985). *Annual health and safety reports, 1982-1985*. Washington, DC: Author.

American Red Cross. (1988). *Infant and preschool aquatic program: Instructor's manual*. Washington, DC: Author.

American Red Cross. (1992a). *Guide for training instructors*. St. Louis: Mosby Year Book.

American Red Cross. (1992b). *Swimming and diving*. St. Louis: Mosby Year Book.

American Red Cross. (1992c). *Water safety instructor manual*. St. Louis: Mosby Year Book.

Ammons, M. (1984). The challenge of teaching. In B.J. Logsdon (Ed.), *Physical education for children* (2nd ed., pp. 455-457). Philadelphia: Lea & Febiger.

Arcand, P., Gauthier, P., Bilodeau, G., Chapados, G., Abela, S., Desjardins, R., Gagnon, P.P., & Guerguerian, A.J. (1984). Post-myringotomy care: A prospective study. *Journal of Otolaryngology*, **13**, 305-308.

Arnheim, D., Auxter, D., & Crowe, B. (1977). *Principles and methods of adapted physical education and recreation*. St. Louis: Mosby.

Arnold, L.C., & Freeman, R.W. (Eds.) (1972). *Progressive swimming and springboard diving program*. New York: National YMCA Program Materials.

Balan, C., & Langendorfer, S. (1988a). Developmental and biomechanical descriptions of adult beginner swimmers. *AAHPERD Abstracts—1988*. Washington, DC: AAHPERD Publications.

Balan, C., & Langendorfer, S. (1988b). Effects of different teaching techniques on developmental changes in adult beginner swimmers. *Abstracts of Psychology of Sport and Motor Behavior—1988*. Champaign, IL: Human Kinetics.

Barrett, K. (1984a). Educational games. In B.J. Logsdon (Ed.), *Physical education for children* (2nd ed., pp. 193-240). Philadelphia: Lea & Febiger.

Barrett, K. (1984b). The teacher as observer, interpreter, and decision-maker. In B.J. Logsdon (Ed.), *Physical education for children* (2nd ed., pp. 295-355). Philadelphia: Lea & Febiger.

Baumgartner, T., & Jackson, A. (1991). *Measurement for evaluation in physical education and exercise science* (4th ed.). Dubuque, IA: Brown.

Bayless, M.A., & Adams, S.H. (1985). A liability checklist. *Journal of Physical Education, Recreation and Dance*, **56**(2), 49.

Beach and Pool. (1947). *Aquatic games, pageants, and stunts*. New York: Hoffman & Harris.

Becker, G.D., Eckberg, T.J., & Goldware, R.R. (1987). Swimming and tympanostomy tubes: A prospective study. *Laryngoscope*, **97**, 740-741.

Beckwith, J. (1982). It's time for creative play. *Parks & Recreation*, **17**(9), 37-42.

Beckwith, J. (1983). Playgrounds for the twenty-first century. *Cities & Villages*, **21**(5), 22-26.

Beckwith, J. (1988). Playground equipment: A designer's perspective. In L.D. Bruya (Ed.), *Playspaces for children: A new beginning* (pp. 49-102). Washington, DC: American Alliance for Health, Physical Education, Recreation and Dance.

Bennett, H.J., Wagner, T., & Fields, A. (1983). Acute hyponatremia and seizures in an infant after a swimming lesson. *Pediatrics*, **72**, 125-127.

Berlyne, D.E. (1958). The influence of complexity and novelty in visual figures on orienting process. *Journal of Experimental Psychology*, **55**(3), 289-296.

Big Toys. (circa 1988). Checklist for installation, assembly, and maintenance warranty validation. Tacoma, WA: Author.

Bory, E. (1971). *Teaching children to swim*. New South Wales, Australia: Paul Hamlyn.

Bowers, L. (1976). *Principles of design for playgrounds* [Film]. Tampa: University of South Florida Film Library.

Bowers, L. (1988). Playground design: A scientific approach. In L.D. Bruya (Ed.), *Playspaces for children: A new beginning* (pp. 29-48). Washington, DC: American Alliance for Health, Physical Education, Recreation and Dance.

Bredekamp, S. (1987). *Developmentally appropriate practices in early childhood education.* Washington, DC: National Association for the Education of Young Children.

Brown, C. (1986). *Workshop games.* United States Swimming Foundation workshop, Fort Wayne, IN.

Bruya, L.D. (1979). The play environment as an effector of mobility and communication in deaf-blind children. In D.M. Compton, M.G. Burrows, & P.A. Witt (Eds.), *Facilitating play, recreation, and leisure opportunities for deaf-blind children and youth* (pp. 81-99). Denton: North Texas University Press.

Bruya, L.D. (1985a, April). *Comprehensive risk management for play environments.* Paper presented at the meeting of the Illinois Parks and Recreation Association, Chicago.

Bruya, L.D. (1985b). Design characteristics used in playgrounds for children. In J.L. Frost & S. Sunderland (Eds.), *When children play* (pp. 215-220). Wheaton, MD: Association for Childhood Education International.

Bruya, L.D. (1985c). The effect of play structure format differences on the play behavior of preschool children. In J.L. Frost & S. Sunderland (Eds.), *When children play* (pp. 115-120). Wheaton, MD: Association of Childhood Education International.

Bruya, L.D. (1985d, April). *A seminar on liability and risk on the playground.* Paper presented to Reese Industries, Chicago.

Bruya, L.D. (Ed.) (1988). *Play spaces for children: A new beginning.* Washington, DC: American Alliance for Health, Physical Education, Recreation and Dance.

Bruya, L.D., & Beckwith, J. (1985). Due process: Reducing exposure to liability suits and the management of risk associated with children's play areas. *Children's Environments Quarterly,* **2**(4), 29-35.

Bruya, L.D., & Buchanan, H.E. (1977). *An evaluation of a play environment and the effect of changing structural complexity on the observed motor behavior of preschool age children* (Research Grant NTSU 35718). Denton: North Texas State University.

Bruya, L.D., & Buchanan, H.E. (1978). The effect of changing structural complexity on the observed motor behavior of preschool age children. In C.B. Corbin (Ed.), *Symposium papers: Teaching behavior and sport history* (Vol. 1, pp. 72-76).

Washington, DC: American Alliance for Health, Physical Education, Recreation and Dance.

Bruya, L.D., Carter, C.S., & Fowler, C.L. (1983, June-July). *Position effects as an indicator of play routes on a play structure.* Paper presented at the International Conference on Play and Play Environments, Austin, TX.

Bruya, L.D., Franklin, L., Langendorfer, S., & Reid, A. (1984, November). *Establishing a preschool aquatics movement program.* Paper presented at the Biennial Conference of the Council for National Cooperation in Aquatics, Fort Worth, TX.

Bruya, L.D., & Langendorfer, S.J. (Eds.) (1988). *Where our children play.* Washington, DC: American Alliance for Health, Physical Education, Recreation and Dance.

Buell, C., Pettigrew, F., & Langendorfer, S. (1987). The effect of the strength of perceptual preferences on learning a novel motor task. *Perceptual and Motor Skills,* **65**, 743-747.

Canadian Red Cross. (1984). *Water safety instructor guide and reference* (Vol. 5). Toronto: Canadian Red Cross Society.

Carter, C., Bruya, L.D., & Fowler, C.L. (1983, June). *Positive effects as an indicator of play routes on a play structure.* Paper presented at the International Conference on Play and Play Environments, Austin, TX.

Chapman, D. (1980). Swimming and grommets. *Clinical Otolaryngology,* **5**, 420.

Cool, L.M. (1992). *Longitudinal changes in the aquatic locomotor patterns of twin boys.* Unpublished video data: personal correspondence.

Council for National Cooperation in Aquatics. (1965). *Water fun for everyone.* New York: Association Press.

Council for National Cooperation in Aquatics. (1985). Aquatic activity programs for children under the age of three. *National Aquatics Journal,* **1**(2), 12-13.

Cureton, T. (1943). *Warfare aquatics.* Chicago: Stipes.

Cureton, T. (1949). *Fun in the water.* New York: Association Press.

D'Alesio, D.J., Minor, T.E., Allen, C.I., Tsiatis, A.A., & Nelson, D.B. (1981). A study of the proportion of swimmers among well controls and children with enterovirus-like illness shedding or not shedding an enterovirus. *American Journal of Epidemiology,* **113**, 533-544.

Dawson, B. (1986, May). The history of swimming. *American Swim Coaches Association Newsletter,* 6-10.

Dawson, C.G. (1990, January). *Remarks about child-*

hood drowning. Presentation to the 1990 National Fox Seminar, New Orleans.

deBarbadillo, J., & Murphy, M.M. (1972). *Teaching the very young to swim*. New York: Association Press.

Dennis, W. (1940). The effect of cradling practices upon the onset of walking in Hopi children. *Journal of Genetic Psychology*, **56**, 77-86.

Desterbeck, R.A., Clement, P.A., Kaufman, L., & Derde, M.P. (1986). The effect of swimming on nasal patency and tubal function in children: A prospective 24 week cross-over study on 154 children. *Acta Otorhinolaryngology Belgetica*, **49**, 606-614.

Diem, L. (1957). *Who can?* Frankfurt, Germany: A/M Willhelm Limpert.

Diem, L. (1982). Early motor stimulation and personal development: A study of four to six year old German children. *Journal of Physical Education, Recreation and Dance*, **53**, 23-25.

Ellis, M.J. (1973). *Why people play*. Englewood Cliffs, NJ: Prentice Hall.

Ellis, M.J., & Scholtz, G.J.L. (1978). *Activity and play of children*. Englewood Cliffs, NJ: Prentice Hall.

El Silimy, O., & Bradley, P.J. (1986). Bacteriological aspects of swimming with grommets. *Clinical Otolaryngology*, **11**(5), 323-327.

Erbaugh, S.J. (1978). Assessment of swimming performance of preschool children. *Perceptual and Motor Skills*, **47**, 1179-1182.

Erbaugh, S.J. (1980). The development of swimming skills of preschool children. In C. Nadeau, K. Newell, G. Roberts, & W. Halliwell (Eds.), *Psychology of motor behavior and sport—1979* (pp. 324-335). Champaign, IL: Human Kinetics.

Erbaugh, S.J. (1981). The development of swimming skills of preschool children over a one and one-half year period. *Dissertation Abstracts International*, **42**, 2558A.

Erbaugh, S.J. (1986a). Effects of aquatic training on swimming skill development of preschool children. *Perceptual and Motor Skills*, **62**, 439-446.

Erbaugh, S.J. (1986b). Effects of body size and body mass on the swimming performance of preschool children. *Human Movement Science*, **5**, 1-12.

Erbaugh, S.J. (1987). Parent-child interactions during an informal swimming session. In J.H. Humphrey & J.E. Clark (Eds.), *Advances in motor development research* (Vol. 1, pp. 61-74). New York: AMS Press.

Fiske, D.W., & Maddi, S.R. (1961). *Functions of varied experience*. Homewood, IL: Dosey Press.

Fluegelman, A. (1976). *The new games book*. New York: Doubleday.

Fowler, C.L., & Bruya, L.D. (1983, June). *A comparison of a play environment with play events with dependent measures of ON, OFF, UNDER, and TOUCHING EQUIPMENT*. Paper presented at the International Conference on Play and Play Environments, Austin, TX.

Franklin, L., & Bruya, L.D. (1983, June). *An aquatics curriculum based on play structure use*. Paper presented at the International Conference on Play and Play Environments, Austin, TX.

Franklin, L., Bruya, L.D., & McWilliams, M. (1984, November). *Novel equipment used in aquatic programming*. Paper presented at the Biennial Conference of the Council for National Cooperation in Aquatics, Fort Worth, TX.

Frost, J.L., & Klein, B.L. (1979). *Children's play and playgrounds*. Boston: Allyn & Bacon.

Gabbard, C., LeBlanc, E., & Lowy, S. (1987). *Physical education for children: Building the foundation*. Englewood Cliffs, NJ: Prentice Hall.

Gabrielson, M., Spears, B., & Gabrielson, B. (1960). *Aquatics handbook*. Englewood Cliffs, NJ: Prentice Hall.

Gentile, A.M. (1972). A working model of skill acquisition with application to teaching. *Quest*, **17**, 3-23.

German, L.W. (1978). *North Canton preschool handbook*. North Canton, OH: YMCA.

Gibson, E. (1969). *Principles of perceptual learning and development*. New York: Appleton-Century-Crofts.

Gilliom, B.C. (1970). *Basic movement education for children: Rationale and teaching units*. Reading, MA: Addison-Wesley.

Goldberg, G.N., Lightner, E.S., Morgan, W., & Kemberling, S. (1982). Infantile water intoxication after a swimming lesson. *Pediatrics*, **70**, 599-600.

Graham, G., Holt/Hale, S., & Parker, M. (1987). *Children moving* (2nd ed.). Mountainview, CA: Mayfield.

Greene, J., & Horne, D. (1969, Summer). *Variability technique for presenting question stems*. Paper presented as a movement exploration workshop, Seattle: University of Washington.

Greensmith, C.T., Stanwick, R.S., Elliot, B.E., & Fast, M.V. (1988). Giardiasis associated with the use of a waterslide. *Pediatric Infectious Diseases*, **7**, 91-94.

Groscott, J.K. (1975). *The basic swimming guide*. Mountainview, CA: World.

Hackett-Layne, C., & Jenson, R. (1966). *A guide to movement exploration*. Palo Alto, CA: Peek.

Halverson, L.E., & Williams, K. (1985). Developmental sequences for hopping over distance: A prelongitudinal screening. *Research Quarterly for Exercise and Sport,* **56**(1), 37-44.

Harper, C.J., & Struna, N. (1973, April). *Case studies in the development of one-handed striking.* Paper presented at the National Convention of the American Association of Health, Physical Education and Recreation, Minneapolis.

Harrod, D.K. (1991). *A scalogram analysis of the American Red Cross Beginner swimming skill items.* Unpublished master's thesis, Kent State University, Kent, OH.

Harrod, D.K., & Langendorfer, S. (1990). A scalogram analysis of American Red Cross Beginner swimming skill items. *National Aquatics Journal,* **6**, 10-16.

Harter, L., Frost, F., Grunfelder, G., Perkins-Jones, K., & Libby, J. (1984). Giardiasis in an infant and toddler swim class. *American Journal of Public Health,* **74**, 155-156.

Herkowitz, J. (1980). Developmentally engineered equipment and playspaces for motor development and learning. In C. Nadeau, K. Newell, G. Roberts, & W. Halliwell (Eds.), *Psychology of motor behavior and sport—1979* (pp. 299-313). Champaign, IL: Human Kinetics.

Herkowitz, J. (1984). Developmentally engineered equipment and playgrounds. In J.R. Thomas (Ed.), *Motor development in childhood and adolescence* (pp. 139-173). Minneapolis: Burgess.

Holt/Hale, S. (1988). *On the move.* Mountainview, CA: Mayfield.

Hopkins, R.S., Abbott, D.O., & Wallace, L.E. (1981). Follicular dermatitis outbreak caused by pseudomonas aeruginosa associated with a motel's indoor swimming pool. *Public Health Reports,* **96**, 246-249.

Hutt, C. (1976). Exploration and play in children. In J.S. Bruner, A. Jolly, & K. Sylvia (Eds.), *Play—its role in development and evaluation* (pp. 202-215). New York: Basic Books.

Jackson, A., Jackson, A., & Frankiewicz, R. (1979). The construct and concurrent validity of a 12-minute crawl stroke swim as a field test of swimming endurance. *Research Quarterly for Exercise and Sport,* **50**, 641-648.

Jackson, A., & Pettinger, J. (1969). The development and discriminant analysis of swimming profiles of college men. In *72nd Annual Proceedings of NCPEAM Meeting* (pp. 104-110). Minneapolis: National College Physical Education Association for Men.

Jeffries, R. (1984). *Unpublished materials from First Annual Ashland Family YMCA Silly Relay Meet,* Ashland, OH.

Johnson, B., & Nelson, J. (1986). *Practical measurements for evaluation in physical education* (4th ed.). Minneapolis: Burgess.

Kelly, K. (1986, March). *Workshop games.* United States Swimming Foundation workshop, Fort Wayne, IN.

Kiemele, D.G., & Bruya, L.D. (1978). *Elementary physical education methods manual: Preparation for decision making.* Los Altos, CA: Kiemele & Associates.

Kirchner, G., Cunningham, J., & Warrell, E. (1978). *Introduction to movement education* (2nd ed.). Dubuque, IA: Brown.

Kochen, C., & McCabe, J. (1986). *The baby swim book.* Champaign, IL: Human Kinetics.

Kropp, R.M., & Schwartz, J.F. (1982). Water intoxication from swimming. *Journal of Pediatrics,* **101**, 947-948.

Langendorfer, S. (1974). *The effects of tactile stimulation using water and general motor activity on the motor development of six to nine month old human infants.* Unpublished master's thesis, Purdue University, West Lafayette, IN.

Langendorfer, S. (1984a, February). *Aquatic assessment instrument and individualized educational plan.* Paper presented at the Annual Midwest AHPERD Conference, Indianapolis.

Langendorfer, S. (1984b). Health and safety concerns in preschool aquatics. In L. Priest & A. Crowner (Eds.), *Opportunities in aquatics* (pp. 57-59). Indianapolis: Council for National Cooperation in Aquatics.

Langendorfer, S. (1986a). Aquatics for the young child: Facts and myths. *Journal of Physical Education, Recreation and Dance,* **57**(8), 61-66.

Langendorfer, S. (1986b). Health and safety concerns in preschool swimming. *National Aquatics Journal,* **1**(3), 8-9.

Langendorfer, S. (1987a). Children's movement in the water: A developmental and environmental perspective. *Children's Environments Quarterly,* **4**(2), 25-32.

Langendorfer, S. (1987b). Facts and fiction in aquatics for the young child. *National Aquatics Journal,* **3**(1), 2-4.

Langendorfer, S. (1987c). Prelongitudinal screening of overarm striking development performed under two environmental conditions. In J.H. Humphrey & J.E. Clark (Eds.), *Advances in motor development research* (Vol. 1, pp. 17-47). New York: AMS Press.

Langendorfer, S. (1987d). A prelongitudinal test of

motor stage theory. *Research Quarterly for Exercise and Sport*, **58**, 21-29.

Langendorfer, S. (1989a). Aquatics for young children with handicapping conditions. *Palaestra*, Spring, 17-39.

Langendorfer, S. (1989b). Evaluating the risks and benefits in aquatics for young children. *Pediatric Exercise Science*, **1**(3), 30-43.

Langendorfer, S., & Bruya, L.D. (1988). Common sense principles for administering aquatic programs for young children. *National Aquatic Journal*, **4**(2), 12-14.

Langendorfer, S., Bruya, L.D., & Gray, D.P. (1989). Aquatics for the young child: Managing the risk. *Parks & Recreation*, **24**(2), 10-12.

Langendorfer, S., Bruya, L.D., & Reid, A. (1987). Facilitating aquatic motor development: A review of developmental and environmental variables. In J.H. Humphrey & J.E. Clark (Eds.), *Advances in motor development research* (Vol. 2, pp. 219-235). New York: AMS Press.

Langendorfer, S., German, E.W., & Kral, D. (1988). Games and gimmicks in aquatic programs for young children. *National Aquatics Journal*, **4**(4), 11-14.

Langendorfer, S.J., Gray, D.P., Sharp, L.A., & Bruya, L.D. (1989). The single most important legal problem in infant/preschool aquatics: Managing risk in the aquatic environment. *Legal Issues in Sport*, **1**(1), 59-75.

Langendorfer, S., Roberts, M.A., & Ropka, C.R. (1987). A developmental test of aquatic readiness. *National Aquatics Journal*, **3**(2), 8-9, 12.

Langendorfer, S., & Willing, E. (1985). The impact of motor development research upon issues in infant and preschool aquatic development. *National Aquatic Journal*, **1**(1), 14-15.

Logsdon, B.J. (1984a). Educational gymnastics. In B.J. Logsdon (Ed.), *Physical education for children* (2nd ed., pp. 241-294). Philadelphia: Lea & Febiger.

Logsdon, B.J. (1984b). Physical education: A design for direction. In B.J. Logsdon (Ed.), *Physical education for children* (2nd ed., pp. 9-23). Philadelphia: Lea & Febiger.

Logsdon, B.J., & Barrett, K.R. (1984). Movement—the content of physical education. In B.J. Logsdon (Ed.), *Physical education for children* (2nd ed., pp. 123-143). Philadelphia: Lea & Febiger.

McGraw, M.B. (1939). Swimming behavior of the human infant. *Journal of Pediatrics*, **15**(4), 485-490.

McGraw, M.B. (1963). *Neuromuscular maturation of the human infant*. New York: Hafner. (Origi-

nally published 1943 by Columbia University Press)

McGraw, M.B. (1975). *Growth: A study of Johnny and Jimmy*. New York: Arno. (Originally published 1935 by Appleton-Century)

Miner, M.F. (1980). *Water fun*. Englewood Cliffs, NJ: Prentice Hall.

Morris, G.S.D. (1976). *How to change the games children play*. Minneapolis: Burgess.

Mossten, M. (1966). *Teaching from command to discovery*. Columbus, OH: Merrill.

Mossten, M. (1972). *Teaching physical education*. Somerville, NJ: Wadsworth.

Munnsinger, H., Kessen, W., & Kessen, M.L. (1964). Age and uncertainty: Development of variations in preference for variability. *Journal of Experimental Child Psychology*, **1**(1), 1-5.

Murray, J. (1981). *Infaquatics*. West Point, NY: Leisure Press.

Newman, V.H. (1983). *Teaching an infant to swim* (2nd ed.). San Diego: Harcourt Brace Jovanovich.

Oka, H., Okamoto, T., Yoshizawa, M., Tokuyama, H., & Kumamoto, M. (1978). Electromyographic and cinematographic study of the flutter kick in infants and children. In J. Teraudo & E.W. Bedringfield (Eds.), *International series on sport sciences* (Vol. 8, pp. 167-172). Baltimore: University Park Press.

Orlick, T. (1978). *The cooperative sports and games book*. New York: Pantheon Books.
on sport sciences (Vol. 8, pp. 167-172). Baltimore: University Park Press.

Orlick, T. (1978). *The cooperative sports and games book*. New York: Pantheon Books.

Osment, L. (1976). Update: Seabather's eruption and swimmer's itch. *Cutis*, **14**, 545-547.

Owen, A.H. (1968). *Swimming for schools*. London: Pelham.

Penman, K.A. (1987). Safe sports equipment and facilities. In S.H. Adams (Ed.), *Catastrophic injuries in sports: Avoidance strategies*. Indianapolis: Benchmark Press.

Piaget, J. (1963). *The origin of intelligence in children* (M. Cook, Trans.). New York: Norton.

Prudden, B. (1974). *Teach your baby to swim*. New York: Dial Press.

Ratnam, S., Hogan, K., March, S.B., & Butler, R.W. (1986). Whirlpool-associated folliculitis caused by pseudomonas aeruginosa: A report of an outbreak and a review. *Journal of Clinical Microbiology*, **23**, 655-659.

Reid, A., & Bruya, L.D. (1984, November). *Assessment of developmental motor patterns in preschool aquatics*. Paper presented at the Biennial Conference of the Council for National Cooperation in Aquatics, Fort Worth, TX.

Reid, A., Bruya, L.D., & Langendorfer, S. (1985, April). *Developmental motor pattern sequences in the aquatics medium: Research findings*. Paper presented to the Centennial Conference at the American Alliance for Health, Physical Education, Recreation and Dance, Atlanta.

Robb, M. (1972). *The dynamics of motor-skill acquisition*. Englewood Cliffs, NJ: Prentice Hall.

Roberton, M.A. (1977). Stability of stage categorizations across trials: Implications for the "stage theory" of overarm throw development. *Journal of Human Movement Studies*, 3(1), 49-59.

Roberton, M.A. (1978). Longitudinal evidence for developmental stages in the forceful overarm throw for force. *Journal of Human Movement Studies*, 4(2), 167-173.

Roberton, M.A. (1990). The weaver's loom: A developmental metaphor. In J.E. Clark & J.H. Humphrey (Eds.), *Advances in motor development research*, (Vol. 3, pp. 1-15). New York: AMS Press.

Roberton M.A., & Halverson, L.E. (1984). *Developing children—their changing movement*. Philadelphia: Lea & Febiger.

Roberton, M.A., & Langendorfer, S. (1980). Testing motor development sequences across 9-14 years. In C. Nadeau, K. Newell, G. Roberts, & W. Halliwell (Eds.), *Psychology of motor behavior and sport—1979* (pp. 269-279). Champaign, IL: Human Kinetics.

Runta, N. (1980). *Pre-school swimming instructor's manual*. Findlay, OH: YMCA.

Ryan, J. (1960). *Learning to swim is fun*. New York: Ronald Press.

Safrit, M.J. (1986). *Introduction to measurement in physical education and exercise science*. St. Louis: Times-Mirror/Mosby.

Sage, G.H. (1984). *Motor learning and control*. Dubuque, IA: Brown.

Schliehauf, R. (1986). Swimming skill: A review of basic theory. *Journal of Swimming Research*, 2(2), 11-20.

Schmidt, R.A. (1975). A schema theory of discrete motor learning. *Psychological Review*, 82, 225-260.

Schmidt, R.A. (1977). Schema theory: Implications for movement education. *Motor Skills: Theory Into Practice*, 2, 36-48.

Schmidt, R.A. (1991). *Motor learning and performance: From principles to practice*. Champaign, IL: Human Kinetics.

Scholtz, G.J.L., & Ellis, M.J. (1975a, April). *Novelty,*

complexity, and play. Paper presented at the International Seminar on Play in Physical Education and Sport, Wingate Institute, Israel.

Scholtz, G.J.L., & Ellis, M.J. (1975b). Repeated exposure to objects and peers in a play setting. *Journal of Experimental Child Psychology*, 19, 445-455.

Seattle Public School District. (1984a). *Seattle Public School District recommendations based on high risk study*. Unpublished manuscript, Seattle Public Schools Athletic Department, Seattle.

Seattle Public School District. (1984b). *Warning, agreement to obey instructions, release, assumption of risk, and agreement to hold harmless*. Unpublished manuscript, Seattle Public Schools Athletic Department, Seattle.

Seefeldt, V. (1980). Developmental motor patterns: Implications for elementary school physical education. In C. Nadeau, K. Newell, G. Roberts, & W. Halliwell (Eds.), *Psychology of motor behavior and sport—1979* (pp. 314-323). Champaign, IL: Human Kinetics.

Seefeldt, V., & Branta, C.F. (1984). Patterns of participation in children's sport. In J.R. Thomas (Ed.), *Motor development during childhood and adolescence* (pp. 190-211). Minneapolis: Burgess.

Shaffer, L. (1969, Summer). *Vocabulary for movement education*. Paper presented at the EPDA Institute in Elementary Physical Education, Western Washington State University, Bellingham.

Shank, C. (1983). *A child's way to water play*. West Point, NY: Leisure Press.

Shapiro, D.C., & Schmidt, R.A. (1981). The schema theory: Recent evidence and developmental implications. In J.A.S. Kelso & J.E. Clark (Eds.), *The development of movement control and coordination*. New York: Wiley.

Shaw, L.G. (1976). *The playground: The child's creative learning space* (Report No. MH 20743-04A1). Gainsville: Bureau of Research, College of Architecture, University of Florida.

Sheffield, L. (1927). *Swimming simplified*. New York: Barnes.

Siegel, S.E. (1987). Swimming with antibiotic drops. *Ear, Nose, and Throat Journal*, 66(11), 469-471. (Letter)

Steele, B. (1985). *The incomplete book of training games and gimmicks*. Chicago: Printing Plant.

Swimming Pool Data and Reference Annual. (1960). *Aquatic games, pageants, and stunts*. New York: Hoffman & Harris.

Thomas, D.G. (1972). *Swimming pool operators handbook*. Washington, DC: National Swimming Pool Foundation.

Thomas, D.G. (1976, November). *Pool chemistry and pre-school swimming programs.* Paper presented at the Council for National Cooperation in Aquatics Preschool Aquatics Workshop, Champaign, IL.

Timmermans, C. (1975). *How to teach your baby to swim.* New York: Stein & Day.

Twardus, B. (1982). *Seattle Public Schools memorandum: Safety guidelines.* Unpublished manuscript, Seattle Public Schools Athletic Department, Seattle.

Wagenvoord, J. (1980). *The swim book.* New York: J. Wagenvoord Studio.

Weilbacher, R.M. (1980). *A comparison of kindergarten girls' social and motor behavior in a static play environment and in a dynamic play environment.* Unpublished doctoral dissertation, The Ohio State University, Columbus.

White, B. (1986). *The first three years of life* (2nd ed.). Englewood Cliffs, NJ: Prentice Hall.

Wielki, C., & Houben, M. (1983). Descriptions of the leg movements of infants in an aquatic environment. *Biomechanics and medicine in swimming* (Vol. 14, pp. 66-71). University Park: University of Maryland Press.

Wight, R.G., Jones, A.S., Connell, J.A., Buffin, J.T., Bull, P.D., & Chapman, D.F. (1987). Three year follow-up (1983-1986) of children undergoing bilateral grommet insertion in Sheffield. *Clinical Otolaryngology*, **12**(5), 371-375.

Williams, K. (1980). Developmental characteristics of a forward roll. *Research Quarterly for Exercise and Sport*, **51**(3), 703-713.

Willing, E. (1986). *A review and reference guide to aquatic games and learning experiences.* Unpublished research paper, Kent State University, Kent, OH.

YMCA of the USA. (1972). *Progressive swimming and springboard diving program instructors manual.* Chicago: National YMCA Program Resources.

YMCA of the USA. (1983). *Aquatics for special populations.* Champaign, IL: Human Kinetics.

YMCA of the USA. (1986). *Splash.* Champaign, IL: Human Kinetics.

YMCA of the USA. (1987). *Y Skippers.* Champaign, IL: Human Kinetics.

Zelazo, P. (1983). The development of walking: New findings and old assumptions. *Journal of Motor Behavior*, **15**(2), 99-137.

Index

About the Authors

Stephen J. Langendorfer, an associate professor and chair of kinesiology at Bowling Green State University, has been involved in aquatics both as an instructor and a participant for most of his life. He has more than 25 years' experience as an infant/preschool swimming instructor and water safety instructor and has been a competitive swimmer for more than 30 years. Langendorfer's introduction to infant/preschool aquatics came in 1971 when he studied at the Deutsche Sporthochschule in Germany under Liselot Diem, who was then conducting an innovative baby swim program and longitudinal study. In 1972 Langendorfer followed suit and established his own toddler swim program in Ithaca, NY.

Langendorfer received a PhD in motor development from the University of Wisconsin-Madison in 1982. He is a member of the Council for National Cooperation in Aquatics (CNCA), the American Alliance for Health, Physical Education, Recreation and Dance (AAHPERD), and the North American Society for Psychology of Sport and Physical Activity (NASPSPA). In addition, Dr. Langendorfer was chair of the American Red Cross Swimming Advisory Committee from 1990 to 1994.

Lawrence D. Bruya is a professor and assistant dean in Washington State University's (WSU) Department of Physical Education, Sport, and Leisure Studies, for which he was department chair from 1988 to 1994. He has taught at the college level since 1976. Before coming to WSU, Dr. Bruya taught at the elementary level as a physical education specialist, worked as an elementary school principal, and held the position of associate professor in the department of physical education at North Texas State University (NTSU). While at NTSU he developed and directed a preschool and elementary children's gymnasium and aquatics program, which helped him understand what effects the design of environments and use of equipment has on children's play patterns. In addition to teaching, Dr. Bruya is a playground design consultant. He also has written extensively about child development and playground design and is the author of the book, *Playspaces for children—A new beginning: Improving our elementary school playground.*

Bruya received his PhD in motor development from Purdue University in 1976. He received the Outstanding Teaching Award presented by the Bureau of Indian Affairs in 1971, and in 1985 he was given the Meadows Teaching Award by North Texas State University. Dr. Bruya is a member of AAHPERD, CNCA, and the American Association for Leisure and Recreation.